WORDS ARE EAGLES

Gregory Day

Gregory Day is a novelist, poet and musician from the
Eastern Otways region of southwest Victoria, Australia. He
lives on Wadawurrung tabayl. Gregory has published five
novels to date and has won many awards, including the
Australian Literature Society Gold Medal, the Elizabeth
Jolley Prize, the Manly Artist Book Award and the Alfred
Deakin Medal. In 2019 Gregory's most recent novel *A Sand
Archive* was shortlisted for the Miles Franklin Award. In
2020 Gregory received the prestigious Patrick White Award
for his ongoing body of work, and in 2021 he was awarded
the Nature Conservancy Australia Nature Writing Prize for
'The Watergaw', an essay contained in this volume.

Also by Gregory Day

Melaleuca Perfumeries

The Black Tower: Songs from the Poetry of W.B. Yeats

Trace (with photographs by Robert Ashton)

The Patron Saint of Eels

The Flash Road: Scenes from the Building of the Great Ocean Road

Ron McCoy's Sea of Diamonds

The Grand Hotel

Visitors (engravings by Jiri Tibor Novak)

Archipelago of Souls

A Smile at Arm's Length (engravings by Jiri Tibor Novak)

A Sand Archive

Rejectamenta: From Real to Imagined Seaweed (soundtrack)

Gregory Day

WORDS ARE EAGLES

Selected Writings on the Nature & Language of Place

UPSWELL

First published in Australia in 2022
by Upswell Publishing
Perth, Western Australia
upswellpublishing.com

ISBN: 978-0-6452479-5-4

NATIONAL LIBRARY OF AUSTRALIA

A catalogue record for this
book is available from the
National Library of Australia

Cover artwork: Sian Marlow
Cover design by Chil3, Fremantle
Typeset in Foundry Origin by Lasertype

This book was written on Wadawurrung tabayl and Gadubanud country.

Contents

In dreams begin responsibility

W.B. Yeats

Where the Songs Are Made

The printed word can be both a wonderful and a terrible thing. Once it is out in the world it can never be reclaimed and, unlike wounds and injuries of the body, no amount of surgery or rest can help. I've learnt this over the years by publishing novels that are largely set in a small town not unlike the one where I live. The sentences and paragraphs of these novels, their characters and the characters' actions, declarations and opinions, are all beyond my control now. In a strange way, despite their roots in my family's home and imagination, they live quite independently of my desires, in the hands of readers who get to make of them what they like. Accordingly, these days, if I really want an idea, inkling or piece of knowledge to remain in my control, I won't write it down. I may say it, but only within earshot of the birds and creatures (including humans) that I feel I know and trust.

Someone once said that every story is a local story, and the air of my local world, the very oxygen that both gives us life and takes it away, the air I can hear moving through the trees outside my window as I write, is the same air that floats the sonic units we call words out of the singularity of our bodies and into the realm of the social contract. The Wadawurrung and Gadubanud people, who have lived in my part of the world for thousands of years, seem to know this well. Prior to the European invasion they did not fix or memorialise by writing words down. They understood how cultural and emotional meaning was indivisible from what their invaders conceived of platonically as 'nature': the air they breathed and voiced, the sea spray and land-lift, the sky-shine and its darkening, the rhythmic circadian and sidereal movement all around them.

The title of this book, *Words Are Eagles*, is derived from a passage in my essay 'One True Note' concerning the Cheshire writer Alan Garner's novel about William Buckley. For better or worse, William Buckley is generally the first port of call in the written historical record for non-Indigenous people wanting to gain a better understanding and connection with the Wadawurrung cultural landscape. His story is so amazing that it is a hard one to tell, but perhaps part of the problem is that it is almost always told as an 'Australian' story. For my fellow topophiliac Alan Garner, however, the tale of the two-metre-tall convict who escaped from the temporary 1803 colonial settlement near the Port Phillip heads and lived for thirty-two years with the Wadawurrung before the British invasion, is as much a story about a kindred Cheshireman as anything else. Garner's Buckley novel, *Strandloper*, celebrates a sense of deep sylvan dreaming on both sides of the colonial divide. It seems to be saying that even despite the brutality of the illegal British invaders, we should not make the mistake of divesting the first Europeans in the Wadawurrung landscape of their humanity. The myths of colonial 'Enlightenment' and the Lamb of God, these figments of superiority that were licensing their behaviour, allowing them to march into another people's home and take and destroy what wasn't theirs, were myths nevertheless. For the invaders to believe and participate in these potent paradigms of mythic belief they required imagination (however docile) as well as the living sense of an abstract ideal that, as far as we know, distinguishes human beings from many, if not all, other species – though I'm not prepared to concede that animals other than humans don't have a space in their being for intuitive visions of ideal behaviour.

One definite distinguishing factor between Buckley and his Aboriginal hosts in *Strandloper* was what Garner describes as 'cutting sand', i.e. writing. In a telling scene that I discuss in 'One True Note', an elder of Garner's imagining, who he calls Nullamboin, comes upon Buckley writing in the sand on the beach at Beangala, these days called

Indented Head. Nullamboin is horrified with the unritualised ease of access to knowledge that such writing can bring. After Buckley writes various words in the sand by way of demonstration, including Bundjil, the Wadawurrung word for the powerful and important wedge-tailed eagle, and after he explains how ideas and information can be transferred in this way, Nullamboin becomes apocalyptic. 'Then all will see without knowledge,' he cries, 'without teaching, without dying into life! Weak men will sing! Boys will have eagles! All shall be mad!'

From Garner's perspective the issue of the written word, and the idea that its utility could completely destroy the timely pathways of ancestral knowledge and landlore, was at least one gulf that remained between Buckley and his Aboriginal lifesavers. If knowledge was something to be attained through highly regulated and ritualised techniques, then the process of inheritance and experience, *events in the landscape*, became the true living etymology of the oral language that served as one of the carriers of this knowledge.

Where that leaves us today in the era of the internet and social media is an obvious next question. Extreme porn viewed on phone screens by children going back and forth to school on the bus is one futuristic scenario that Garner's fictional Nullamboin surely could not have foreseen. What he did sense, however, and what so horrified him, was the violent chaos that ensues from a carelessness caused by the lack of connection to the memorial contours and emotional topographies of place. The idea of a young boy having access to a creature as powerful as an eagle was his equivalent to the phone-screen porn. And as I wrote the pieces in this book, pieces that describe at least some of the complexities involved when you use a recently introduced but now dominant language in a continent that was not so long ago one of the most linguistically diverse on earth, the potential indelibility of what my own young boys might see over someone's shoulder on the bus as they travelled up the coast each day to school felt every bit as scary as them being savaged by a giant eagle. The power of the potential predator is, and has always been, everywhere embedded in our relationship to both language and place.

So writing in this polyphonous country that is now called Australia has always been a complex act. The minute you fall in love with the place you're in, you're on the path towards it becoming who you are, and the other way around. Thus a thrilling and tortuous process begins. How to describe it without betraying it. How to love it without destroying it. How to learn from it and listen to the lessons it has to impart. As W.B. Yeats said, 'in dreams begin responsibility'.

Narrandjerri elder David Unaipon, scientist, inventor, musician, preacher, who, absurdly enough, earned the title of the first official Aboriginal 'author' in the 1920s, believed that human beings were originally not of this earth at all. In his *Native Legends* of 1929 he describes how when the great decision was made to come here from the Spirit Realm it was the animals – the insects and birds, marsupials and reptiles, vertebrates and invertebrates alike, each and every creature – that taught us how to be here. Every creature had a different lesson to impart, so that we might live on the earth in a balanced way that allowed everything to continue. Unaipon's is a totemism for our times. Of course it is; it is a totemism for all times. Writing wasn't one of the lessons the animals in his legend taught, but it was nevertheless Unaipon's gift for writing that allows us eternal outsiders to better understand how to belong. Inevitably this process of understanding leads us to a country that has always existed, both before and after any Western notion of Time. In my experience this is the place from which language comes, and where all the songs are made. It is a regenerative place, of drama, stillness, sound and feeling. A place with no beginning and no end, where words are eagles.

One
The Colours of the Ground

The Watergaw

Driving slowly on the flat newly green plains near Inverleigh we saw
a tangled knot of silver-grey weather railing in the mid-sky from
the south-west. We both commented on this clear view the plains
afforded us, as if the low earth itself had become a high observatory.
As we drove further we watched the knot develop tendrils and ragged
fabric edges and then eventually a broken swatch of rainbow could
be sighted in it. I looked through the windscreen of the car, nodded
by way of acknowledgement in its direction, but said nothing. It
reminded me of Hugh MacDiarmid's watergaw.

It was a glimmer the poet wrote about, but distinct to him, and as with
all things so personal it felt unique and required a new language. A
new language tempered in an old forge. That's of course what I was
doing out at Inverleigh in the first place: getting reacquainted with
the foundry of atmosphere and clod that shaped my early ancestors
James and Mary and Antonio, and no doubt all of us after them. The
swatch of rainbow afforded by the flat plains was from that ancestral
forge. And yes, it reminded me of the watergaw.

Hugh MacDiarmid, Scottish poet, friend and mentor to many other
poets, Seamus Heaney among them, was obviously a blazing original.
He refused all artistic standards but his own, and gave and copped
a lot of flak for it. He fished deeply in old Scots, particularly in a

Griffith Review (2021)

little monograph entitled *Lowland Scotch as Spoken in the Lower Strathearn District of Perthshire*. It was not long after reading that monograph that he applied its numinous sonics to his own name, changing himself to Hugh MacDiarmid from Christopher Grieve. And with that his writing changed too. He became the poet the world is sometimes glad to know him as.

One of the first poems MacDiarmid wrote, with his new name and his new sense of what was required of his existence, was 'The Watergaw'. No doubt it came as a bolt out of the blue and required much fastening to the jinker, but it reads like a bit of the earth's speech. It's a burn steadily chanting over the brae, as they'd say in his part of the world.

But now it's entered my world, and so far away; or rather, I've traced a passage back: the big gamble taken by the farm servants James and Mary when in 1841 they got the hell out of Offaly and Westmeath in Ireland, made their way to Plymouth, and crossed the risky seas. They landed at Point Henry near Geelong, spent a few years ploughing, shodding and sowing near Moriac and in the Barrabool Hills, before envisaging the farm on a low ridge, with rivered pasture and a long view south towards the Otways, across sanctified country, back when it was still moist and beautifully clothed in groundcovers from being entrained, cultivated and worshipped thus by the Wadawurrung. I've entered their world, slipped between the layers of James and Mary and the Barrabool, let blood's story lure me away a little from the gravity feed of my home coast and into this nearby back-country of reversed creation, of rifled waterways, penetrating absences, ostentatious farm gates, and GPS-programmed harvesters.

And there, in the gnaw of it all, alights the watergaw.

There's a nonsense between fathers and sons, no matter how close. In a sense they are always at cross-purposes. For the elder, the son is a fish successful enough to be born out of his life's stream, with flesh tinted and flavoured by the master-habitat; whilst for the younger, the old man will always be somehow fixed as a source, a headwater issuing in the high country of the past, a cleft mixture of role-play, DNA, expansive love and restrictive law. In 'The Watergaw', MacDiarmid put paid to all speculation on such a theme, saw off Abraham and Isaac, the Holy Trinity, Job and the prodigal sons. Instead of a legend, a narrative, or a moral imperative with phoney nodes across time's landscape, he captured an ordinary patrilineal moment. One ordinary moment. Not to mention its bewilderment. He let that moment, and the bewilderment, capture him. The way all the rest of time fell into it. In the close thudding form of verse with an air of predestination, he allowed the ancient mismatch of blood love, of father & son love – where one plus one doesn't quite equal two but rather something closer to the original one – to come right on down like that waterchant over the brae.

It couldn't be done, let alone sung, in anyone else's language. Every deathbed is the same, some more successful than others. He had to decode the dross, sort it, the words and the tropes of thoughts, the inauthentic cadence of emotions that had been foisted upon him, or merely absorbed by him, from the seeming inevitability of imperialistic society and culture. He had to divine the previously unutterable, the misinterpreted, untangle the message, the look in death's eye, the eye of the father farewelling the son, signalling to him, or merely looking, at the broken rainbow, 'brinbeal' here in Wadawurrung country, the hatching, transformed, but saddened light across the sky. Farewelling that light. He had to quest but never find, to let sound find him, and find him it did, like a glimpse behind the veil.

And the country as we drive, and as we've driven about all day, is gleaming with that farewell of broken light. It's as if James and Mary, my great-great-grandparents, and Antonio Denerio, my Sicilian great great grandfather who washed up mysteriously in Geelong at roughly the same time, are now tumbled up like a Mologa roly-poly into my one-and-the-same dad. I'm driving back away from the sea cliffs he bred us to, back inland only forty kilometres onto the plains towards a time before him, from which he was bred, to come around the back of time and see him from behind, as creation itself sees him, in the hope that what has gone from my earth – his personality and foibles, his walking self, perhaps even his voice – will come back a little closer. For death affects distance, not only in space but in time; death's vacuous finality creates a similar vastness in the sky, a deeper horizontality on the land, so that the minimalist aftermath of the volcanic plains seems suddenly more appropriate than the ongoing drama of the ocean: appropriate, appropriately quiet, yes, an appropriate place at least to be your little self. Your little self with a licence to see the watergaw.

When Hugh MacDiarmid turned from writing purely in English to writing a Scots creole or pidgin, he sometimes called it Doric, sometimes 'my Scots', but assuredly it tapped closer in to the heartbeat of his land, to its structural braes and burns, its geologic fogs and onomatopoeic sleet. In such shrouded weather the currencies of light that shine through become discoveries, and not by the reader's and writer's eye alone. But in the decipherment of the poet's words there is a pact, a filling-in of the outline, the embodying of the glow, a musical process wherein chaos is revealed as harmony, a vision shared but private, personal but universal, quotidian but mythical, flesh and spirit, real and imagined, as in the lines of 'The Watergaw', which tell us of the night his father died:

> Ae weet forenicht i' the yow-trummle
> I saw yon antrin thing,
> A watergaw wi' its chitterin' licht
> Ayont the on-ding;
> An' I thocht o' the last wild look ye gied
> Afore ye deed!
>
> There was nae reek i' the laverock's hoose
> That nicht—an' nane i' mine;
> But I hae thocht o' that foolish licht
> Ever sin' syne;
> An' I think that mebbe at last I ken
> What your look meant then.

He admits that his pidgin Scots of 'The Watergaw' will be 'quite unintelligible to all of you, unless I explain', but this is not of course to apologise. Quite the contrary. He goes on to say: 'A watergaw is a broken rainbow, a broken shaft of a rainbow that you can see sometimes between clouds.'

The broken shaft of a rainbow. This too describes the place we *discover*, as we are pulled by some gravitational force of the lyric towards the honourable charge of decipherment the poet has thrust upon us.

And there, look, there it is above these drained yet still greening plains so close to my ancestors' town with its Scottish name *Inverleigh*, just west a little of *Bannockburn*, at the bottom arc of the globe, and now delivering unto me from its sky of so much more a broken shaft indeed, a glimpse yes, a severed light, gleaned amidst fraying knot and glancing squall, a site terrifyingly specific but, as MacDiarmid's poem shows, a site that like all places is also and always an everywhere.

As we take the slow curve of the grass-and-mushroom-freckled bend, I'm hopeful the knitting-up of my brow is the forerunner to satisfaction. I peer through the windscreen looking inexorably for the rest, the lost section of the arc, the James and Mary of the thing, the continuation of the colours, the reason Papa Antonio arrived, the rest of the rainbow, just as I was compelled to listen deeper into the sense in broken Scots of MacDiarmid's poem, and uncannily now of course into the last looks, indeed into all the looks my father gave and were given to him.

MacDiarmid kindly translates the opening two lines of his own poem as such:

> *One wet, early evening in the sheep-shearing season*
> *I saw that occasional, rare thing –*

He knows as he goes that this translation is sadly inadequate, nothing more than a linguistic Bailey bridge, a trussed-up paraphrase of what the Scots expresses and what is unattainable in English. Like any retrieval from the past there is a built-in insufficiency to the task, an inevitable failure, which is of course due to the singular beauty and power of the organic poem, the living thing, and which gives the past its myth and romance.

And thus, we keep driving about.

Likewise it goes on these plains that were once painted with the full flower spectrum of the various Wadawurrung tuber and root vegetables and medicines: the gold of the 'murnong' or yam daisy, the purple of the vanilla lily, the yellow of the 'parm' or bulbine lily, the purple-blue of the grass lily, the striped white and purple of early nancy, the mauve of the fringe lily, the pale brown of cinnamon bells, the greenhood orchids, the cream of clematis or 'tarook', the blush of bindweed, and the pink of crane's bill. Now, above the once multicoloured land from which it rises, the watergaw can seem the broken shaft of a cultural and metaphysical message, a dray or chariot ascending but stalled mid-sky, and thereby implying not only the fall but a definitively tragic landing on hard, hoof-compacted, colour-leached, colonial ground. For a moment the whole world feels a jumble of such fucked-up things, all smashed up, cast out and flung into a corner. My corner of the world. Broken blood, broken words, broken land, broken bodies, broken colours of the sky and earth, broken time. The layered strata of geology here are not just underground mutton after all! It's in the poet's words, the veils of time that we journey through in quest for the tang of our blood, the truth of our situation, the spirit's GPS that is the real pith of place.

So hollowed-out English would not suffice for MacDiarmid, and so often also it won't suffice for me. Not when there is a language that comes from here, is of here, that sounds of here, in timbre and noun, beat and retroflex, and that we were never taught. The next two lines of MacDiarmid's fatherless fatherful poem he translated thus:

> A broken shaft of a rainbow with its trembling light
> Beyond the downpour of the rain
> And I thought of that last, wild look you gave
> Before you died

Here then is both the motif and its explanation. I've driven out of the forested littoral, over and away from the 'nyooroo', or ochre, of ocean cliffs, back up onto an optically level world that might level with me about the tragedy of belonging and love. The broken stalk of colours, the fabric fray of wispy edges, so epic yet ethereal over these tractored plains, so sweet yet sawn-off, so ambient and quiet yet so charged with history's noise, is the love we feel. The fact we have to physically be here to receive the motif is not lost on me. Beware all substitutes. Beware any archive but the land, any page more static than the ever-fluent sky. I've driven out of the 'ngangahooks', or ironbarks, through the tweedy heaths and lakelands to travel into a timelessness that forms the heart of any such motif. The watergaw. Busted brinbeal. The blunt and the vivid. What makes it so. Spontaneity is always born from the long-unconsidered prelude. In each line of mine, James and Mary's risk and Papa Antonio's mystery provides an epigenetic score. In the run of life I strain their genes through watered-down paint but here, looking out through the windscreen, I sense a return to the complex palette of their fate. Is this my vanity's ransom? I consider this seriously until there, *there!*, through the streaky glass, is the watergaw.

So high that rainbow stalk, yet there is nothing so dun-ordinary as ancestral ground, nothing so ordinary as Dad. Families are daggy, all families, but deep family history is where this dagginess merges back to the magic fables of land. For land is not place without sky, without the dark underneath, without the lit air of story and fable. Place, of which soil chemistry is but one smear of taste on the tongue, one component. All families narrate. All families are an opera, so all place too. In our case these are some plotlines: how they bashed the country on arrival, how they inserted their farm, how they sowed their crops between ghoulish censuses of the Wadawurrung in Geelong that saw numbers dwindling between 1835 and 1877 from 3240 to ten, dwindling like the groundwater. How they ate instead the papery colours of nasturtium sandwiches and married that early enigmatic Siciliano. This is us. The us of which we are never transcendent. As if a rainbow could never be broken.

By the western district rail line, the lonely silent rails, the sleepy sleepers and the blue volcanic shards in between, we stop at the cemetery and my child, just a three-year-old, wails under the Italian cypresses like he's haunted. His name is also James, and already he rolls his r's like an Italian. We see how the weather works at his namesakes chiselled on the headstones. I can almost hear the sphagnum creeping beneath our feet as we observe how other mosses and lichens seek our ancestors, find their groove. I see the words then, the letters and numbers – JAMES MARY 1841 1874 1898 – as the curves and bends of guzzles and rivers and creeks, moist habitats for fungal life and tendril, debossed shelter-shapes from wind and direct sunlight. Language provides a melancholy lintel for vegetation's thrive, a brindled language more powerful than words.

In the end what's written there is only statistical. Integers, not rainbows. As James' wailing reminds me. He has the ragged sawn-off sound in his voice. His lungs are strong. Opera-strong. Nor do three-year-olds suffer fools. So it's back in the car and drive on.

Rainbows break in atmospherics, and like memory the sun gives off light rays of many wavelengths. The shorter, quicker waves rise to blue light; the longer slower waves to red light. Yellow and green lie between these, and the total effect is that the light appears white. The whiteness that breaks the rainbow. The watergaw appears at the boundary of air and water, then it breaks as the boundaries blur again, boundaries of life and death.

The car tyres ripple over the train line, across a brief rise then a fall of ridge, until we turn right into Day's Road. It's like the best seat in the house, this view over the fields. I consult the program:

> The skylark's nest was dark and desolate,
> My heart was too
> But I have thought of that foolish light
> Ever since then

And now, in the way of great poems, the words become our own. As if, going by the mossy dates, I have myself been thinking of that *foolish light* ever since 1841. What we did, or didn't do. What we have, and have not done. What events are, and are not, in our blood-libretto. Dad told us all about the meat on a plover's breast, how to flush the quail out of the poa grass, he showed us the knack with two-inch nails and crayfish, told us what the go was with snapper and gummy sharks, but never about the succulence of glasswort or boobialla currant, bearded heath or she-oak frond. Was it women's business to harvest plants rather than meat? I've seen the sketch of the Wadawurrung women with their 'karni', or yam-digging sticks, harvesting the murnong from these once golden plains. It's only women working in the precious image that survives, the colours all leached out by the Westernness of the depiction, a drawing by the colonial surveyor and politician John Helder Wedge. So is that why Dad only talked about the animal meat, not the plant flesh? Not because he was just a beery carnivore, not because he was Wadawurrung by blood (he wasn't, we're not), but because we are all intervolved. In the roles and rituals of nature. We've more in common than otherwise, as is proved by our globally shared stories of the Pleiades, or Seven Sisters as they're called in English, or 'Kuurrokeheaar' as they say in Keerray Woorrong just down the road, or Subaru as they are known in Japan. And that's before we even begin to mention our fingers and toes. Whatever the case, James and Mary fostered no murnong or boobialla for their tucker. As far as I know it was all chops and bacon, apricots and carrots on those formerly spongy slopes down to the River Barwon. That's Barwon by the way, a diminutive of Barroworn, which was a glitchy mishearing of Parrwang, the Wadawurrung word for the maestro of song in these parts, the bird *Gymnorhina tyrannica*, commonly known to us now (most underwhelmingly) as the *Australian magpie*. So Magpie River. The same river that is still the water I shower in, still the main tributary running all the way through the *foolish light* I am thinking of.

The heart must accept its dark inheritance, its skylark nest of place. This is partly what the dying father's *wild look* is always about. The wild damage that MacDiarmid's poem expresses, and the death.

Interestingly, it's groundlarks rather than skylarks that are flushed up when you stop the car, get out, and go walking on these plains. They buzz and fizz. They seem to like the moisture in the level river fields, the tiny tucker available there. We hear them as soon as we've waited long enough, been still for long enough beside the cooling car, and then we go, we walk out towards them. The larks are ancient technologies, and so it amuses me how they sound so much like old dial-up modems transmitting deep from the mystery of the grasses.

James is happier now that we're on the wander. Those curving cemetery paths and Italian cypresses, the peppercorns and headstones, were creepy. But now that we're walking it's the sky that dominates. The prisms of light. It's an aria moment, with not one, not two, but *three* watergaws climbing and terminating in the sky. They're like the transient trunks of trees, soaring old growth severed in mid-air, yet not. Are they the narrative arc unfinished, the motifs of a place still dreaming? For so long I've been thinking of that *foolish light*, for a time that actually feels way longer than my lifetime, my heart dark and desolate, but in the heart of the boy the new adventure's now on, and the arc must continue.

Not long before my own dad died, our ordinary daggy dad who lived not immortalised in MacDiarmid's poem but in our own unperform-able opera, my brother spotted a hare scampering over the rise outside the hospital window. I had had the call that Dad might not have long and had rushed over, only to find him sitting up in his bed eating cash-ews and reading the paper. The *wild look* had not yet come. He might as well have been at the pub. But though my brother had not yet told me what he had seen, the hare had already scampered over the rise. Feeling relieved that Dad seemed ok, I settled into the chair beside his bed. I asked him then if he thought he may come right. *I wouldn't have thought so*, was his reply.

No one can avoid the realism of what has happened here. In this place. Where the truth is both ferocious and plain. Truth of the basalt plain. Volcanic eruptions and then, in their long ongoing aftermath, colonial violations, depravities, and worse. There are still stories told in the Wadawurrung community about those deep-time eruptions of the old volcanoes: the Yawangis (the YouYangs), Buninyong (a suburb of Ballarat), Moriac (fast becoming a suburb of Geelong) and Loolarrungoolak (these days a wind farm on a hill just north of Birregurra but renamed long ago for the Hobart lawyer and land speculator Joseph Tice Gellibrand), not to mention the comparably modern colonial eruptions brought by Messrs Batman, Fawkner, Fyans, Smythe, Roadknight, etc.

There is a saying I like though, which diffuses any false or anxious claims about who qualifies, and who doesn't, as a local around here. Typically such definitions are all about the length of time spent in a region, the *chronos* rather than the *kairos* that makes my Indigenous friends true royalty, but the saying is: *it's not how long that counts, it's how*. Well, let's face it, there are people who have lived their entire life in these parts and don't know a gang-gang from a galah. There are others, whose ancestors are buried far away rather than up close, who can delineate the industrial utility or otherwise of the different grades of quarried local bluestone with the precision of the best wool classers. This is what our little James begins to teach us as he strides out fearlessly into the paddocks. The cyclic quality of time-in-a-place. That Greek word *kairos* is all about quality of time, rather than quantity or duration. Unlike *chronos*, *kairos* is actually more about *timing* than time. Timing, as in the hare scampering over the hospital rise. My brother being there to notice. Timing, like little James Day scampering over what he doesn't even know is his complex ancestral ground.

This is the timing-truth of music, of a poem, the timing beyond word counts or harvest tallies, the timing of rain. Rainbows are of course absolutely suffused with *kairos*, and the blunt edge of the watergaw only emphasises this further. It is like watching a thing achieving itself, a thing failing and succeeding at the same time, a bright exciting thing but a dying thing, a thing half made, in process. Yes, it is like watching a place. Being in a place. Being a place. My great great people's bones lie composting in the ground, just as my boy goes out from us, becoming himself. When MacDiarmid's father gave him that *wild look* he also gave him a new language. Shedding English like a husk the poet took on the challenge of inhabiting the sound of the ground he'd been given. A grounding in truth.

I have been writing in English all my life but in my desire to shed my own local *foolish licht* I have also, for over thirty years now, been slowly learning and absorbing Wadawurrung. Which is the same as slowly learning and absorbing place. My clumsy attempts these days sound like here, the sound of our wider area and its peoples, its continuation, abrupt combinations, uncanny augmentations, and tragic brokenness. This 'impure' onomatopoeia of here is itself an arena in which to gather, and the watergaw feels like the sight of it. It is neither merely sweet to see or hear this language, nor redemptive. It's more like a step towards 'transposing the parochial into the planetary', which is how Seamus Heaney described MacDiarmid's art. Whatever the case, it feels like part of an inevitable process of the heartland, the process of our being here, of our time in the place.

> *And I think perhaps at last I know*
> *What your look meant then*

When Dad died his own sounds became animal, a new dawn in the offing. Like MacDiarmid I remember the wild look he gave, but luckily in my case it was also accompanied by the last two words I remember him uttering in my presence. They came in response to the nurse's offer of morphine, which I had agreed she should give to him. *Natural pain,* Dad said, looking at me as if I were some kind of criminal. Despite how confronting this was at the time I was proud that he said that, and have been ever since. After that, if I ever asked him anything in the few days he had left, all I remember hearing in response were the magpies outside his window. The parrwang opera. That's 'parrwang' by the way, with a decidedly Sicilian rolling of the rrrr's.

Summer on the Painkalac

I swim around the riverbends with a childhood friend. The water is fresh but ancient, silken, sepia, then golden when catching the western light. It holds a mirror under our chins as we breaststroke and talk.

My friend lives these days in Hong Kong, a city that until recent government crackdowns he called the New York of Asia. He looks for patches of good humour in a seriously busy life. He also looks out for cul-de-sacs of nature in his *Blade Runner*-ish city: an Atlas moth on his doorjamb, a Chinese porcupine on the small patch of forested hill behind his apartment building.

As we breaststroke towards the new jetty the shire has recently installed at the wide riverbend, three goggled holidaymakers, evenly spaced across the river, freestyle towards us. They're obviously not past masters at this, as their strokes make quite a foaming splash and racket. By comparison our breaststroke seems almost stealthy.

Something however alerts them to our presence because suddenly, just as we're beginning to divert towards the reeds, their arms stop flailing, their heads spring up, and they remove the goggles from their eyes. They express complete surprise at our presence.

Nature Australia (2019)

'Get back in your lane,' my friend jokes. The holidaymakers scan our faces, computing, assessing us for balances of irony and seriousness; then, laughing, one joins in on the mirth: 'Sorry,' he says, 'I couldn't see the line on the bottom.'

This 'silly season' banter is disarming. They regoggle, we pass on by their commotion, with only the paddocks and the northern sky above the hills ahead of us now. We continue slowly towards the wide riverbend where in the aftermath of the humour swallows begin to duck and weave between our ears. The swallows' movements are expert, balletic, hi-tech. They are the rivertop connoisseurs, we are a visitation from another world, a world of ingenious but often fearfully excessive infrastructure.

Now we are swimming into the middle of the wide-open bend we have both known since we were born. It is more an elbow than a bend actually, as its turn is something like a hand-drawn ninety degrees, but a bend is what we've always called it. A close family friend drowned himself here as an old man to avoid social services. He got up one night in his pyjamas and dressing gown, walked down the little slope from his house behind the pub, folded his nightwear on the bank as he had been taught as an orphaned child, and jumped into the water like the swaggie in the song. Sometimes these days people use this man's name to denote the bend. Butler's bend, they say. But not Butler's elbow. Through his long and quiet life here in town, Joe liked often to wander in for a stout at the pub, so to use elbow would be confusing. For those in the know it would most probably conjure up pictures of him on his stool at the bar. Or behind the bar back in the days when he was publican. So Butler's bend it is.

As we enter the expanse of the bend we see what a fabulous spring it's been for grass. It stands tall in its multishades of green, hale and happy along the far paddock bank. We breaststroke smoothly through the riverskin. We look and discuss modern life as we go – family, politics, work; we are a bit like two banjo frogs twanging along in old and familiar water.

On the southern uncultivated bank to our left, a bank that only recently was rife with boneseed, ragwort and flax-leaf broom, but where now, thanks to a group of local weed-haters, native herbs are aspray and beaded glasswort prospers in its segmented succulence, we watch for the kangaroos who usually browse on that spot at this time of evening. I tell my friend how the roos make me nervous at times, because of the story of old Reg Vowells and his curly retrievers. Back in the day, those soft-mouthed dogs loved nothing better than to swim across to the wild bank and hound the roos around and around amidst the acres of sedge, boobialla, weed and tufted reeds, as if they'd stumbled into some ideal canine video game. Then one day the curly retrievers' fun came to a halt. One of the dogs, in full slobbering chase, was led on by a big buck roo to the river. The roo jumped in and the excited retriever followed, whereupon the buck promptly swivelled about and drowned the dog with a breathtaking deftness.

These days when I am swimming alone and I see the roos right there, first feeding them periscoping their ears as they register my sibilant approach, I imagine the horror of them jumping in beside me. Wincing, I visualise the rip and tear of those prehistoric talons, my pale skin sliced open, my crimson blood spilling into the sepia stream. I sense the atavistic defence of their domain, their mastery of a habitat that I, as a house-dwelling human swimming in boardshorts, am still at least one remove from.

Anyway, today there are no roos down amongst the brookweed tendrils, no threat amongst the palette of glaucous goosefoot and the summer-reddened glasswort. And so we swim smoothly by.

A few minutes beyond Joe's bend we arrive at the pomaderris hut, on the southern bank about halfway along the next straight stretch of river. The Wybelena hill is straight in front of us in the west: pyramidal, ironbark-clad, with these days the town mobile-phone tower perched jagged and grey in a roughly dozed gash at its apex. We can hear the roar of ocean off beyond the hummocks in the south. Treading water I peer through the foliage and point out the hut to my friend. My kids and their friends built it over the quiet winter months, hiding it deep inside a copse of boobialla. It's in a great spot, out of sight of any house or road or pathway of town, unless you bother to leave the land and swim or canoe upstream. What looks like a random pile of bosky bush is actually watertight cladding on a knobbly frame, worked on secretly all through the snakeless time, and now left unattended through the warmer months, when those same sleeping snakes are awake and weaving like Celtic lace in the sun.

I can see that my friend – whose name is John – is happy that the hut exists. Its dishevelled existence seems a long way from the sheep-like tourist traffic of this time of year, when police helicopters hit the sky, and the crowds come like the Peterburgers and Peterburgenkas swarming to their summer dachas in Dostoyevsky's *The Idiot*. John is happy because, despite the naysayers, the kids' hut is proof that free-range childhoods still do occur.

We tread water there for a few minutes, discussing the ins and outs of hut-form, as memories upmerge in us from the depths of our middle-life. We begin to talk of when we were young on this same riverflat, young and 'free' and *brutal*, cheeky and ignorant, but as fit as the roos. We laugh at some of those old events: the daggy new year's eve square dance we boated to upstream, the day we chucked yabbies all over the kitchen walls of some girls we liked (such an elegant way of expressing our attraction!).

Then we swivel in the dark layers of the water, and stretch out, silently kicking our feet down low and spreading our arms to propel us back into the rhythm of our swim.

Now, amongst the pastoral grass on the opposite bank to the hut, the cultivated paddock bank, we notice three welcome swallows perched superlightly on the tender stems. The swallows make a tiny vignette amongst the vertical clusters of the grass. It is like haiku but in three dimensions, like something you might see under a Japanese glaze. The way the swallows are positioned also reminds me of music, of bird-notes on a grass-stave, a small living notation.

I say nothing to John but am filled with pleasure at the scene. Despite everything that is going on in the world, we are but two seeing-bodies in the river after all, ninety per cent immersed, with no visible appendages, only our heads poking out into the clarifying light.

I see John looking at the three grassperching swallows as we go by. The way they sit so nimbly there. 'That's pretty,' he says. In the normal run of life John is never without his mobile phone, just like I'm pretty fond of my iPad. We both agree that these so-called 'devices' are actually much more. They are supercomputers, augmenting our bodies, our memories, fragmenting the ancient constraint of our geographies. Because we are in the river, in only bathers and skin, I am aware that John's normal impulse to grab for his phone and photograph what has pleased him is thwarted. Swimming by his side, I feel that despite the difference in our lives these days, we are already retuning to each other. I almost inhabit my old friend's skin as I intuit his impulse to reach for the impossible technological adjunct.

Still looking at the three welcome swallows as we swim quietly by – their russet throats, their Prussian-blue wings – I say:

'You know the best thing about that scene, John?"

'No, what?'

'It's not on Instagram.'

He smiles, then says, 'I was just thinking what a great photo it would make.'

We leave the swallows behind and swim on. We swim past the small bunch of persistent blackberry bushes that I've been checking regularly for the annual harvest. The flower has just turned to hard budding fruit, so it shouldn't be long. We swim past the slowly dying riverflat redgums where the old kangaroos, or 'go-im', as they were once called in these parts, seek the morning shade on particularly Moolacenic summer days. We swim past the stately black ironbarks at the base of the Wybelena hill, which, despite still wearing the char from the 1983 bushfires, look as if they've lived forever. Perhaps they have. In the past the ngangahook was possibly used by the Wadawurrung as a sepulchre tree. When local squatters like my own ancestors defined the pastoral lease around here during the nineteenth-century land grab, they named the lease with that word but left off the glottal *ng* sound at the beginning. The trees, the place, the river, the sea, were all now being looked at with faraway eyes, the sounds they made were heard with different ears, named with a different configuration of the mouth, tongue and throat. With a European alphabet. Beginning with *a*.

We swim into the ngangahook shadows and rest for a time, chatting. Like when we were kids we don't talk about the trees. We joke, make each other laugh, and comment on the houses crowding the eastern hill-lines of the town.

Finally we turn and swim back the way we came. It's strange how, when you're breaststroking along at water level, some stretches of the river seem to be flowing uphill and some downhill. The stretch flowing south back out of the ironbarks seems to be going up and the stretch that runs back past the hut seems to be going down. How does that work? No matter how many times my mariner friends explain it to me I'll never understand. All I know is that illusions are everywhere in the landscapes of water, and that fact alone has always made them somehow talismanic to me. The imaginative world never exists in itself, but always as a collaboration with our senses, and with mood and feeling.

When we get back to the wide-open water of Butler's bend, we see that, while we've been upstream, three humans have taken up positions on the new shire jetty on the town bank. Three people: one man, two women. The man is dressed in a rather debonair fashion: light linen jacket, shoes with heels, a summer trilby. The women are also looking fine. One of them films with her phone as the other two sit on the picnic rug they have lain over the jetty planks, clinking their champagne glasses in a festive new-year mood. In that moment the newfangled shire jetty is a celebratory jetty, and I make a mental note. The thing is, when the jetty was built a few of us who live with the river as a store of defragmentation and joy, and who want the riverbank to remain 'natural', decried the jetty as unnecessary, an excess, an environmental tautology.

John and I swim along a little more self-consciously now, like a couple of Top End crocs with the potential to break the happy tourist moment on the new jetty.

But no, the voice of the woman with the phone splits the air. 'Good evening!' she calls, glancing at us out of the corner of her eye while continuing to train the screen on her friends. Her words ring out across the water.

'Hello,' John says in bass response, from our stealthy level in the wet brown water.

And then, perhaps because I'd mentioned Instagram to John upstream, and therefore had the phone issue rattling about somewhere in my mind, I couldn't help myself.

In suddenly pointed yet quite affable cheer, with the jetty-three still clinking their champagne glasses and the filming woman capturing it all on her supercomputer held at arm's length, I call out cheekily: 'What do you think would happen if you weren't filming that?'

The woman with the phone is surprised. She pauses, factoring everything in. Even in the soft evening light I can see her face cogitating. I want to say then that it's not because I don't battle my own digital urges that I've asked the question. No, it's just that in the free motion of the river the words came flowing out of me before I could throw up a weir.

The river waits. How will this turn? I wonder.

Eventually I notice her face relax. The question draws closer to its answer. What would happen if she stopped filming her happy moment with her friends? Opening her arms wide, she finally replies: 'Well, it wouldn't exist!'

What I say next is not exactly true but because of her good cheer I call it out anyway. 'That's what I thought you'd say.'

Of course that wasn't actually what I thought she'd say, but something in me did think that that was what she may, somewhere in the currents of her being, actually suspect. Or fear. It's likely too that from time to time my own feet in the river have given a little extra scissor kick at the thought that if all this wasn't recorded, edited, posted or published, it simply wouldn't exist.

Anyway, now that we'd come this far and had enough ebullience to communicate as strangers across the unifying river, I took an even bigger gamble and said: 'Well. It puts a new spin on Descartes, doesn't it.'

The mind is as quick as any galaxial beam. I had decided, in the time it takes a 'go-im' to drown a dog, or a swallow to land on a grass stem, to make the quite unlikely move of bringing the French philosopher into it. Looking back, I suspect this may have been partly because the woman was, either consciously or unconsciously, referring in her phrasing to his most famous maxim, but it was also because I had decided that it wouldn't matter in the end if a bunch of visitors on the jetty had no idea who Descartes was or whether or not they thought I was barking mad. Perhaps though, such a decision had something more to do with the playful confidence we are afforded by the gravity-free zone of river swimming.

So yes. 'Well. It puts a new spin on Descartes, doesn't it,' I said.

The woman holding the supercomputer looked nonplussed at first, but before she could put words to her disorientation it was the dapper man in the summer trilby and cream linen jacket who took up the baton. He saved the moment from veering flat, he deepened the open riverbend even further. Laughing, with champagne glass in hand, and nodding in acknowledgement, he said, 'Yes, yes, I *film* therefore I am!'

My smile spread easily above the river. The woman with the super-computer seemed to relax again then too, and even to understand, as if some distant undergraduate memory had been jogged. It was the same with John. He remembered as well.

But then the dapper man went one better and managed to improve upon his initial response.

'No, no,' he cried, triumphant and full of panache, '*iPhone* therefore I am!'

We continued on our way then and the man wished us a lovely evening and thanked us for decorating what was already for him a happy scene. We continued on beyond Joe's bend, heading due south, finding our way back into the always uphill-seeming home stretch of the river. We were two childhood friends breaststroking in sync, past the lemon-scented gum where the landrail lives, past the striated stumps of the original jetty site of yore, where we used to fish on baking timbers as small children in the 1970s, in the days before we knew any of the ancient local names for things, let alone what the word tautology meant.

Eventually we arrived back at the river-rope, which hangs from a battle-scarred manna gum opposite the Carrolls' old house. A big tiger snake's been living in the bushes there since just before Marg Carroll died, so we know to give it a wide berth. I have swum with the snake in the river there though, and so have my children. Its name is 'kaan'. Or 'kangalang'. I tell John how when a new resident put up handmade texta-drawn signs alerting visitors to the snake it had the happy effect of keeping people away from the river. An old-fashioned quiet had temporarily returned. Kaan and us were free to swim in peace. Even fear can sometimes have wonderful consequences.

John and I stopped just there but rather than climbing out and swinging from the rope like we might have done once, we treaded water and peered into the opposite bank, where over the previous few weeks I'd watched a white guano nest being secretly fashioned amongst the boobialla branches by a willie wagtail couple. *There*, I whispered to John, nodding my head but not wanting to point in case anyone walking by on the river road might see me and be alerted to the nest. John peered in the direction and then we both could see the female wagtail, the thin white markings of her glossy black brows, sitting snug but wary in her pottery nest.

I was keen to look but not to linger, to observe the nest but to move slowly by, so as not to distress the mother bird unnecessarily on her eggs. John was more inquisitive. Because he lives a long way away nowadays and was only visiting his family home for the new year, he hadn't seen the nest being constructed like I had. Thus he was enchanted, and naturally super curious. He veered off on a slow diagonal towards the musty aqueous shadows of the boobialla fronds.

By this stage I'd gone on ahead a bit, and was quietly willing him to realign to the centre of the river and to come on up beside me and swim on. I didn't want to say anything though, I wanted him to sum it all up for himself. I was confident he would. John's father Hec had been a great champion of the river birds when we were young, a real classic twitcher complete with binoculars and stats. I felt sure that the son of Hec wouldn't trespass much further.

And so it went. Once again two old friends were tuned in by the river and *voilà!*, John veered away from the tableau of nest and frond, tree and stream, mother and child. He stroked his way back towards me. Then, with our chins resting on the soft ledge of the rivertop, we swam on side by side for the last little stretch we had remaining.

Finally approaching the spot under the pines where we'd begun our swim an hour or so earlier, we caught sight of John's sister and her farmer-husband walking along the river road. John had told me earlier that he was expecting them. They were coming down for the new-year celebrations from their grape farm in northern Victoria.

'G'day,' we called.

'G'day,' they replied.

'Have you done a lap?' his sister Anne called then, with smiling ironic eyes, as if a lap of such an intricately curling thing as our eely river would ever be possible.

John and I chuckled, causing micro-flurries of humour in the stream. Then I saw the insignia of a familiar football team on John's sister's farmer-husband's cap. Immediately I made a jovial remark across the water, as if to say: despite how things may have changed around here and in the world at large, despite the rise in the price of everything and the gap between rich and poor, and how that means the old town seems at times to have been invaded by cold fish and stressy gentry, despite the fact that barely known French philosophers are these days being discussed openly from the centre across to the edges of the stream, we still know how to extend a down-to-earth gum branch of camaraderie.

A half-shouted conversation thus ensued, about John's brother-in-law's footy team, the season just gone, the season ahead, me in the river, he on the bank, moving us along towards the end of our swim. Though he didn't have a loudhailer we were I suppose a little like a rower and his coach, calling across the divide between water and land. It was fun, and we seemed to agree on the important things.

Suddenly then, before we knew it, John and I had arrived back at our starting point. Suddenly too we'd emerged from the waters and were standing upright in the somehow less rarefied and certainly cooler air of normal life.

John's sister and her farmer-husband came over and shook our hands warmly by way of saying an official hello. Perhaps, if you were watching all this from a distance, you might have imagined this shaking of our hands as a form of congratulations for some great river swim John and I had just completed. We had swum the English Channel, hadn't we? We had forded the wild Orinoco. Surely we had braved the eye of the needle and crossed Bass Strait?

No, we had merely performed ordinary feats in familiar summer waters. We had swum our way back into the magic of our childhood river. As one year was finishing and a new one beginning we had managed not to drown in nostalgia. We had allowed ourselves instead to be carried side by side in the old current, letting the place and its multi-storied spirit touch our skin. We had refreshed the past to use as ballast for the future. We had allowed the river, for an hour or so, to retune our receptors and detune our limbs. Temporarily at least it had washed away what ails us all, the glary politicking on dry land, our click & swipe addictions, all the unnecessary distance we put between one another.

As I walked back to my house I thought of that willie wagtail on its pottery nest and the old Wadawurrung name flew into my mind. 'Yellpillup'. The tail wags for sure, but that alone could never describe the whole bird.

The Colours of the Ground

'Men with orange shovels
Arrive at the so-called "dawn of life"'
Peter Minter

'the smell of the road'
Marcel Proust, as translated by Lydia Davis

I

It was just a moment, a single moment, but it contained so much. The bubbly little Getz in front of me was definitively, synthetically red. It seemed fast too, and intent, so I got a surprise when at the end of the overtaking turn-out it stopped almost to a complete halt so that I could go by. I was not in any mood of urgency or impatience, I had not been harassing it to go faster, I'd been thinking of things other than the road I was on.

The red Getz left me no choice though so I veered around it, accelerating, and shot clear to the north-east.

Rounding the bend where the road pulls further away from the ocean, and where I always peer left through the trees to catch a glimpse of the defunct Alcoa coalmine that used to spew its toxins into the Anglesea River, I saw new roadwork speed-limit signs, like bullseyes in front of me: **40**, they said. Roadwork ahead.

Every year here on the Great Ocean Road, after the long community winter, we are inundated with vehicular steel, a longer ribbon

Cordite magazine (2020)

of reflective glare. Thanks to the deadly efficacy of the recently constructed Geelong Ring Road, more and more cars are coming out of a heated-up Melbourne towards us. Understandably so. Spring in these parts is now not only the customary season for orchids and ripening glasswort, but also for roadwork, by way of preparation for the upcoming wear and tear. As birds nest and the wattle blossom recedes into the rustier tints of bush and parrot peas, the VicRoads crews mend, patch, and lay treacly tarmac. At a pinch, and if it didn't stink so much, the freshly laid bitumen could remind me of the glossy blue-black of the male satin bowerbird that spends the winter months in our garden. Alas, the road's acrid reek wafts off infernal machines. I am always impressed by how the workers never seem to even flinch. They wear ear muffs but not masks. They guzzle polymers and surfactants. They even lop overhanging tea-tree in full flower. Amazing what we can get used to. But like all of us, they've got accounts to pay, bills that pile up.

As I approached in the car I saw that this time the road crew were multi-tasking, both laying the new paste of bitumen *and* widening the carriageway. I looked out my driver's side window at a visual chaos: men and women in hi-vis bibs, heavy machinery at modernist angles, disrupted ground.

It was the disrupted ground that most caught my eye, because of its colour. In piles and heaps in the foreground of the trees, vivid earth lay about amongst the machines and the workers in bibs. The piles and heaps of earth were bright orange, or blood-orange, or orange-red, or ochre-red, or rose-gold; moist clumps and sods of coloured ground exposed now that the tourist-pummelled macadam had been machined up.

The reason for the either/or imprecision of my colour list is threefold. Firstly, the earth's colours always seem to escape the capture-language and spectral grids we lay upon them. This is partly because there is something essentially kinetic and alive in organic colour that no single word can entrain. In their constant dialogue with the light, the earth's colours exist in time as well as space.

The second reason is related to the way descriptive language so often springs from a seed of comparison and simile. Take 'orange', for instance, a word whose derivation goes right back through France, Italy and Persia to the Sanskrit. It is the name of a particular citrus fruit, of course, but it has actually only been used as a colour-word in English since the early 16th century. So what were all the orange-like things called before that? Even now, unless 'orange' is used as a noun it often fails to describe all the many and subtle varieties of what it is attempting to describe.

The third reason for the inexactness of my list is that I've never actually known the right name for the unmistakably dominant pigment of the coastal landscape in my part of the world. It is a pigment well evident in the ocean cliffs and in the immediate hinterland, also on the exposed road cuttings along the shore, and on the unsealed off-roads, roads that are much loved locally because they are generally quiet, but also because of the hue of the gravel with which they are covered.

This gravel is sometimes called Barrabool gravel, 'Barrabool' being our old shire name, before we were eventually swallowed up during the Jeff Kennett years by the corporate muzak of the 'Surf Coast' supershire. As it turns out though, the word 'Barrabool' only confuses the question of what might be the right name of the local pigment, for it is a Wadawurrung word co-opted by white settlers, an ancient word, not for ochre or pipeclay, or any such brightness of the ground, but possibly for oyster.

These days, amongst laconic earthmovers, local plumbers, landscape gardeners and other 'soul-surfer' tradies, the ground – or at least the part of it that manifests in the surface gravel of the back roads – is more commonly known as Gherang gravel. 'Gherang' is one of the Wadawurrung words for the yellow-tailed black cockatoo. It's also the twangy place name of a small area around Lake Gherang Gherang, a rather secluded patchwork of farms and forest near where the controversial Cheshire convict William Buckley sighted a bunyip that scared the living daylights out of him back in the early 1800s.

Gherang is also the area where the gravel pits that supply the local road surfaces began their operations in the early 1900s.

In the 1920s, at the same time as the gravel pits at Gherang were beginning to prosper (they even had their own railway siding back then), there was a jarosite mine just a few miles further south towards the ocean, in the ironbark basin between Bells Beach and Point Addis. As I approached the roadworks, I was driving right between the still working gravel pits and the redundant site of the jarosite mine. 'The old paint mine,' as it is sometimes called locally, was an ambitious but ultimately unsuccessful venture started by a geologist and weekend prospector named George Affleck, who, when scouting around the beach at Point Addis one day, noticed jarosite-rich beds up to three metres thick in the cliffs. After a little bit more investigation, and figuring there was a buck to be made from mining the cliffs for the manufacture of a red oxide-based paint, he teamed up with a financier and a chemist, took a crown lease of more than 200 acres of the ironbark basin abutting the coast, and for a time sold the pigment to the Victorian Railways, which used it to paint their once famous 'red rattler' trains. So before our intricate and largely forgotten local Otway railway network was decommissioned to make way for the independence and convenience of motor cars and trucks, the small trains that would wend their way along the saddle of Moriac, Layard, Gherang, Wormbete and Wensleydale were painted in predominantly endemic tones.

Affleck's jarosite mine came to an abrupt close as the Great Depression kicked in, but what is interesting is how he had attempted to capitalise on the quality of the ground that had been so prized by Aboriginal people for millennia. Notwithstanding the economic downturn of the Depression, and the critical lack of freshwater on the site of his mine, the term he used to describe the mineral he wanted to cash in on – 'jarosite' – can perhaps give us a clue as to a deeper reason why his venture was ultimately unsustainable. What interests me is how this geological term itself fails to do justice to the local material it names, very much the same material that was exposed amongst the hi-vis and machinery as I drove by on that otherwise unremarkable day.

A dictionary in common use in George Affleck's day, the *Century Dictionary*, defines 'jarosite' as 'a native hydrous sulphate of iron and potassium, occurring in ochre-yellow rhombohedral crystals, and also in granular masses'. It's interesting though that the rather generic suffix of the word – 'ite' – often serves to transform a noun into an adjective in order to denote some kind of connection or belonging to a place or thing, as in 'Israelite', or 'Carmelite'. In the case of 'jarosite' the suffix turns out to connect the mineral to a specific area in Almerian Spain, the Barranco del *Jaroso*. So 'jarosite' the word is *of* the Barranco del Jaroso, on the shores of the western Mediterranean. It goes without saying then that 'jarosite' is certainly not a precise, let alone an autochthonous descriptor for the endemic brightness of our local ground here on the edge of the Eastern Otways in southern Australia.

For millennia before the word 'jarosite' was ever uttered on these shores, the pigments of the littoral had been ritually used by the Wadawurrung and their neighbours on-country, up-country, and beyond. It had been traded along ancient routes as far north as the Murray River, and probably further. I've spoken to knowledgeable elders from the Wadawurrung, and I've also combed the tragically fragmented archives of the remnant language of the region in search of the original word, or words, for the pigment. I've also run through the exotic names of the European paintbox, in search of the right term. Burnt sienna and raw umber, these are two that come to mind straight off the top. Which, once again, takes us to other faraway geographies, 'sienna' coming from the Italian *terri di Sienna*, or 'earth of Siena', and Umber from *terra di ombra*, 'earth of shadow', with its topographic implication of 'earth of Umbria'.

So it's frustrating. There would once have been exact local words for this vivid earth I've been walking on and dreaming about all my life. Back when my ancestors arrived in the area from Ireland and Sicily in 1841, it was treasured by the Wadawurrung as a currency of significance beyond the value of diamonds.

For the time being, however, and with much Wadawurrung language reconstruction continuing apace, we can't be exactly sure what the right term is. There's a word collected by the early colonial Protector of Aborigines, William Thomas, in the vicinity of Bacchus Marsh in the 1840s: 'nyooroo nyooroo', meaning ochre or paint. And there's 'paapool', or 'paapul', meaning chalk, or mud, or pipeclay, collected also by Thomas in the Melbourne area, denoting a lighter-coloured hue. But what was the term here amongst the Turaltja clan of the south-western Wadawurrung littoral? Through talking to local artists who use this local dirt for renders and pigments I know that, like anything of substantial beauty, the colour I am thinking about is not just one thing, or in this case one tint, hue or tone.

From the Gherang gravel pits on the north side of the Great Ocean Road to the 'jarosite' beds between Bells Beach and Point Addis on the south, there is a range of earths that make up this complex local brightness. Amongst the ochry tones, for instance, is the substance known as kaolin, or china clay, a pale talc-like material whose elastic properties are useful for anything from the making of cosmetics and porcelain to the sealing of farm dams. The word 'kaolin' comes from the Jiangxi province of China, a region famous for its porcelain. My brother Peter, an artist who often works with the local clays and pigments, shows me how when you hold this kaolin in your fingers you can't help but notice its beautiful pliability, its feather-like softness, and the smoothing effect it has on the skin. You also can't help but be fascinated with the way it mixes with and marbles the ochre tones around it.

When the Gherang gravel is first laid out on the roads it has a deep and rich reddishness that over time fades towards the pale tones of the kaolin (or perhaps 'Jiangxi-ite'!) it lives with. They are quite literally bedfellows, perhaps nyooroo nyooroo and paapool side by side. Therein lies our locally specific spectrum. This is variegated earth we are talking about, hybrid ground, as complex and rhythmically integrated as the rituals of the Wadawurrung in which the pigments play a central part.

II

As I drove past the roadworks that day, I wondered if any of the workers standing by the machines (most of whom presumably lived in Geelong and surrounds, if not in this specific coastal area) had been struck by the colour of the ground as they exposed it from under the stiff black icing of tar. In spring morning light, after a long Bass Strait winter, and with the twinkling leaves of messmates behind, they would have had to be visually impaired, or severely preoccupied, not to have registered the vividness of the colour, at least in the privacy of their own thoughts.

The mind plays its games though. As we dip our oar in the water it ceases to be straight. I once dreamt of the bitumen of one of my favourite local roads being rolled back like a hallway runner for two or three miles along the riverflat here in the place the Wadawurrung call Mangowak. In my dream the earth under the road was on full display again, the soil sighing under the sky like an innocent person just freed from jail. The dream finished with a smile for the knowledge that it wouldn't be long before the grubs and ants and soily macro-invertebrates reappeared and began to thrive.

But as I drove past the roadworks and the clumps of exposed ground, I was reminded not only of that dream of the road peeling back but also of the way the world becomes untethered from our soundings of it. So the local colour drifts up into the forefront of my mind, my dream, my imagination, but only as a visual phenomenon somehow adjacent to language, not as something that I have the tools to translate, or describe. Is this then pure psychogeography? I wondered. Or does it speak ironically of the way in which long-ago poets like Mallarmé and Rimbaud unhooked language from the drudgery of our expectations, untethering words from the objects they were conventionally meant to describe? Whatever the case, the local colour as I experience it, the ground under my feet, teems with inaccurate flailing sounds. Opposites of the *mot juste*. Remember my list: 'bright orange, or blood-orange, or orange-red, or ochre-red, or rose-gold'. The place these words are attempting to capture, or to be emissaries of, has similarities to other landscapes of other parts of the earth, other countries and their geologies, even to other planets and moons (indeed, jarosite has been discovered on Mars), but they are only that, similarities. Sure they are kin within the parameters of a somatic and networked concept like Gaia but, like myself and my brother, they are not the same.

I believe this constant 'missing' of our language makes us even more vulnerable than we already are in a Moolacenic climate. We feel the need to ameliorate the situation, if not to outright revolutionise it. Out with 'jarosite' and the paint mine, and in with ...?

This is the silence that as a nation we are only just beginning to properly hear.

As I drove off down the road past the piles and exposed heaps of *orange-blood-red-rose-gold-ochre-jaroso-kaolin-jiangxiite-barrabool-foxhued-nyooroo-nyooroo-papool-paapul-jarosite*, I had one last unbidden thought upmerge in my mind. I was reminded not only of my dream of the rolled-back tarmac, not only of the way we've unleashed this teeming vacuum of language (at the same time as our industrial colony has gone about de-teeming the biota and landscape), but also of a thinker I'd been becoming increasingly annoyed by in the previous few days, the Ancient Greek philosopher Diogenes of Sinope.

When it came to language, Diogenes himself was a minimalist. He was the master of the Greek *chreiai*, or one-liner. He is sometimes known as Diogenes the Cynic, due to the fact that he was a founder of the Cynical school of philosophy in Ancient Greece. My interest in him had been initially pricked by how he prized frugality, or *euteleia*, both in lifestyle and in thought, and also by how he was something akin to an Ancient Greek hobo-poet, living rough on the pale streets of Athens after being exiled from his native Sinope (in current-day Turkey) for, amongst other things, debasement of the currency. But why, I now asked, had he suddenly sprung into my mind in direct response to the uncovering of my local ground?

In Athens, Diogenes snubbed his nose at the conventions, excesses and illusions of the society around him. He often slept in a ceramic barrel on the street. He was famous, among other things, for rebellious and humorous acts, like eating food loudly during Socrates lectures, and telling Alexander the Great off for blocking the sunlight when he came to visit him in his barrel. But during his lifetime he was perhaps most famous for requesting that his body be simply tossed over the city wall when he died, for the beasts to devour. This attitude was radical then, and perhaps would be even more so now. Indeed, I think it holds the key to why, after my initial fascination, Diogenes had become so downright annoying to me. Which also, as it turns out, could explain why he came to mind as I drove by the roadworks in my car.

The question of why the word 'jarosite' won't satisfy as a term describing our local ground is for me not one of mere nomenclature or linguistics, but of metaphysics, of ceremony and ritual. Sure, jarosite, kaolin, and the rest, can suffice in a functional sense as commonly agreed upon terms, or repeating sonic agreements, but not in a deeper, more psycho-geological sense that will connect to the landscape of my/our dreams. A philosopher who claims then to have no regard for how spiritually fragile humans are, how we are peltless, clawless and often clueless in the face of the mystery of death, will likewise have no understanding of why we need ceremony and ritual to cope with that vulnerability, and why the quality of certain substances of the ground where we have lived and loved would become critically important to such ceremony and ritual. A man who insouciantly requests that his corpse be thrown over the city wall, even if he is just being an egoic provocateur, would, within the confines of that role he has defined for himself, most probably scoff at the recent increase of our yearning to connect with the hydrosonic, terraphonic language of the First Peoples of this land.

For myself this yearning began as a teenager and over the last twenty years or so it has become not just a key issue of my writing life, but of my life more generally. I realise now, thanks in part to the unlikely trigger provided by those roadworks last spring, that it is a yearning that actually springs from a place beyond ideas of justice, reparation, mending, preparation, responsibility or ethics. It concerns an issue that, in an Enlightenment sense, defies such rational or 'worthy' motivations. But it is a human and creaturely yearning that cannot itself be tarmacked over. Despite Diogenes the Cynic and his anarchic bitumen-thinking, I am not embarrassed to admit to my need for a richly variegated and ceremonial road to travel on. Sure, it will be messy, marbled, striated, smelly, rutted, puddled, abrasive and dusty. It will wear out our expensive chariots of steel and slow down our facile momentum. But it will be bright, vivid, recursive, season-sensitive and full of life. Well over 200 years after the European invasion of this continent, and all the sounds and sights that have been covered over as a result of it, it seems the only kind of road that will take us home.

Whoo-hoo Thinking

1.
Whoo-hoo

2.
Whoo-hoo

3.
It is strong but with soft acoustic edges, a voice with the breath of a creature grown in high tree hollows.

4.
The Powerful Owl, the thought of it roosting high in its demesne. The thought of violence, the lethal grip of its talons, stripping, tearing a ringtail possum, gorging and disgorging.

5.
It is also known to hunt wallabies.

6.
Capture – to take into one's possession or control by force – mid-16 century French, from the Latin *captura*, from *capt* – seized, taken.

Meanjin (2021)

7.
Its eyes bore into me, sharp as talons.

8.
Is this solace or terror? Or the way they coincide?

9.
Not worn-out castles but composting tree hollows. I'm looking for living royalty, a sense of nobility and dignity, not undeserved privilege. Apolitical power on my doorstep.

10.
Beyond the riverflat.

11.
Up into the bush, along a moonlit path.

12.
In mid-air, the mid-air ballet of the canopies of midnight. The owl, wings out, for balance, grasping the possum whose feet are also out, but in terror, and its ringtail too. White curl against strong midnight. Caught in the camera flash of my eyes.

13.
The Powerful Owl is uncompliant.

14.
Our scale of importance in the context of the landscape can only be measured against the scale of eternity. We are tiny moments in the deep *Whoo-hoo*.

15.
'The heart of standing is you cannot fly.'
William Empson

16.
Under its spell all my thoughts are like possums seized in its grip.

17.
It is the largest owl in Australia. For it to take up lodging in your mind you must make room for it.

18.
Once I took a group of people interested in writing out into the *Whoo-hoo* and they came back silent. With empty notebooks.

19.
Another time I took a friend who had just lost his father.

20.
My friend and I recorded 4 minutes and 33 seconds of 'silence' in the *Whoo-hoo*. It was all about the bird we did not hear, the father that was no longer there.

21.
Given its hunting range, for me to accommodate the Powerful Owl in my thinking and feeling means that my head has to be at least 1000 hectares wide. It flies beyond bone and arterial structure, flies nightly, silently, into the patternlands of myth.

22.
Small spaces are important too. Tree hollows for instance. Where the owls dream through the daytime, where they lay their eggs in early winter, where they are first born into moonlight.

23.
Small spaces are born of slow time. Tree hollows are more frequent in forests of large old trees.

24.
Any *Whoo-hoo* thinking I do is hollow-dependent.

25.
Hollows can be husks of old ideas.

26.

By stealing old habitats we simplify the land. Science, despite its aversion to emotion, the subjective, and the pejorative, might even call it *extreme simplification*.

27.

Make sure to leave hollows in your life. It's almost impossible to find nourishment without finding a space at the very heart of things.

28.

I write to another friend who is grieving – in this case the loss of his wife – to tell him the largest, most epic and compelling creature I know needs a hollow to be born, and thereafter to flourish. A dark hollow at the centre of things can house a god in high manger.

29.

Without these dark hollows the world would be entirely bungaloid. A state that will not last for long.

30.

Sometimes the old-growth forest of grief can make you feel terribly vulnerable, like a possum caught in talons. Mantled by a fluttering gory pinion.

31.

The Powerful Owl stands up to well over half a metre tall.

32.

It is speckled with feathered scales of moonlight-white and soily sepia.

33.

It roosts in high trees above the rusty pomaderris bushes, otherwise known as the hazel bush, which in turn overhangs the speckled thrush.

34.
In far-off Scotland, Robbie Burns sang in his autumn-song 'Now Westlin Winds': 'the hazel bush o'erhangs the thrush'. Burns left a hollow in his song for the Powerful Owl to roost and call.

35.
The song within the song, the *Whoo-hoo* forest between the human notes.

36.
Darkness hides in the daytime, as does the owl. But does darkness also dream, of other darknesses? Or does it lie there, under the fallen mossed spar or deep under stones, cooler and stiller than a life in exposure, and not even waiting or wanting, and certainly not yearning, for the kinship of nightfall?[1]

37.
The days leading in to the winter solstice are an unnamed micro-season. In its still hush, generated by a world leaning more towards darkness than light, the mycelium floor of the *Whoo-hoo* monarchy is sprung and quietly teeming. Under the overhangs and beneath the high hollow and boughs on which the talons rest, the solstice-season blossoms into gill, capulet and woodfrill.

38.
Within this unnamed season there is yet another season without a name: the bolting days of high southerlies that whisk the treetops and quiet the owl. I picture the huddling, the deep coverage. As roots clutch the gully soil and cling to the slopesides.

39.
When the agitation of the wind passes, the still night-depth underneath the surface returns. We stand. Ear becomes lens. There it is, the code of entry, the biophonous portal, the deep breathed

---

1 'God becomes a preoccupation in the landscape more easily than in the town.'
Christopher Neve

Whoo-hoo. It is as if the wind shared its purpose, as if its call is built from the wind that has blown onto land from the ocean.

40.
A song battery recharged.

41.
Wisdom or terror, what does the owl represent to you?

42.
Still, and stealthily, it comes, and then *clutch*! And *snap*!

43.
No wonder the possum takes up lodging from time to time in the roof of our house.

44.
Science uses mist-nets to catch *Ninox strenua*. It also uses recorded calls as baits. To tag the royal personage, ostensibly to protect the monarchy, but also to democratise.

45.
The owls are easily caught at first but soon the mist-nets are empty. The nets fill haplessly, and ironically, with nothing but forest mist.

46.
The Powerful Owl remembers.

47.
Thought there was something not quite right about those calls.

48.
The scientists are *mist*-ified.

49.
The owl-range remains a slurry of estimates; in other words a *mist*-ery.

50.

In the aftermath of the 4 minutes and 33 seconds of silence for the father of my friend, I begin to imagine how the *Whoo-hoo* ghosts his passing on.

51.

In its own quiet way my friend's father's life was epic; but now it is more so.

52.

Now his spirit consorts with the Powerful Owl.

53.

When composer John Cage wrote his 'silent sonata' in 1952 – 4 minutes and 33 seconds of silence scored in three movements and performed for the first time by David Tudor in the Maverick Hall amongst the forests of the Catskill Mountains – it seemed to open a two-way door, or hatch, to the future and to hidden histories of the past. It lay down a sonic welcome mat for everything that was not there; or rather, everything we'd ceased to hear, and therefore forgotten to imagine.[2]

54.

Whoo-hoo, Whoo-hoo

55.

I wonder: how many o's actually describe the owl's call? 2 & 2? 4 & 4? Or more?

56.

oo oo

57.

oooo oooo

---

2 'Slowly, we have the feeling we are getting nowhere. That is a pleasure which will continue.' John Cage, 'Lecture on Nothing', *Silence*, 119

58.
ooooooooo ooooooooo

59.
Or is 'o' the wrong sound – does the owl possess its own vowel?

60.
At the time of writing this there are 184 recorded versions of 4'33"
pinned to the map of Australia on the app created by the Cage Estate.

61.
Plus one 'In Memoriam 4:33' for my father's friend.

62.
Though famous as a musician, John Cage once said that he was
ambivalent about music. He said he found it too predictable. He
preferred to open his apartment window in New York City and listen
to the street.

63.
I stand upon the forest track and listen to the street in the trees.
Ancient taxis under the light of the lunar lamp.

64.
Even something as apparently uniform as traffic is different every day.
Especially ancient traffic.

65.
It is like a drawing turning into a painting, then back again.

66.
Architectural stone returning into the ground.

67.
Those supersoft wings wending through the felt of darkness.

68.
An image in the ear.

69.
Voluminous photosynthetic air surrounds the tree hollows.

70.
The call within it is an inverse fable: not the boy who cried wolf but the owl who cried *Whoo-hoo*.

71.
'Call' is not quite the verb.

72.
Whoo-hoo is its own verb, made up of its own vowels.

73.
We cannot know the exact state of the Powerful Owl's amorousness or whether it is sounding in the same way old village bells were rung in 18th-century French villages.

74.
There were often no official physical markers of the boundaries of those villages – when you could no longer hear the bell you were outside the town.

75.
The *Whoo-hoo* feels out the contours of its range. The ridge above the gully, the way sound moves up and out and over and beyond.

76.
Not so much a *call* as a way of being.

77.
The sound of being there.

78.

In the deep pre-solstice days the *Whoo-hoo* becomes an overture to the still point at the centre of everything.

79.

Sometimes it sounds like the *Whoo-hoo* is full of aqueous breath, sometimes as if it's speaking with its mouth firmly shut.

80.

It is at one and the same time a greeting, a feeling, and a summoning to the svelte quality of darkness.

81.

As if the air is filled with soil.

82.

Seeds begin to grow where the bodies of our loved ones rot and decompose.

83.

Not so much the boy who cried wolf but the vowel of truth.

84.

There is no fake news in this kingdom.

85.

For a long time I was scared of owls. I still am. But now I'm not only scared of them.

86.

When an owl sculpture was erected in our town without consultation I was upset. The bird is not an ornament for retired burghers to play with.

87.

It is a symbol, a potency that our sub-selves understand, even if our hobby-selves have forgotten.

88.
To shape it up in wood like that and plonk it by the road seems a flippancy.

89.
No longer do we agree any more on the matrices of myth.

90.
One person's owl is another person's bollard.

91.
Until we re-enter the kingdom.

92.
Re-entering the kingdom is to re-enter the dreaming, or what W.E.H. Stanner approximated with the term *the everywhen*.

93.
Being outside the kingdom is to remain ensnared in the mist-nets of Western philosophy.

94.
'Philosophy, as the thought of the world, does not appear until reality has completed its formative process, and made itself ready.'[3]

95.
In *the everywhen* the 'formative process' is never completed. The creation of the world is ongoing, just as 'virginity renews itself like the moon'.[4]

96.
I think I know this or that part of the bush – specific places where I have walked all my life – until I am reintroduced to them all over again by a new noticing.

---

3 Hegel wrote that.

4 W.B. Yeats said that.

97.

I can recognise fungi, bark, grass, branch, thrush, stone, sap, wallaby, ephemeral wallaby tracks, creeks both wet and dry, falls both running and bare, and a whole lot more, but still there will be new rejuvenations.

98.

The Powerful Owl, for instance. The way it *Whoo-hoos* above it all.

99.

The way it seems an intermediary of the moon.

100.

Politeness becomes exaggerated in a community existing without a shared philosophy. That common matrix of mythology. We are careful then to not speak directly, unsure as we are of what even our friends and family members might stand up in: their skeleton of belief.

101.

The owl though cannot be too careful. Politeness is another country. In the broad hushed gully of tall standing gums, of greened hollows and charred hollows akin to Notre Dame of Paris, life is simultaneously subtle and direct. The *Whoo-hoo* says it plain.

102.

By this it is our fellow creature. Saying what we often can not. Or will not. Or don't have the language for.

103.

Just as a bud makes a sound when opening, so too do I hear the *Whoo-hoo*

104.

Whoo-hoo

105.
For as long as it still has biological life a place can never be lonely, nor can the weather ever be absent from it. We sometimes feel it to be lonely but it is us, not the country or the weather, that possesses such qualities.

106.
Our unconsciousness of such distinctions makes us dangerous, and capable of devastating the land. The more we edge the land towards lifelessness the more it becomes our tragic form of self expression.

107.
A lack of distinction in our soul begins to bleed into the environment.

108.
We become a leaking chemical, a running dye.

109.
Tree hollows are replaced by hollow estates.

110.
If the *Whoo-hoo* falls silent has it flown away to the moon?

111.
I wonder this sometimes in the space between the v*owels.*

112.
It is a decorative thought, not a genuine fear.

113.
The kind of human filigree that distracts us from the darkness.

114.
The Powerful Owl is powerful, but it could never fly that far.

115.

Yet how on earth can we relinquish our prerogative to imagine and to dream?

116.

Are we not the most powerful owl of all? The most powerful shark, tiger, spider, whale?

117.

Yes, perhaps we are too many things. As if like Zeus we have swallowed the world.

118.

But listening for owls, or owling, can be a lonely activity.[5]

119.

It often requires solitude, and the quality of silence it involves provokes large amounts of introspection, which sometimes can make you gloomy.

120.

Sometimes, when I'm in the middle of the process, I think it's these factors that have caused the owl to become a symbolic battleground in human history, of good and evil, wisdom and terror.

121.

The Ainu of Japan believed that the great owl was a god of plenty, shedding tears of gold and silver over the land.

122.

But why was he crying?

123.

In one ancient Arabian treatise the owl laid two eggs. One held the power to cause hair to fall out, the other held the power to restore it.

---

5 'I remember loving sound before I ever took a music lesson.' John Cage

124.

I stand alone in the gloaming, beside a Notre Dame tree, with dew descending onto my beret and shoulders.

125.

Or I walk out with others, in moonlight, thinking about how pointless human language can seem in the demesne of the Powerful Owl.

126.

We chit and chat, point and gape, speculate and laugh.

127.

We look ahead into decolouring light, we also look to the side of the track, as it rises above and runs alongside the broad creeked gully, allowing us to rise too, to access deepening sightlines through the bigger trees.

128.

We see then through a quilted perspective, and the conversation continues.

129.

People tend to be happy on an adventure, buoyant on a walk in the forest, so someone cracks a joke. Did you hear that they've discovered sound coming from Beethoven's crypt?

130.

I turn, very interested, as if towards the owl.

131.

Yeah, they reckon he's decomposing.

132.

The owlers giggle, splutter, scoff, and as they do I wonder how on earth we will ever hear the *Whoo-hoo.*

133.
It wasn't until the punchline that I realised it was a joke.

134.
Sometimes it is as if human society is forever crossing a bridge that then rots and decays immediately behind us, preventing our return.

135.
But why do I think this way? Surely we don't *return* to the owl, surely it is always there, up ahead, in the future?

136.
Sometimes the *Whoo-hoo* can resemble a heartbeat.

137.
That's also when you hear the o's extend.

138.
oooo oooo

139.
But with their lips shut tight.[6]

140.
No one sees a church more clearly than when it is burning.

141.
Sometimes it is the Notre Dame trees that are chosen by the *Whoo-hoo* as its manger. But mostly it's the slow-rotting and rising trees, the cycle of Sun and Moon in their composted architecture, the natural decomposing of Time.

142.
We notice the uncanny things. How so often we first hear the owl's call at the very moment we have mentioned it. Walking along, one of

---

6 If you can *call* them 'lips'.

us will pause and look from the track through the sightlines of the gums, and say: 'You know this all fits *exactly* with what they say the Powerful Owl likes best. A healthy habitat is a perfect recipe.'

143.
At which point we will hear it. At first like someone making a sound in another room. A heartbeat deep in a chest. Then a hand goes up, an ear is cocked. Our heads all tilt. And we listen strongly.

144.
Or, we pause on the track as someone demonstrates the sound of the *Whoo-hoo* for someone else who hasn't heard it before. And immediately we hear the real thing.

145.
It is then that the o's seem to multiply and become most numerous.

146.
ooooooooo ooooooooo

147.
Or, as we walk along, beginning to doubt whether we will ever hear 'the call' again, we stop to describe these very anecdotes of the uncanny – the synchronicities of owling. Whereupon the owl will begin – *Whoo-hoo*[7]

148.
It is waking up after the sleep of the day. And so are we.

---

7 **Call** (of an animal, especially a bird) make its characteristic cry: *overhead, a skylark called.* • shout out or chant (the steps and figures) to people performing a square dance or country dance. • *Bridge* make (a particular bid) during the auction: *her partner called 6♣.* • *North American informal* claim (a privilege) for oneself, typically by shouting out a particular word or set phrase: *I call first dibs on the bathroom.* • cause (someone) to have a strong urge to choose a particular career or way of life: *he **was called to** the priesthood* | *I think teachers, really good teachers, are called to teach.*

149.
First a gentle *whoo* … No capital letter. It sounds almost like it's coming from round a corner. Then silence.

150.
Then another soft and breathy *whoo*

151.
Then one more, a little louder, before silence again.

152.
We are wide-eyed, entranced by the way what seems like the end (dusk) is always the beginning.

153.
And then – the full owl: frequency, amplitude, timbre, duration.

154.
When I write 'wide-eyed' I can't help but think of the possum and the glider.

155.
It is as if suddenly, in the thrill of listening, we too have become prey to the owl.

156.
Our thrill feels innocent, childlike.[8]

157.
The eyes of possums and also of gliders are often described as innocent.

158.
Perhaps this is because when we see their eyes clearly enough to ascribe them a quality it is when we have blazed a torch in their face.

---

8   'I remember as a child loving all the sounds, even the unprepared ones.' John Cage

159.
Otherwise their eyes are only visible to us as sharp bioluminescent pins in the darkness. Not vulnerable or innocent at all. They share a kinship with phosphorescence, glow-worms and glowing fungi, even the stars.

160.
Just as we do when we come face to face, or ear to *Whoo-hoo*, with the Powerful Owl.

161.
Such is our dominion as an apex maker-predator that this world of the *Whoo-hoo* gives us a pleasurable thrill. But the innocence of this thrill is not the same as when a torch is shone in a possum's face. Unlike them, we feel safe.

162.
Or do we?

163
Still the *Whoo-hoo* has a power over us.

164.
There is a feeling behind our looking, behind our listening, behind this writing. An unresolved ratio of sensory fact to emotional truth.

165.
The Powerful Owl is powerful but nevertheless remains undoctrinaire.[9]

166.
In the Monarchy of *Whoo-hoo*, such contradictions are the sign of life.

---

9 'We cannot doubt that animals both love and practise music. That is evident. But it seems their musical system differs from ours. It is another school.' Erik Satie

167.

The tone of everything is so subdued in the forest. It is almost as if it is covered in a foreign blanket of snow.

168.

But there is no snow here where the *Whoo-hoo* reigns.

169.

Just frequency, amplitude, timbre and duration.

170.

Ratio of place and mind, vision and seer, mass and maker.

171.

Not all or nothing, not one thing or another.

172.

N.B. The birds have not stopped singing and the land is not lost.

173.

Whoo-hoo

Mere Scenery and Poles of Light –
Four Pre-historical Walkers of the Moolacene*

Through a suddenly lit arch in the cave of the mind images of salt-dusted plains open up; winding paths along cliffs torn high above acidic tides; desire-lines scrawling away through serrated uplands and beyond to a tar horizon.

The cave of mind we leave, so dense with bats and thoughts, a subterrain of the senses, has offered us this:

Our two legs, scissors cutting away the dross;

Our feet, padded sensors returned to the earth's slow philology;

Our heart, cradled in its basketry of ribs, sending and receiving prey and game from the brain.

Where the journey begins the aperture widens, the shadows are strong, even the base granite and ironstone beneath us begins to become liquid and rhythmic, to spiritualise, to reappear.

We see a high sky, a knife glare, a space into which formula and intention dissolve. As we go we use a genetic chrysalis as passport and

---

* My neologism. 'Moola' is a Wadawurrung word for shadow, and also a US slang word for money.

Island Magazine (2017)

fuel. The finite earth, with its archival geologies, its climate maps and forest fables, all of these respire through us. Like Zeus, Krishna, like all the carbon gods, we are turned inside out as we breathe.

Inhaling our predicament step by step we let it out again just the same. The things that hold us low, or render us anxious on unaccustomed heights, become perforations, etiolations, so many anachronistic pages left outside in the air.

We walk along a stone synapse of generative recircuitry and perpetual arrival. The wind whispers, information waits, as if for centuries in ironbark glades; or it brushes suddenly up out of the scented garrigue, gathering its knots before it, only to untie the light.

The body, our plastic carrier, is as it should be. But our nursery-landscape isn't. We are forced to see, instead of just looking. We are arriving. En masse. We are always arriving ...

———

My dear Paul,

I am afraid that I am very late in thanking you for sending me your biographical volume, because I am at l'Estaque, the home of the sea-urchins. The copy that you were kind enough to send me landed at Aix and fell into the hands of my impure relatives. They took good care not to mention this to me. They stripped it of its envelope, cut it, went through it in every sense and I was waiting under the harmonious pine tree. – But at last I found out. – I demanded it, and now here I am in possession and reading.

Paul Cézanne to Paul Alexis from l'Estaque,
15 February 1882

Given the romance of his much-fabled outdoor childhood in herb-aceous Provence, where he roamed and grew perceptive as a child, it is tempting to speculate that each of the seemingly hundreds of paintings Paul Cézanne did of the sea at l'Estaque – the small village some thirty kilometres from Aix where his mother rented a fisherman's cottage – is a sentimental return, a portal through trees and oblique rooflines to the hackneyed peace of blue water.

The very image of the sea in Cézanne's l'Estaque pictures can seem created to balance the tight whorl of schizothymia he was commonly struck by as an adult. Each painted biome of piney hill and each chalky blue bay, executed from the many different prospects among the slopes above the village, can be felt as a private absolution, a breathing-out, a sigh of relief on behalf of a deeply rooted but troubled local boy.

The fact is, however, that Cézanne was not a cathartic artist. And though at times he could be wistful in his correspondence – especially near the end when the penny of his art finally dropped for the younger generations – in his pictures he was a sworn enemy of pictorial nostalgia and a relentless warrior against mere scenery.

The more profound perspective (the deeper notion we get to after many miles of thoughtful walking) is that Cézanne himself was like one of the prickly sea urchins of l'Estaque. As a personality he certainly took some handling, precisely because as a creature he was so sharply armoured. His allegorical physiognomy was inside out: the scented hills and glary littorals of Provence his flesh and organs, the granite shards and astringent shore his mirror and alter ego. Also, in the hard clench of countless dark escarpments in the Provençal hinterland we see the slow depth of his attitude; in the cracked masonry of an abandoned farmhouse we feel the long increments of his germination.

At this distance in time, of course, he can only be a figment for us, a kind of granitic motif, but nevertheless I place him in the grip of a retinal environmentalism, striving towards an objectivity of the senses, working to understand the world he saw and breathed in, to outflank the onset of mass consumption, to surpass the culturally absurd by embodying the aeration rather than the mere motion of the

Mediterranean breeze, the phenomenological process of truth rather than the abstracted data of the earth, the visual synergy and gusting osmosis of the sea.

Thus his relentless iterations: up before dawn traipsing the miles of literally thousands of painting days, setting up his easel among the insects and weather, on a rock or amongst the tufts of roadside thyme (he believed we can *see* odour), immersing himself in the silent chill of a gorge or the spook of an abandoned aqueduct.

Like the combs of wild bees he'd come across, the pictures he walked to paint were revolutionary without the 'r', each one of them both a visual laboratory and a primitive hunt, an attempt to deal with the prismatic complexities of space, its elusive nourishment and prey. He made a daily raid upon the solidity and fluency of the world, the land and upslopes and skyscapes, as they merged in his senses with his trunk and legs and arms and head.

Time and again Cézanne risked the opaque, in media as analogue as coloured mud and hog's-bristle brush. Whether his paintings succeed or fail (like a number of great artists – Frida Kahlo and Bob Dylan come to mind – the humanity of his failures are intrinsic to the overall effect), they do always have a psychological tint about them, but even more than that, plumbing deeper down into the watertable, Cézanne's famously inanimate human figures, in their *woodenness*, were a clear indicator of what he was attempting. In his hand the hierarchies of dominion as put forth in the biblical Genesis, and re-trumpeted through nineteenth-century inventions such as the daguerreotype – which was actually invented in the year of Cézanne's birth – were made level again. Humankind, even with its outsized brain and cultural facilities, its ability to photograph the moon, was not set above or apart. A human was no different from an apple or a chair.

Accordingly, as if his skin were made of local glass, his eyes of quartz, his legs and arms the trunks and burls of trees, Cézanne called the world of scrub and sea and sky to move through him. He became the weather, an aesthetic cat flap for his habitat, and it was due to this two-way seeing, this marriage of perceiver and perceived, that he coaxed along the key ingredient of his originality: a passion for fidelity.

Hence his echinoid spikiness, his gruntmanship and awkwardness amongst the social interactions of his day. Hence also the irony of him being so rightfully seen as a progenitor of modern art, with its worship of the self-obsessed and subjective view.

My dear Achille,

I have not been able to achieve anything, neither in the Batignolles, nor anywhere else. If I have delayed writing to you for so long, the reason is that up to the last moment I had some hopes.

See the pollen filaments as he walks along, on his dark clothes and in his beard. See the cloudcover cross his face as he serrates conversations.

Believe me, the hour always comes when one breaks through and has admirers far more fervent and convinced than those who are only attracted by an empty surface.

It is a very bad time for selling, all the bourgeois jib at letting go of their sous …

The paternal pressures on Cézanne's experiments, we are told, were of an intense compression. He was the only son and thus his face (occluded, Italianate) was not strictly his. Rather, it was a mask of suntanned skin to be stretched over the family structure; any beard was meant to be grown only for mercantile gravitas, tonsured precisely for the pride and transactions of the dealing street, not left wild to resemble the banditry of klephts or the austerity of saints.

With a father conservative not just from the anxiety of his own rather extemporised financial model (Louis-Auguste Cézanne was a hatter who became a banker who wanted his son to be a lawyer) but also from the viciousness of village talk, the son developed a need to be *outside.* Like Calvino's *barone rampante*, he needed to be away from the Sunday table and out amongst it. He needed to climb out the middle-class window, to walk, to bring the background to the front.

He also had to express the law that had been overlooked, the law he felt had been cast off into the lower case, the only law that he deemed worthy of the capital 'L'. This is the law that is now, over a century later, not so much being overlooked but habitually ignored. It is the arrangement that has been *given*, not on the paper of a father's ruled ledgers, but sown into the relationships between volume and light, between ambulacrum and soil, scratched out in dirt by the ants of the woody scrub, the law that secretes perfume and wine, and that is carved into the human history of the earth for all time, with Cézanne's own ruthless palette knife.

Famously he would return again and again to the same motif, the stolid yet transient cone of Mont Sainte-Victoire. With every circadium of light he spent out there, with every near-success and failure, any remnant bourgeois comportment he had diminished. His eye despaired as his palette and brush striated and strove, not to *reproduce* the world in the manner of a Cook's Tour photographer, not to *own* or to *capture* it like the banker or the real estate agent, but to *represent* its truth.

He became, therefore, not unlike a Rachel Carson or James Lovelock, an emissary of difficult things. Consequently his paintings, seen properly from our Moolacenic century, seem more divination than exhibition. In their silent technologies they are the action that is louder than words.

The landscape thinks itself in me, and I am its consciousness.

Inevitably Cézanne has taken his place in the realm of tourism but more importantly he has found a genuine place in the realm of myth, not so much as a god, or even as a human figure, but as a being at one with the cave of Hypnos or the rocks of Orpheus. All the walking to and fro, his gear strapped to his back, his footwear worn and coming loose, was immensely practical. The walking was as basic to him as the stretching and framing of the canvas, the preparation and reflection necessary on either side of his sustainable world.

And so, to perpetrate the opposite view, the almond-eyed view: it was not so much the cliché of social anxieties and tortured temperament that contorted the painter into a sub-brusque recalcitrant genius, but rather his dedication to joy. His pictures are a response to a vision of a possibility not just for art but for life.

From every overhang and dry limestone jut ran the song of an unspoken language, a chthonic language unreckoned by Roman annexation and mis-curated through the medieval era when Provence was a papal colony of cultural patronage, mannerist politics and pious guilt.

Any hills outside the limits of aqueduction and irrigation, let alone the resonance of the village bell, had been deemed, as it were, *unpasteurised*.

And yet, on his walking out, from Aix to Mont Sainte-Victoire and as far as l'Estaque, and in the generating barefoot mantras of his outdoor childhood, he saw the reality-base, the coming-into-being, the *mouvement perpetuel*, the subtle craquelure behind the flat sturdy edifice of his father's industrious way.

As a result, the painter's walks were not artist's escapes or spiritual retreats but confrontations. He became not only urgently industrious but, as a consequence, determinedly anti-social, not only anti-bourgeois but, in the proto-yuppy era of the Second Empire, anti-imperial. His great friend Pissarro's cry to 'Burn the Louvre!' was actually a call to go walking. The whole *plein air* impulse of the 1870s was not an optical issue alone, nor one for the linearity of canons or the modernity of which he is now seen as the father. The garrigue had permeated the child, and it was while walking, while looking at giant cubes of stone spilt on cypressed ledges and the green moisture of gullies in the sea's brisk shadow, that he best understood how to overcome our now dangerously attenuated sense of time and sylvan space.

He knew also the repression of instinct and truth involved in mediocre iconography, what we might call these days 'greenwash'. But did he presage an earth we now fear we have lost? Perhaps. Cézanne seemed assured in fact that the original multi-timbre and deep state of nature would always outlast the monologues of fashion, capitalism, the Republic and the father.

———

Sometimes, during the long and caustic summer, the walking begins in bed. Unable to sleep I stroll out in my mind along the banks of the home river. I begin inland from the ocean, deep in the glasswort of the riverflat, and drift as if suspended along the reeds and glaucous goosefoot of the banks. In critical moments I've walked here wide awake, rescinding from a life more hectic, contentious, volcanic even, to pace my way towards equilibrium. These river walks have been anguished at times, beseeching. So it goes. A life is not a walk around the corner, it is a huffing and puffing, a scaling of uplands and a sudden falling down sharp escarpments. Green pasture with the sound and vision of water flowing nearby feels like a historical pleasure, it is not always reality, not always the tint of a walker's consciousness, even if it is a pasture he walks through and a gentle river he walks beside. In this way our eyes and ears, all our senses, are not just portal and lens, not just antenna and radio mast for the two-way exchange of the world and the walker. No, sometimes they are all bottled up, hunched in and around our consciousness. We walk through paradise even when it feels as if we are walking through hell.

But in the bed, in the altered hierarchy of sleepless night, the walker walks the river from a place where the imagination and the memory gather all senses into one. This night walk needs ingredients: succulents, nutrients, memories, all the things the land needs. We float in our sheets. We walk our way into the made body of the world

until the riverscape, the glasswort, the reeds and goosefoot, the
clutches of blackwood, the musseled jetties, the sable flow, become
a physiognomy. Our breathing mouth becomes the river's spring, the
lungs and heart its watershed, the stomach and bladder its estuary, the
penis or vagina its debouchments into the greater sea. We understand
then, as we lie there, what this walking is all about. Deep existence in
the universe where all things are alike but different, where there is no
true beginning or end.

When the young J.S. Bach set out in 1705 from Arnstadt to walk to hear his hero Buxtehude play in the Marienkirche of Lübeck some 250 miles away, he was wildly upset. Twenty years old, an orphan, he had taken on the role of cantor at St Boniface in Arnstadt as an expedient first posting in his plying of the Bach family trade. The position was well salaried and the duties light. He had only to see to the workings of the organ and play the instrument himself each Sunday in the church. But in reality his employers expected more. No matter his dreamings at night, with the coming of each day his visions were mired in disputation as, under the orders of Herr Olearius, the superintendent of the Consistory, he was required to direct cloth-eared instrumentalists in the process of learning the following Sunday's cantata.

Imagine the young Sebastian standing, hands on hips in the little courtyard of St Boniface. His hair is long, russet, his body lean. He has just come slamming out through the side door of the nave, his normally eloquent hands fisting not with contrition for having just called one of these instrumentalists a *Zippel Faggotist!* but from what incited such abuse: an unforgivable blotching and blurting-about in the music. His created notes have been doused, not by the tempests of Thuringian wood and reed, but by the cross-purposes of a bassoonist's lazy flatulence.

I see the young Bach grimacing among the hard surfaces of the claustrophobic Mitteleuropean courtyard. He begins to pace, high walls echo his step, the side of the church, the consistory offices consonant in pale stone. And as he paces back and forth, he recollects again those barging notes that slurred the cantata. He lets fly once more with the streetwise curse.

'*Zippel Faggotist!*' he cries.

He pauses then, pauses in midstep to listen to the effect. The yard takes up his youthful curse, the words rising like swirling forest leaves: the crisp and larchy Z lifts, the insidious beechy *tist* cymbals out upon the spiralling air.

The courtyard space ensembles, his own angry tenor refracts like the town's gossip. There are ears behind the walls, the ears of his employers, the whispery old clerics of the Consistory of St Boniface.

The decay of Sebastian's outburst subsides within the walls as he feels his ill-temper floating away, like a bird from a spire. He hears too that inside the church the shocked players have all departed. With their absence his face settles. He becomes clear again.

The truth is, he could pace back and forth in that ricocheting courtyard his whole life, develop a hobby perhaps, so that music would become just a duty and a wage. Or alternatively he could take the risk of departure and exertion, 'go the extra mile', and immerse himself in both the structure and freedom of the music that would become his ultimate home.

———

Bach was ten when he was orphaned. What first must have appeared as an inhospitable road turned out to be a miraculous path. A place was found for him as a student in the Michaelisschule. The music came easily. It was during that time, on a thirty mile walk back from

Hamburg where he had gone to hear Reincken play, that an image of his own deep luck swam before his eyes. Outside a wayside inn, in the roadside grass, he saw a vision of fish moving about, threshing and weaving amongst the green blades, with coins glinting in their mouths. Here was he, a poor musical pilgrim in a picaresque fable. He launched, swooped up the fish, and the coins, and felt the hand of providence in an uncanny way. He felt it then and so he would for the remainder of his life, his feet on the road, his fingers on the keyboard.

So it was that he decided there in the courtyard of St Boniface some ten years later, in the glow of such luck and with his preternatural antennae hoisted to catch the music of the world. He decided to walk.

The year was 1705. Johann Adam Reincken's good friend Dietrich Buxtehude was the Kapellmeister at the Marienkirche in Lübeck. Buxtehude was an old man, and the twenty-year-old Bach had always wanted to hear the master at work. And so, in lieu of duelling the *Zippel Faggotist*, he applied immediately for special leave from Herr Olearius to undertake the journey to hear the great Buxtehude play.

The leave was granted and Sebastian was unshackled. He set off, with no doubt an ostinato or two of his own redoubled pilgrim's melody already forming in his mind.

His exact route is unknown, although with everything taken into account – the common byways of Thuringia, the distance he had to traipse in order to arrive in time for Buxtehude's Advent concerts, the geographical network of his associates – it is reasonable to suggest he tramped alone through the pre-Enlightenment towns of Gotha, Northeim, Seesen, Braunschweig, Lüneburg (where he had studied at the Michaelisschule), and then via the well-worn salt route to Lübeck on the Baltic coast.

Like any woodland animal, the young Bach carried no musical device to coax him along. He had only his own chorister's voice, the sonic lure of his destination, the invigorating prospect of his journey's end, when he would emerge from the sepia tones of the dense Thuringian forests to enter the old Hanseatic town of Lübeck, stroll across the River Trave, step across the threshold of the Marienkirche, and hear the majestic artifice of the *Große Orgel*, the Grand Organ.

Until then he had only the crisping of his own tread to listen to, the leaves speckling the cart-tracks of the autumn forest, the trebley sluicing of waters through glades and village mills, and undoubtedly the beat of his own blood in the permutations of putative cantatas dancing through his imagination as he went. Perhaps at night he read upstairs in a public house. Perhaps he carried a writing instrument and manuscript paper, and perhaps he may have stopped over at Lüneburg, where he had studied, to enjoy some music-making with friends. All this we can only surmise. But what we do know is that he walked.

It is said that Buxtehude had his eye on Bach as a husband for his daughter, an engagement that seems also to have been an unofficial requirement for any would-be successor to the great man in the Kapellmeister post at Lübeck. Apparently Handel had already been there, and did not fancy the measuring-up. The fact that Sebastian arrived in Lübeck on time but was late in returning to his own post at Arnstadt, seems to have had nothing to do with romantic dalliance and far more to do with the excitements of what he heard there. He was meant to return by December but after the long walk he stayed on in Lübeck right through to February, to observe the master at work and to hear, and even participate in, Buxtehude's famous annual series of Advent concerts. It is likely that by the time he re-entered the forest tracks of the return walk, he carried the scores of this season along with him. We don't know how on earth he kept them dry among the damp and dripping of the late-winter beeches, but it seems that he did. It is reported in the minutes of the Consistory of St Boniface that upon his return the young Sebastian began to inject several controversial innovations into his arrangement of the church cantatas.

As he treads the path from Arnstadt to Lübeck and back again, the low hum of detail that is available to us about Bach's life becomes positively silent. The walker interrogates his own landscape, beyond the cupped ear and the prying eye. We are left again, as he himself was so many times, both at the keyboard and on the track, with our own imaginations. We know that on the outgoing journey he was walking north towards both spring and the Baltic, but we don't know in what shape, timbre or form his walking visions came. Was it on this pilgrimage that the Fibonacci patterns in the scales of the lucky roadside fish of a few years before began to morph into possible inventions within the aesthetic mathematics of musical scales? Was it as he walked through the weather that he began to divine the repeating tonal relationships that would sustain him through the endless tragedies (the early passing of his first wife, the death of ten of his twenty children before adulthood) that were to come later in his life? How many times did the unfathomable composer-to-be descend from solitary and complex mental choristries to observe the given architecture around him – the Escher in the beeches, the Gödel in the clouds – and to casually hum or whistle, as a forest creature himself, along the way.

Free of the bureaucratic admonitions of St Boniface, with only the orchestra of bird, rain and tree in his ear, surely those walks, conducted for the twin catharses of music and freedom, were intrinsic to the sound that was slowly building within him, even at such a young and truant age.

It is possible, of course, that the very forces that were constraining the young Bach in Arnstadt were in need of a good walk themselves. The village burghers taking their daily constitutionals and all that. Dignitaries power-walking around the block of their hotel. But the kind of walking I'm thinking of here is not around the block. Nor is it up and down on a treadmill.

In Cromwellian times, in the little village of Carrick-on-Suir in Tipperary in the south-east of Ireland, the Earl of Ormonde had his own treadmill of sorts, a stone treadmill as it turns out, in the eponymous castle he built on the edge of the town. If the clerics of Arnstadt had the freedom to take their walks in fresh air, the Earl of Ormonde, being so unwanted in the land, had a far greater restriction.

On the first floor of his castle was, and still is, a ninety-nine-foot-long narrow room in which the earl would pace up and down for his daily exercise, being unable to take the air down in the town or along the nearby flowing waters of the black Suir due to the fact that he would be shot, if not garrotted, on sight. In the silence of his great abstracted height, encased in the airlessness of the treadmill, the earl would walk purely for exercise, in the manner of a twenty-first-century resident of high-rise Hong Kong. And, unlike the young Sebastian at St Boniface, the earl's confinement was not due to the immanence of his genius. On the contrary, the Earl of Ormonde on his treadmill makes Herr Olearius and the other respected denizens of the Arnstadt Consistory look enlightened before their time. Why else would they possibly have given that young man leave to go traipsing across the land purely in search of inspiration?

Many times I've walked the ironbarked hills around the mental riverflat. From vantage points and nodes of minor physical conquests I've been able to get outside and look across and down at what it is our imagination creates. The cluster of houses on the nyooroo clay. Their micro-polluting. These are the walks where past walkers can be felt. In a flush of health I become not only hosted by the eucalyptus aerating my muscles and blood but also by the personal lineage

lineage *linea* (Latin – a line) *lignage* (Old French)

or **trail** *traillier* (Old French – to tow) *trahere* (Latin – to pull)

which has been created through the magnetic field of cultural interests. The histoires sacrées *they have created in me.*

And so, as I climb the steep, silver-sandy and sardonically named Gentle Annie Track, just inland of a landbrow abutting Bass Strait, I hear the music in faraway Sebastian's head, the ideal music he was walking towards on that long journey to Lübeck. My own gait sheds statistics and staves, takes on the propulsive zest of a cantata, the mind grows recitative, but nothing that I speak or sing to the trees sounds in any way baroque. And yet it is the thought of Bach that lifts me along, the thought of a music fully realised in the placing of one foot in front of the other, one note before or after or under or above the next.

As I climb the difficult slope, my thoughts drift towards the acoustics of a former world, a world where alps had to be crossed, dark forests risked, just to hear a concert. It is as I wish that some such appreciation-determination-inspiration could enter me, that I have given over part of myself, literally, part of myself: a shoulder perhaps, an arm, a thigh, my hair, to Sebastian. He has in part created me and thus, in the way of the natural reticulation of these things, is being reinvented in return. This is not some glib simile. It is as real as the bushels of grain and cords of beech that were delivered to his door as part of his salary at Arnstadt. It is as real as the clanging watertanks of the dry Moolacene. It is a simple truth, the walk we are on, a truth of a walker.

———

William Buckley's walking was not driven by vocation. He had grown up across the water in Cheshire some one hundred years after Johann Sebastian Bach and was apprenticed to a bricklayer before joining the King's Own Regiment and leaving to fight Napoleon in the Netherlands. His crime when he returned to England was stealing a bolt of Irish linen, and by the time he was traipsing alone on the foreign shores of what was to become south-west Victoria in Australia, he had more pressing issues on his mind than a vocation. But in his struggle to survive extreme circumstances, his life was to become one of those rare spans of human value. An epic destiny was thrust upon him by an encounter with the local people of the littoral through which he was walking. Mistaken as the returned spirit of a much-loved tribesman, Buckley was inducted into Wadawurrung cultural life and spent the next thirty-two years in an integrated cohabitation with his generous saviours.

These were the years of walking. This time in a walker's land. How else could the country be known, the spirits be heard, the plants be nourished and digested? The seasons dictated campsites, ochre trading routes, the ceremonial nodes. The Bellarine Peninsula, as it has become known – from 'bella wein', 'where we lean on our elbow beside the fire while looking out over the sparkling sea' – would have been, like Provence once was, a paradise. Though Bach was dead and Dante's choirs of western angels were not to be heard, the sound of tides pounding into the river mouths at night were. If a Christian soul was to leave purgatory for paradise, it might be commemorated with a rain-drip falling through moonah fronds. Hell was a tribal infraction, the blood-retribution that ensued, but also the potential of encountering the mythologies of the land, the bunyip for instance, come to haunt the solitary wanderer beside the sloped horizons and fresh waters of Lake Modewarre ('modewarre' – musk duck). What to others may appear to be a *Purgatorio* par excellence – those three decades of dissimulation and reidentification with the unpaved earth – to William Buckley must have in time seemed like an end in itself.

He married into the Wadawurrung patrilineage, had a child, was taught their language and forgot his own. He learnt to trap 'boonea' (eel), to endure the chill insinuations of Bass Strait winters. He became tattooed for life, by the diet of 'kooderoo' (abalone) and murnong (yam daisy) he grew accustomed to, the mimetic brolga dances he was privy to, and literally, with his initials WB, his totem 'barrawarn', or 'parrwang', a crescent moon and a rising sun, carved into the skin of his arm.

Buckley had walked to an unexpected freedom; with one foot in front of the other he had unpicked the process of incarceration and colonisation and, in the image of his tattoo and his story as he told it, we see an alternative history of the Australian continent, how it might have been if, like Buckley, we had chosen not to grab and ride, to drive or fly, but to walk communally through the land.

Buckley in fact met a sadly ironic end when, disillusioned with the Machiavellian brutality of Port Phillip, he moved south to the place he had so badly wanted to avoid in the first place, Van Diemen's Land. It was there, at Greenpond near Hobart, that this walker of history fell off his horse & gig and died. But not before making his feelings known.

When he had been rediscovered by the redcoats of the Port Phillip colony after his thirty-two years with the Wadawurrung, Buckley's English seemed initially to have disappeared on the Bass Strait winds. With the ships inshore, among the shellfish and succulents of Corio Bay, and Buckley nervous about being remanacled as a long-lost escapee, he managed to muster his courage and face the redcoats on the grounds that the duration of his exile meant that his penance was surely paid. Face to face with the bristling muttonchops, he put his hand out to receive the bread on offer to him. As he did so he remembered the word. *Bread.* Ever so slowly more of his native tongue came back to him, until eventually he was deemed of use and granted a pardon by the authorities. He was enlisted as a go-between to help smooth the transition between the Wadawurrung and British imperial worlds. It was a role he saw a purpose in. Perhaps he could be the bridge between the world in which he grew and the one that he had come to know. Between an unsustainable Europe and a culture that could prosper for thousands of years. Perhaps this hope was the closest he ever came to a sense of divine vocation.

Hanging around the makeshift camp at Beangala (Indented Head), he wandered between his former tribe and the armed invaders: passing messages, answering questions and offering advice. Caught between, in the pincer movement of expropriation, he tried and failed over the following months to build the bridge of understanding between two such disparate world views. If a bridge was to be built it would have to constitute a unique collaboration of social engineering. Not only would it have to span depths and overcome geographical difficulties, it would also have to withstand the flack of cross-currenting cultural weather. Thus it would have to be made of pliable materials – reed not steel, tea-tree and roo sinew rather than cement and iron. The interlock between the possum-cloaked peoples of the Kulin lands and the high-collared men of the ships would have to be ingenious, patient as any worthwhile craft, poetic even, with the imagination widened on both banks of the divide.

But time and again Buckley was forced to understand how conditional his role must be. He was after all a public servant of the Crown, and any reconciling to be done with the people of the basalt plains was only in order to dispossess and subjugate them to the law of the gun and the rule of a British Christ. As a result, like a weathered parchment, Buckley's vision etiolated, the ideal image he had in his heart became weakened and worn, stippled and pocked. His disillusion grew, with his own self and with the world, and as it did his face went grim and surly. A cloud passed over. He fell from favour with all parties, colonists and colonised alike.

Enter Foster Fyans, the carbuncled war veteran who would eventually set up his own personal fiefdom stretching all the way from Geelong to Portland, across the world's largest volcanic plain, an area half the size of England. Fyans ruled this demesne from a ford over the Moorabool River, the site known these days as Fyansford. He was brought into the colony from the penal settlement of Norfolk Island as a liquidator, in order to assist the chagrined land squatters in their dispossession of the native peoples from the rich soils and waterways of the plain. Upon Fyans' arrival, Buckley was given the role as his walking interlocutor and guide. He was to walk with him from Melbourne to Geelong, show him the lay of the land and, more importantly, introduce him to the Wadawurrung. By this stage it had been nearly two years since the day at Indented Head when Buckley had remembered the word for bread, and by now he had had enough. As poet Barry Hill has pointed out, after thirty-two years with the Wadawurrung 'the frontier that Buckley knew was the frontier where the white man did the assimilating'. The transition from member of the Wadawurrung to coercive public servant was not one he could achieve easily.

He refused to walk with Foster Fyans, just as he would not dine with him. In the end he was destined to do again as he did when his companions left their camp across the water from Sullivan Bay back in 1803. He walked alone.

And this is where he still walks, at the foot of the You Yangs (home of the Yawangi clan), across the border country of the Wadawurrung and Wurundjeri, through the tussock and tea-tree, the leucopogon and murnong. Is he, at this point, as he refuses to chaperone Fyans to Geelong, as he turns his stare away into the folds of the land, the loneliest walker in history? Estranged from his wife and child, scorned by the countrymen of his British childhood as a subhuman degenerate, isolated in a land he'd been inducted into and was now enlisted to scarify. He must have wondered about the extraordinary hand of fate he had been dealt. Was it disingenuous of him to accept the role the Wadawurrung had bestowed on him all those years ago, when they first found him wandering alone around what is now the surf industrial complex of Torquay? He had been carrying a spear he found on a burial place, the spear, as it turns out, of a deceased warrior, Murrungurk. The story goes that the Wadawurrung had presumed, because of Buckley's white skin and immense stature – he was six feet six inches tall in an era when the average height of an Englishman was five feet five inches – that he was the ghost of Murrungurk. They had embraced him and welcomed him as such. But of course he was no such ghost, no such warrior. He was a Cheshire bricklayer who had fought against Napoleon and stolen a piece of Irish cloth. He was a terribly long way from home, and when those ships finally came into the bay thirty-two years later, he proved it to be so by his sadly obsequious need for their approval and pardon. But what choice did he have? And how could he have rebutted the Wadawurrung keenness to celebrate his hallowed spirit-return as Murrungurk? Where would that have left him in the land? And what choice does he have now, in our own minds, as we go on re-creating him, as he continues walking through the historical landscape at our disposal?

Perhaps he is not so much the go-between of the colonial moment as the cautionary antidote to a dangerously convenient Romanticism.

For here was a European man honoured as a native, a man of fact not fiction, but fated through an almost sci-fi style misunderstanding to survive in sympathy with nature; a man who'd been taught, as we would say now, to walk in both action and reflection, to both hunt and to sacralise the hunt, to live sustainably within the behests and laws of his adopted habitat. And how did it end for him? Where did his walking take him to? Just to despair? Or also to that secret place where the author of all the songs resides? Buckley said in fact that he was shown such a site during his time with the Wadawurrung and that he also knew the place where the being dwelt who was in charge of the pole that kept the sky up off the earth. The pole of light. It is right there, in that awareness, that he begins to walk the page with Cézanne and Bach, who sought such an arrangement out for themselves, alone, on foot, in the media of paint and music.

The being in charge of such a wonderful pole must still exist of course, somewhere in the southern landscape of the Bellarine Peninsula, or out the back near Modewarre, or further south-west towards the Otway Ranges, in Gadubanud country. In every tribal ground there is a version of this being, but in what is nowadays sometimes called Buckley country, it is, for the time being, literally lost.

And yet somehow, by walking, we feel we are approaching it. The column of light where creation's structure is revealed. For us, and perhaps for Buckley in the end, and all his surviving countrymen, it is the single most important sustaining figment of the mind, a star fallen from the sky to nestle in behind our eyes and light the way. This is the mental leap and fresh blood-flow that we are afforded when we step outside and walk.

And so it goes, imagined in both the chiastic patterns of sleeplessness and in the kinetic reality of a physical daylight. When Buckley left his anxious fellow escapees to continue south-west into an unknown littoral he was soon exhausted. He didn't know what he could and couldn't eat and any provisions he had were soon used up. It was when he got to Mangowak, to this river I call home, where he discovered the small estuary sheltered by its tide-born hummock, that he finally had some luck. There had been recent burning, either natural or cultural fire, and its embers were still glowing. He found a billabong of fresh water not far from the estuary and sea, and thus he could finally rest and replenish, cooking fish and crustacea and drinking his fill. His bones began to thaw, his muscles relaxed, his anxieties abating, at least momentarily, in this sheltered spot.

I go with that sense of Buckley's relief and the depth of his personal restoration, each time I walk the river down to the estuary, through the rusted sedge and fire-retardant boobiallas to the dunes. He spoke of how he held this spot as a talisman in his mind, those healing days he spent when all had seemed lost and without reason or succour. From time to time in his years with the Wadawurrung he would return alone to the billabong and river mouth and hummock of Mangowak – to take his sabbaticals if you like – and as I walk I am conscious of that line. My bare feet squelch in the silty ground of the banks until I stop to lean on an upslope of dune. It is quiet, perhaps midweek. I let the sun's rays warm me, as he would have done. I watch the ants going about their micro-industries; and then I walk again, giving over perhaps an ankle or a hip, perhaps half of my face, to the idea of Buckley. He walks with me, just as Sebastian does, and Paul, after all this time, and in all this space.

'An earth of ashes which physically nourishes the plants and brings back the life the voices of the dead within those plants.'
Andrea Lauterwein

When David Unaipon, Narrandjerri elder, entered the realm of the volcanic plain's forested uplands and long deep valleys, he came with rare knowledge. Unaipon, the son of the first ordained Narrandjeri church deacon and the grandson of Pullami, the great chief, or Mungkumbuli, of the tribal grounds at the embouchement of the Murray River, was a man unusually suited to building a bridge between black and white cultures. He had a lifelong obsession with the scientific problem of perpetual motion, a cornerstone of his passion, his urgent need, to demonstrate the confluence between Western science and Aboriginal cosmology. This was a driving force behind his thousands of miles of walking, behind his immense and varied activity, and his eventual fame, a fame that persists today through the image of his face on the Australian fifty-dollar note.

It is claimed that Unaipon was the first official Aboriginal author of a book in Australia, an absurd notion in itself given how the patchwork of nations across the continent had been a living palimpsest – *the* canonical continental text – for thousands of years. It follows from such absurdities that the British colony, and subsequently the federated nation, was without either spiritual truth or true scholarship, and it is within that context that Unaipon's official authorship should be acknowledged.

> *'Thus and thus spake Nha Teeyouwa (blackfellow). Nhan-Garra Doctor: Children, I have many strange stories to tell you. All came to me whilst I slumbered in deep sleep.'*
> David Unaipon, *Native Legends*

Unaipon's first book, *Native Legends*, was printed and published in Adelaide and contained Narrandjeri mythologies and cultural beliefs all spelt out in his King James Bible prose style. The small essay on Totemism, subtitled 'The Companionship of Earthly Creatures', describes the belief that human beings in fact originally came from a separate spirit realm to this material earth, after observing from afar how the creatures of the earth could guide, instruct and caution them as to how to live in this physical habitat.

It was with such lore in his head that for decades Unaipon walked the south-eastern landscapes of the continent in a three-piece suit, stopping to preach at church services or in homes, always polite, often humorous, and always, *perpetually*, nutting things out, writing and thinking. When he showed up at a pastoral station in the eastern Otway Ranges not far from where I live, he walked up the driveway to the homestead with intimate knowledge of burial sites on the land. How a Narrandjeri man from some 1000 kilometres away could know this is mysterious, but, even as late as the 1930s, the communication networks between the dispossessed families, bands, clans, tribes and nations of south-eastern Australia were still operating in extremis.

Unaipon moved through the land as a divining rod, and he came with a forked message, one contained within the yarns of the bound and official Bible he held in his hand and the other a message in danger of being cauterised to silence by the white invasion: the knowledge of the spirit realm, where the song still dwelt, the pity and sympathy, the knowledge and laughter still flowing through the land.

Can you hear his feet shuffling along, as he turns in under the windbreak pines, in his road-dusted black suit, along the polished grooves of the driveway? Can you hear him coming on up to the house for scones and tea?

He comes respectfully, along a hallway I imagine to be brindled with knick-knacks, Gulidjan testaments, china plates and grinding stones, cloisonne ducks and throwing spears, basalt flints, parrying sticks of yore. He sits as requested upon an upholstered chair, nervous, but civil and assured. And there begins the cup-to-saucer conversing, the suspicious looks, the exchange of names, the nods and frowns, the gracious smiles, the mindful engineering of the cultural bridge he was intent on building. Eventually, inexorably, as the room begins to like him and to relax in his presence, a strange event occurs. Right there in the watery daylight the stars of ancient galaxies begin first to spill then to pour from his mouth, issuing from his lips in a pointillist stream of light, falling down over his waistcoat and fob watch to glitter in his lap where his hands rest on the holy book. The streaming galaxies reflect back up into his face, illuminating the spirit in his eyes, before rising to swirl like braided phosphorescent rivers around the architraves and jambs of the colonial room.

In his mind the cogs and wheels are greased and turning, his heart is beating, and he begins to speak of the things he has thought about as he has walked: the fascination of universal mechanics, of perpetual motion, how the mind of creation will never cease, how we are all of us strangers from another place, strangers in a strange land. He speaks of animals, Kangaroo, Emu, Goanna and the Insect Life, how he believes they were all watching on, the birds and fish as well, when Christ appeared to the two disciples on the Road to Emmaus.

It is then perhaps that he turns to smile kindly at the little boy staring with his mouth agape nearby. It is then that he makes the joke, the joke as deep and black as the spaces between the stars, the joke he keeps for the children, the joke that the black of his skin 'won't come off'.

It is then that he again tastes the creek on the light southerly fluttering the lace curtains of the homestead. The joke has worked its magic, as has the child. And so the time has come to invite his hosts outside, to show them around their own 'property', to show them the burial grounds.

Stand at the spot. After so much wandering. Feel the southerly breathing.

Hear the humming of groundcovers underfoot, listen to the voices of the leaves in the breeze.

Say solemn prayers. Remember Grandfather Pullami and his great shield. The shield that protected the shining ideas, the river of stars, the moon and sun. The shield that keeps the universe moving, the people's knowledge as they walk through the land, the shield that protects the laughter of the living and the dead.

If the sky was overhead it now ceases to be so. As they stand at the burial place, the stranger in the three-piece suit, the farmer, his wife, their son, they all feel it. There is no barrier. If they were to look up they would see more than the birds, more than magpie or cockatoo, more than the pace of clouds or the time of day. And when they look down, at the ground, where the bones are interred, and from where the spirit flies, all is as clear and transparent as water.

The boy is young enough to remember. He will never forget. He will measure his growth as a man by the way he thinks and feels about this moment. His parents will remember also. This day will become for them a secret measure of the immense tragedy that is hidden in their local earth.

When Unaipon leaves, his book returned firmly to the inner pocket of his black jacket, they farewell him warmly and stand to watch him go down the ruts of the drive. Above his head the eucalypts reach.

When he turns out into the road they wait, as if hypnotised by the air he has passed out of, the way it seems to shine and buckle at the homestead gate. It reminds them of the stars that poured from his mouth.

Eventually they turn, without a word, and go back inside.

———

The pen steps across the page in pursuit of the trail. The cursor flies. As if the world is indivisible so I can see myself, the walker, as an assemblage, with Buckley's tattoo on my tongue, with the score of Bach's English Suites written onto my skin, with a vision of the sea at Cézanne's l'Estaque lifting me to the top of the climb. My whole body is transformed by the journey into a condition resembling the circular breathing of the didgeridoo player, or David Unaipon's perpetual motion machine. Fears become faded prints of the mind, old habits to evolve and traduce, maledictions without clout. I am untethered from the street of tombs, the grids of città the prattle of atria, the salt on a cocky's tongue. I forget the panic of the traffic of the dead, and the coagulations of the library.

The human being is made of stars and ash, one foot in front of the other. The path under our feet is polished by fresh images and returning motifs. The track creates its own melody and the ribbon dances upside down right way up.

We are walkers, heading to and from our maestri, heading for fish, flesh and fire, heading for home. Some make for the joyous fugue, some for the image, the sound, the freedom, the perpetual mythology.

At least one thing is common to us all. En masse.

We are arriving, we are always arriving ...

Moonah Mind

My life was confusing, I felt tangled as the moonahs, nothing so organised and purposeful as a coherent essay would evince. And yet, the tangle of those trees right there, the copse of moonahs I was thinking of, and writing beside, was beautiful for all its tangle. Its weird and wonderful shapes and sinuosities.

But wait. *Evince* – what kind of a word is that? And *sinuosities*, for that matter, what kind of a word is that? Wasn't this meant to be a piece of writing that helped clarify my confusion? Are these the right words – *evince, sinuosities* – to include in the family of such concerns, or are they too hoity, too arch, like some exotic or even imperial thing, some colonising span, laid across the honest, the messy, the organic and eternal?

Well, let's go deeper then into the tangle, this tangle of words, by quickly putting the spotlight on *evince*, just to try to ascribe a scale of worth where precision of language is at one end and familiarity of language is at the other. Once we've done that, we'll resume our exploration of the tangle.

Meanjin (2021/22)

So yes, *evince* sounds old-hat, and it is, though it's no older than *tangle* itself, and it does have its role. It means, firstly, to *disprove*, or *confute*, and it originates from the rhizome of Ancient Latin where its root word, *evincere*, means *to conquer, subdue, prevail over*, or *prove*. Thus its late-eighteenth-century meaning in English came to be *to show clearly*. Needless to say, *evince* doesn't exist in the *Australian National Dictionary*, where words like *whacked, bonza*, and *corroboree* hold sway, but the fifth-listed definition of *evince* in the *Oxford English Dictionary – to be an indication or evidence of*, the sense in which I used it in the opening of my piece – cites as its earliest known written usage the year 1790. That was also the year when, in the published account of his voyages, the great mariner Captain Cook wrote: 'Their pacific disposition is thoroughly evinced, from their friendly recognition of all strangers.'

Given that Cook was eventually murdered by Pacific islanders, we could perhaps add to this quote that the nature of our death can sometimes *evince* the excessive nature of our own positive disposition.

But what would we mean by that? That it proved that positive disposition was correct to be excessive, as if by contrast, or that it refuted it? And can *evince* in this case imply both roles? Ah, yet another dilemma or, dare I say, *tangle*.

Whatever the case, the question remains, why *evince*? Why not *indicate*, or *show clearly*. The answer in my own case must surely have something to do with sound and rhythm, a desire in my ear to end the sentence – 'I felt as tangled as the moonahs ...' – with something like an emphatic *thump* in keeping, ironically of course, with the propensity of the essay form to *conquer*, or *prevail over* its own material. This the essay purports to do via a fluency of prose and a facility of argument, qualities much valued in the aforesaid university which furnished us with the dictionary that gave us the deadly quotation from the Great Mariner. In this way the essay is a mode that achieves an intellectual victory of order over the chaos of its material. Which of course brings us right back to the old Latin root of *evince* – *evincere* – meaning *to conquer* or *subdue*.

So you see then that my ear is not only an auditory organ, but one that also likes to *make sense*. Because of its onomatopoeic hint, *evince* shot through the *tangle* of my writing mind, emerging as the first of many out into the light, or out of the sonic subfusc, to take its place at the end of that particular sentence. 'My thoughts felt tangled as the moonahs, nothing so organised and purposeful as a coherent essay would evince.' And *evince* was victorious because of the way its *sound made sense* in the sentence, the way it embodied my meaning, and not for hoity, arch or imperious reasons after all, even though the etymological source of the word's success – *evincere* – in the triumph of both its rise and then its falling cadence, has something to do with the Romans.

So what then of *sinuosities*?

> **Sinuous** full of turns and curves – 1570s, from the Latin 'sinuosus' meaning full of curves, folds or bendings, originating from 'sinus': curve, fold, bend.

This word is more in keeping with the atmosphere of my *tangle*, but why, might you ask, do I use *sinuosities* rather than the accessible synonyms in the given definition: curves, folds, bendings?

Of course the answer once again here has to do with more than mere semantics, but in this case it also has as much to do with sight as it does with sound. When I look into that special patch of tangled moonahs I see shadow as much as light, the light seemingly dependent on the shadow for its existence. To get that across, to transport my visual sense of the moonahs to you I need therefore some darker words, darker at least than *curve* or *bend*, which have not much atmospheric agency at all, and virtually no sense whatsoever of either light or dark. No, they are very much material adjectives, unlike *sinuosities*, a word whose own curves and bends speak sensually, with all those s's, of the indispensable darkness and shadow via which we see the light.

In a sense we're talking of words as bathyspheres here, language as an immersive vehicle. Another way to put it would be to say we are describing language that is full of what the great Anishinaabe writer Gerald Vizenor calls *natural motion*. For Vizenor the unforeseen metaphoric leaps and lateral movements of creative language are connected to the great animal migrations across North America. The mind moves freely in its realm, following its own seasons, finding and renewing habitats and communities, hunting for its own sustenance, making connections as it goes. This language of *natural motion* is entirely different from a lexicon seeking social status or evoking hierarchical stuffiness.

Tangle itself is a case in point. For this *tangle* in my soul, the *tangle* of which the *copse clutch patch* or *tangle* of moonahs I'm referring to is becoming an emblem, has no hierarchy of exclusive worth but rather a commonality in which it is theoretically impossible to exclude any word or image, sound or sight based on ideas as to whether it's perceived as culturally 'high' or 'low'. I'm open to all the etymological layers and strata, which might be one reason I'm in the tangle I am! Is this state a symptom of what they call contemporary *hybridity*, of what Donna Haraway calls 'making kin in the Anthropocene'? Is this a result of the sudden rights of internet democracy, of how all things are freed by information flow and therefore released as possibilities into our ken? Is that how I come to compare my emotional condition to a patch of *sinuous evincing tangling* moonahs?

Perhaps, but whatever the case, *tangle* itself is a common enough word, whose own provenance and history leads us right back out of the pages of dictionaries and books to the pre-print landscape of the coastal trees.

> **Tangle** verb   mid-14c., nasalized variant of *tagilen* 'to involve in a difficult situation, entangle,' from a Scandinavian source (compare dialectal Swedish *taggla* 'to disorder,' Old Norse *þongull* 'seaweed'), from Proto-Germanic *thangul-* (source also of Frisian *tung*, Dutch *tang*, German *Tang* 'seaweed'); thus the original sense of the root evidently was 'seaweed' as something that entangles (itself, or oars, or fishes, or nets).

Yes here we are then, right back in the phycological (as opposed to psychological) land of the salty littoral. These moonahs (*Melaleuca lanceolata*), leaning, curving, bending this way and that, are specifically coastal trees, endemic in the rooted native retinal language of their *tangle* to this part of the world. I, however, though my ancestors arrived in this area back in 1841 – not such a long time actually, unless it's measured with a white Australian chronometer – am not endemic. And yet surely by now, after nearly 180 years, *I partly am*. So in the *natural motion* of the poetic impulse, the seed that flies on the wind, wherein the barrier between the inner and outer life is no longer, I find that increasingly my metaphors, my understandings and my symbolic talismans, come from *home*, a concept that was once upon a time defined as the auditory range of one's village bell.

My friend saw a kangaroo get hit by a car right by these moonahs once, and she went to its aid as it lay pulsing in agony by the side of the road. The cars went by but the moonahs were still. As if bearing witness. Or not giving a fuck. They had no choice of course. Just by being there, they are witnessing still.

In my mind and heart, my wrists and forearms, my calves and boots, and in my winding songs of thoughts, cut down or not, the moonahs are always there. Here. Out the window, by the side of the road, on the bank of the river. The river of *natural motion*, where the mullet flow like clouds, where our lives grow like trees, where we become the place that we are.

When I walk by the moonahs, or drive past, when I am arrested not by the police (who sometimes do breath tests right there) but by the angles and the tangles of this billowy local tree, which grows as if as a cousin to cumulus, I find it is etched onto me. For what it displays of me, for what, in its complex but entirely effortless and natural *tangle*, it explains.

I am not alone. It is natural, the moonahs tell me, in all this weather of life, to grow into a tangle.

Moth Sea Fog

I talk to the moth caught in the car. Driving past heat-mottled dams whiskered with reeds. I tell him about the fog of the day before. It was not just any fog, but a time-fluxing sea-fog outrolling the waves, creeping over neaptide ledges, tickling the glossy anemones with its smoky edges. It made silhouettes of the gods.

The sunlight was a memory, I tell him. The physical became meta-physical. He bats the patterns on his wings, whirring against the windscreen.

You know in your guts when you've made a friend. And so I tell him more, watching the way his blackwire legs work adhesive, like a dancer in a heavy carpet cape except that his wings have made a shuffling pact with the light-sheaves of the air.

It rolled in, moved in, hefted in, a light-changer seeking the convex of the coves. It greybrushed the ocean, narrowing the spectrum from blue-green and gold to heron-grey and tint of ash. Yet this was not a creaturely dirge, this wasn't death or aftermath, this was *le temps*.

The moth doesn't speak French and nor do I. But when I'm with the moth all languages, like all the cars on the road, could potentially be ours: those bonnets of steel, we could be in any of those glary glass

Best Australian Stories (2016)

and steel chariots, they come from the same marketplace, just as words can be restored to sounds with long histories, joint histories, like the *tempest* in *le temps*, the weather in time.

And the fog, I told the moth, was a new moment cast, a *momento* that rolled in and would roll out again, or uplift, streak and stretch, or disappear, or dissolve like honey in the teacup of the world.

Every late October I wait for the moths, which come in numbers to thrum on the ocean windows. How many springs is it that I've been vigilant? Relative to the time it took to paint those wings, or the time it took to create those honeyed cliffs the fog greyscales into, it's only a few. I tell him that. How the grey sea-fog painted the ocean cliffs … how we were down below on the sand of the cove. The Horseshoe Rock was veiled, the great tower-stack of Eagle Rock was one of the silhouetted gods. The day had been too hot but now it was antechambered, as the great meteorological shift came in.

As I drove out of farms onto the edge of new suburbs, the moth flew in close. And still. It had probably slept between dash and steel armature but was now accustomed to the light. Awake in the daylight. Displaying his totem mirror-wings.

The sound of those wings seems the musical equivalent of the way the fog crept. My boys and I were going to cool down with a swim until we'd noticed the tumbled uneven tendril-edges of the fog moving silently over the cliffs. We decided to go anyway. For the excitement of new phenomena, rather than the cooling down. The invisible air was suddenly visible, as if a billion atoms had clenched into an optical fact, into visible existence.

Things, big things, come unannounced. Like the moths in spring. This single forerunner, companion in the cabin of my ute, did not phone ahead. And before we knew it we were on the path down, the fog's damp hem tingling our skin. We stepped down the steep winding path, moving further under cover, towards the sea-sound, further into the secret.

Another thing I tell the moth is that it was a midweek sea-fog. No other human stick figures materialising out of the spectral air, just us three: me, the eldest, the youngest. We got down to the bottom of the steps, onto the sand of the cove, thrilled to be besieged, so gently besieged by something so much bigger than us. It too was both old and young. An ancient character freshly, wetly, minted. It felt like strange kin, a spectacle we were part of, an unannounced visitation both ghost-ish and real, like the moth's cloud thrumming through each spring. I told him that as I drove over a bridge, how he reminded me of the fog, how they seemed connected.

It's like someone you meet who you know loves travelling. You talk destinations. Or someone who loves to cook. You talk food, or kitchen-ware. To a friend of the stars we talk astronomy, myth. To a friend of the river we talk birds who've roosted in the river-trees. So it was with the moth and the fog. Sometimes we have a hunch, a message comes travelling through the air between us, and we feel we know. And so we raise a subject however unlikely, as if on a whim. But it's not a whim. It's a windlassed knowledge so deep and fast, so multi-sensed, that even the word *intuition*, which after all is a nicely sinuous word, doesn't come close. *Feeling* is better. As in *sensing* and *seeking* at the same time. The fog and the moth would be interested in each other, that's what I felt; they were like family members. Like we three on the beach.

The water was calm, with silky blue-grey waves unpeeling under the blue-grey creature. The world was birdless for an hour. The clifftop bristlebirds did not make their quirky twee-wit calls, the gannets did not glide or dive, the cormorants did not bob up or stand as if sermonising on the rocks. We did not ask where they were though, we did not picture them holding their breath, or becoming overawed. We took this mysterious ethereal birdless cove at face value.

The eldest wanted to swim, I told the moth. The youngest wasn't so sure. He clung to me, as if the fog clung to him. Sometimes in a dream we see the world like this, seldom in reality. Sometimes in a dream we can cross over, as if into other worlds. Perhaps that's what it reminded the youngest one of. He obviously needed, in this waking hour, the world, and my presence in it, to be real. As real as the moth.

I had life on my dash, one dry stalk of slender velvet bush, one wizened stalk of lavender. Still with a faint perfume. To be inside the cabin of my ute, its plastic and steel, could have also seemed a dream to the moth, like the fog could seem to us. The world as you know it changed. A different, unfamiliar hall. But I'd wound the window down to let the moth out if he so desired. I'd left the window open, both when the car was still and moving. But no, the moth was staying. There was something in those dried stalks, those clefts and crannies of the car, that dam-mottled windscreen, that kept him there. Still, or tiptoeing across the glass, or thrumming his wings like a thinking thought. Something kept him there. So I told him the story.

Once upon a time, on an otherwise ordinary day, insofar as a too-hot day can be ordinary these days, a sea-fog rolled in from the endlessness of ocean and gently covered the reefs, the coves, the cliffs and downsloped shoulders and valleys of our town. Every pond was lightly brushed. Every road sign shrouded. One boy went for a swim in the fog, another boy stayed back on the beach with his father. The two of them peered through the dimmed light, through a wispy world, at the swimming boy. Until he was gone. Diving obliquely through the ocean's skin and swimming like a star pulsing under the water. He swam and swam, until he could breathe no more and came to the surface. His hair was plastered wet, he felt that he shone, but they could not see him. He had gone into the fog.

The father yelled, suddenly frightened. The younger boy's face screwed up in fear. But the water lay still, the impervious waves peeling in with what seemed now like stealth, an awful regularity and silence. The father broke clear of the grip of little hands, moving towards the water. He yelled again, but there was only absence now, erasure, an awful clarity on the sea.

The moth thrummed and whirred before standing still at an angle on the dash. Staring at me, as if accusing. No, I said. No, it wasn't like that. But that was my fear as the eldest went in. Like a seal in his black wetsuit, but for the short sleeves and leggings. His pale young limbs outstretched. As he slipped under the skin of the water my fear went imagining. Like the CFA alarm drills used to go sounding over the hills. One day a boy swam into the sea-fog and when the fog had passed over he was not there any more. The sea and sky had merged then unmerged and he was not there any more. Nowhere to be seen. As if he'd been abducted by the fog. As if the world had warped for half an hour, as if fate had held the boy's life between its forefinger and thumb, held it suspended, before dropping it again from its great height. And changing everything.

But this is not how it had gone, I told the moth. It was not like a fable or fairy tale. Though it had such an atmosphere. No, he was there, standing there in perfect form, in the water still, in his short wetsuit, overjoyed to be encompassed by this ocean shroud, this magical blue-grey cape, this smoky secret ... and me calling.

'Come in, come in,' I called, 'we'll walk around the point a way.' Thus forestalling any possibility of what might then be written by the strangeness of the world. Let's write something else old moth, I say, young moth, moth both old and young. Let's write simply of encompassing moments, how small we are in the large world, yet always kindred. Let's walk the cove, moth, father, eldest, youngest, to the dribble of rocks at the point, over the dribble of rocks, pushing our way through the mystery as if through a blue-grey curtain.

And so we went, the moth and I. Along the ordinary roadway. The boys and I too, around the rocky point to the seaweedy beach on the other side.

I seek the seasons, I told the moth then. I seek your arrival as the last of the wattle has faded, I seek the coming of the snakes. I seek the muttonbirds darkening the sky with a texta smudge, the *ficifolia*'s lurid flowering, the coming and going of *le temps*. I seek the new chapter of the budding plums, the wide grassy cast of introduced freesias, just like I seek new light in the morning and the shading of dusk towards dark. I seek the seasons, the season of rainbows, mushroom seasons, seasons of the nesting kites. *Thara*. That's what the men and women like me, the boys and girls like my own, called those nesting kites. Before we white people came like bad weather that would never leave. A fog outside of time. *Thara*, they said. The black-shouldered kites, we say. *Thara*, they say. And they know the seasons, coming on the unbroken loom of *le temps*.

So the fog is like spun air, like wool too, wool unravelling. Unravelling from the giant loom at the end of the sea. It unrolls in. Unrolls in. A memory, a freshly remembered thing. And yes, we go seeking through it, through the clammy wet stench of the seaweed beneath the marbled cliffs. Seeking to reassemble the broken parts of the loom, dear moth. The loom that wove your wings, the turning wheel releasing the fog-skeins, the sound of your whirring. In this deep and secret shroud the truth of seeking is made real. Aren't we always pushing through a fog we can't see? Except here, in the veiling unveiling coves, we can see it. *Feel* it. Our seeking made real. The feeling we have that the world hides and reveals, that the loom spun those patterns on your wings.

So this then, in this season, is our moth country. Not so much car country or road country or radio country or traffic-light country but mothy-foggy country. An ephemeral routine. And in the fog, as I say to the moth, we sense the truth of the deeper season. Season of invisible things. Things not so easily grasped and held. Season of a billion atoms, season of risk, of our disappearing. Our coming and going. *Le temps*. Your season, dear moth. Season of swimming in the fog. Season of driving with the moths.

I'm here to record, as a father must, that the younger one eventually loosened. We rounded the next point all smiles. We looked back. The cliff was not a prop. Nor were the gods. They had almost disappeared, like the past. Into the future.

Two
The Ocean Last Night

The Ocean Last Night

'Who will ever know all that lies in the secret heart of certain works?'
Francis Poulenc

*'To learn how to read any map is to be indoctrinated
into that mapmaker's culture.'*
Peter Turchi

Lorne, Victoria, 1937. Who could say the name of the pollen that was billowing through the air along the road towards the pier? Who could say how many dolphins were in the pod arcing across Louttit Bay? Who was to say how best to catch the purple crays crawling through the pools of the shelving shore, or what was the name of the lemon-browed bird bobbing in the currents between the waves?

But look, here comes a recent thing, a motor car, a dark maroon Standard Tourer, with a soft top, rumbling along through the pollen fibres and beneath the dappled light of the blue gums on the point. The driver of the car has an aquiline nose and a dark complexion under a short-brimmed Stetson hat. He is heading for the Grand Pacific Hotel.

The car slows. Approaching the impressive building it veers off the road and parks out front. Out of the motor car steps the man. He is middle-aged, of middle height, has a dark complexion and is wearing grey suit pants and a casual pullover.

He looks around, stretches his back after the long journey. Leaving his car door flung open he walks slowly then across the quiet road,

Meanjin (2018)

unwinding after the excitement and ordeal of driving the long road from the city and out over the high sea cliffs.

On the ocean side of the road he stands and gazes down towards the long pier reaching into the vast expanse of blue water below the hotel. No ships are tied there but one fishing ketch bobs amongst the deep shadows of the pylons.

It was less than an hour back along the road that through the windscreen of his Tourer the man had laid eyes on the ocean for the first time in his life. Yet nearly one hundred years before, his grandparents had arrived off the boat at Point Henry, just up the coast a little way at Geelong. How could that be? What is one hundred years in a place like this? Is it a long time, a short time, a long enough time to lose sight of what you know?

There are many types of silence, as many as there are sounds. Every silence has the blood of its listener pumping through it, as does any landscape of personal significance. When Archie Roach sings, in his song 'A Child Was Born Here':

> *Be careful where you walk in this land*
> *Because a child was born here*
> *And a child was born there*

he expects to be taken literally. He is singing his people's history. Both *in utero*, and *in extremis*. Just as there is blood in our ears so too are our hearts in the land and sea. See that memory under the tree just there? Remember that morning in the rockpool?

There is no silence without a listener, no landscape without a beating heart.

Nowhere in my life so far have I been without the sound of the ocean, no matter how far I am from shore. And no footstep I have taken on my home coast has laid itself down upon a blank. *Here* is a live screen.

———

All those splash marks on the surface of the bay? They look like a hundred cotton seams stitching themselves across the water into the south-west. If a man has only recently seen the ocean for the first time, how could he know what is causing this effect, whether it has anything to do with the seasons, the currents, the angle of the sun or the phases of the moon? How could he ever understand the language of what the ocean was writing there?

Now, in the distance, beyond the flurry of the dolphin pod, he sights the white architectural stalk of the lighthouse standing sentinel. He knows the name of that headland as Split Point. He passed through it on the Ocean Road only half an hour before. He could hardly miss the lighthouse of course, but he had particular cause to notice the name 'Split Point' on the map because a friend had mentioned it to him before he left Melbourne.

Perhaps a tear comes to his eye. Perhaps he turns away, from the lighthouse, the ocean and the pier. Perhaps he looks up at the ornate filigree of the Grand Hotel's high verandah. Perhaps he wipes his eyes. Perhaps he walks back across the road, closes his car door, and begins to ascend the hotel steps.

———

When environmental music pioneer Irv Teibel went out onto Coney Island in Brooklyn, New York, in 1969 to help record the sound of the ocean for a friend's film, he wasn't expecting what he found. In his studio the next day, as he began to edit and loop his recordings of the waves, cutting out any extraneous human sounds as he went, he began to notice that unlike all the other field recordings he'd worked with, this one didn't start to grate on his nerves in a way that made him want to turn it down as he worked. Instead the opposite was happening. He was becoming more and more relaxed.

From all accounts Teibel was no nature boy. But he was interested in creative technologies, in photography, and in sound, and the effects of sound. After he had made a few more ocean recordings – on Martha's Vineyard, and also in Virginia – he took one of his loops to a friend, Louis Gerstman, a neuropsychologist specialising in speech synthesis. Gerstman fed Teibel's ocean loop into a huge old IBM 360 and began smoothing and modifying what he had captured, just as he would the recorded sentences of his patients. For Irv Teibel the finished result turned on the proverbial light bulb in his head. He promptly formed a company called Syntonic Research Inc. and released the hour-length recording as an LP, complete with a Bauhaus-inflected sleeve design. He called it *Environments 1: The Psychologically Ultimate Seashore*.

Remarkably, for a record of ostensibly unadulterated ocean sounds with no artist listed as its progenitor, *Environments 1* was licensed by Atlantic Records and sold lots of copies. These days it is seen by some, along with Erik Satie's *Vexations*, John Cage's *4'33"*, and Brian Eno's *Discreet Music*, as a pioneer work of ambient music. Less auspiciously it has also spawned a global industry using the sounds of the natural world as kitschy relaxation and healing aids.

Through the remainder of the 1960s and into the 70s, Teibel released a further ten records in the *Environments* series, which included other such curated phenomena as rainforest sounds, sailing boats in the wind, the sound of thunderstorms, etc.

> *'Maybe the nature of a particular can be understood only in relation to sound inside the sense it quickens.'*
>
> Susan Howe

―

In a slew of broken concrete we are attracted to a blade of green grass. It doesn't even have to be green either, it can be wheaten, the colour of bone. When our eye lands on high viridian cliffs with the ocean lapping and roaring at them from underneath we want to sing. At least to speak. Or, if not, to listen as well as look.

Biophilia is the attraction of life to life. When entomologist Edward O. Wilson first coined the term, he would have had perhaps some inkling of the energy his idea itself would attract. Part of his biophilia theory implies that life longs to marry life, to acquaint itself with life, to cohabit with life. For the speaking, singing, dancing, painting human this can be described as the biosphere having a call. The heart lifts, either in fear or wonder, and wants to provide an echo to that call, or, at the very least, an interpretation.

Here then is my position on the map, here then are my coordinates of heart and mind, grief and vision, history and its impact.

Wilson suggests a force of attraction between life and life, which cannot help but remind us of the force of gravity in our atmosphere. And so when the hills above Bass Strait curve down from sky to shore in such grand scale I cup my ear for the correspondence in local human culture. Some song or text or dance or image that those that live here have made in response. But what happens when the human voices of such a compelling landscape, or any landscape, have experienced a rupture more akin to a gravitational attraction to death rather than life? Is that *necro-*, rather than *bio-*, philia? Does our inheritance of that disruption leave us wanting to offer a reply to the life of the place but only capable of making a shrill one?

> **Philia** – (/'fɪljə/ or /'fɪliə/; Ancient Greek: φιλία), often translated 'brotherly love', is one of the four ancient Greek words for love: *philia*, *storge*, *agape* and *eros*. In Aristotle's *Nicomachean Ethics*, **philia** is usually translated as 'friendship' or affection. The complete opposite is called a phobia.

———

Once he enters the Grand Hotel building the man removes his hat. Immediately he sees the golden ribbed horn of a gramophone on a table near the bottom of the staircase at the far end of the foyer. But even before that he hears the sound. Perhaps he actually heard it coming up the steps. The doleful strains of the orchestra. The crackle of the needle. The voice.

> *Caro mio ben,*
> *Credimi almen,*
> *Senza di te languisce il cor.*

It is just before midday. He stands alone with the music.

> *Il tuo fedel*
> *Sospira ognor.*
> *Cessa, crudel,*
> *Tanto rigor!*

Eventually a member of the hotel staff appears through a side doorway. A young man, he comes initially with a bustling gait, but sensing the stillness of the visitor listening there with his hat in his hands, he slows and acknowledges the music with a smile.

It is our visitor who speaks first.

Good day to you.

And to you sir. Can I be of assistance?

Please, yes. The visitor nods towards the gramophone. Can you tell me who is singing?

The concierge smiles once more, but also with the beginnings of a laugh. I can sir, he says. Normally I am no afficionado but Mr —, who owns the hotel, only recently bought this record. He has made sure it is known to us all.

I see.

The singer is Beniamino Gigli, sir. There is a second 'g' in the surname but you don't pronounce it. Italian, sir. At present we are playing the record rather a lot.

Thank you.

You like it sir?

Well yes, I do.

Can I ask then, if you don't mind. Do you understand what he is singing about? That's what always stumps me.

Our visitor frowns. 'Not really,' he says. 'Perhaps a little. My mother was half Italian.'

The young concierge raises his eyebrows in surprise. I see sir, he says.

There is a pause in their conversation, and briefly in the music. *Sish, sish.* When the arias recommence the concierge says: Now then sir, do you have a booking for a room? Or can I help you with anything else?

———

When I was a teenager, making my first acquaintance with what classical scholars call Eros, with its local smell of zinc cream, mosquito coils, dusty leucopogon leaves and, of course, the surf, I found one of its closest cultural correspondences in the songs of the Canadian singer Neil Young. Subsequently I discovered that Young had a house and studio on the Pacific coast, in California, and that both the *Great* Ocean Road (where I write) and the *Grand* Pacific Hotel (where my grandfather stayed in 1937), are in a way scions of that Californian culture in which he lived. Henry Gwynne, who built the Grand Pacific in 1879, had been inspired to do so by a journey he made along the

Californian coastal highway a few years before. *I know a spot*, he must have thought to himself, *where only the wind blows*. Into that assumed 'vacancy' he inserted his plan.

Many years later in 1919, when Messrs Howard Hitchcock and co. of the philanthropic Great Ocean Road Trust were devising the idea of a road that would open up the scenery of the Otway coast, it was the Californian ocean road that provided a template. Its very existence, along with the road through Ilfracombe in Devon, England, gave a real-life imprimatur to their vision.

Why then does the hotel, and the road running to it, inspire something more in us than mimesis? Are we that live in and around this coast:

gannet, myrtle beech, crayfish, bullant, bluegum, wattlebird, sheoak, bandicoot, leucopogon

suffering from our lexicon of borrowed names?

If I call you Susan and your name's actually Joy, do you feel the miss?

—

The hotel's guest is our grandfather. By the time he went to bed that first night in the Grand Pacific it is possible that he had taken Gigli's voice, the melodies and the sentiments of the record the publican had purchased, into the very salt of his bloodstream. If nothing else it had put him in a listening frame of mind. When he went down for lunch after being shown his room it may have been 'Panis Angelicus', 'the bread of heaven', coming from the golden ribbed horn. Later in the day, when he stepped out through the foyer to stroll down the slope and inspect the pier, it may have been Bassani's 'Posate, dormite'. The eternal sleep of heaven. Whatever the case he was caught, in his very own *mappa mundi*, between the two poles of heaven and hell. He died before I was born, so I can only imagine him standing at the end of the pier looking back across the bay towards the lighthouse. The image makes me also think of Jay Gatsby gazing across at the East Egg light. Despite the fact that the very existence of the Grand Pacific Hotel in Lorne was inspired by Henry Gwynne's tour along the North American coast, why in this case does the involuntary association feel like a trivial literary allusion? Is it only because our grandfather's situation is a real-life one, and therefore to be deemed more important than that of F. Scott Fitzgerald's fictional character? Or is there some other reason, something caught not between our judgements of what is real and imagined but between our notions of this world and the next?

For our grandfather there was no Daisy Buchanan to yearn for just across the bay. Quite the opposite. His young wife, Rita, our grand-mother, had only recently died after a long, gruelling illness. William Day was a widow in the midst of his mourning. That's why he had been persuaded to come on his own to Lorne.

> 'All that is told of the sea has a fabulous sound to an inhabitant
> of the land, and all its products have a certain fabulous quality,
> as if they belonged to another planet, from seaweed to a sailor's
> yarn, or a fish story.'
>
> Henry David Thoreau

In 2009, as I was composing the third of my Mangowak novels, *The Grand Hotel*, a consultancy company based in Melbourne called Village Well was commissioned by the Great Ocean Road Coast Committee (GORCC) to produce a document on the future development of Point Grey, at the southern extent of the township of Lorne. By September of that year this document materialised as the 125-page 'Point Grey & Slaughterhouse – Place Essence Report'.

Point Grey, site of the Grand Pacific Hotel and the Lorne pier, along with the nearby former slaughterhouse area of the colonial town, was considered by GORCC, the commissioners of the report, to require fresh 'investigation and planning' for 'future use and management'.

The creators of the 'Place Essence Report', Village Well, described themselves in the document they produced as 'place makers'. The document also incorporated their self-description as specialists in 'the 5Ps of Place Making – People, Place, Product, Program and Planet'.

Is it confusing that the word 'Place' is itself included in the list of ingredients that make up a place? My head hurts. Is the term 'tautological' sufficient to describe this anomaly?

In fact, it begs the question: *Wasn't the place they're purporting to make already there?*

If not, where did the sound of the sea come from that our grandfather heard in 1937? And exactly what void-like absence is capable of producing the luminous pollen filaments that billow along the point every spring?

Due to its apparent failure to account for the place already in existence before the potential existence of the 'place' that they had taken it upon themselves to make, I wonder if Village Well's 'Place Essence Report' isn't a belated corporate manifestation of the dreaded terra nullius. But perhaps I'm being too harsh. Maybe something deeper is going on. Maybe the 'Place Essence Report' actually embodies Village Well's inherently metaphysical view of the world, and the vague imprecision of its language implies the presence of some unseen spirit realm, a possible unexplained foundry that produced all these supposedly indescribable prior phenomena that have been just waiting like sculptor's clay for Village Well's particular skill set to arrive.

Things such as *gannets, myrtle beeches, crayfish, bullants, bluegums, wattlebirds, sheoaks, bandicoots, leucopogons* ...

In David Unaipon's *Native Legends* of 1929, the following explanation is given for the coming of humans to the earth:

> *when the appointed period arrived Spirit Man made the Great Decision and adventure to be clothed with earthly body of flesh*

and blood, his Spirit Consciousness experienced a great change, for he was overshadowed by another self, the Subjective Consciousness, which entirely belongs to the Earth and not to the Sacred Realm of Spirit, Immortal dwelling place, just at the threshold of the Greater Spirit, the Father of all Mankind – Eternal Home. He began to realise that his Spirit Self was controlled by an earthly Subjective Consciousness which bound him to earth's environment with all its blessing, disappointment, discomfort and its pain and sorrow. Being a stranger in a strange land he found it most difficult to adapt himself to earth's environment. His Spirit Self began to fret and pine for its Heavenly Home. The Living Creatures of the Earth saw his plight and were moved with pity and sympathy.

The town of Lorne itself was named in 1871, in honour of the Marquess of Lorne from Argyllshire in Scotland's marriage to Queen Victoria's sixth child, Princess Louise. Point Grey, however (the supposed *yet-to-be-a-place* of Village Well's 'Place Essence Report'), being itself a more noticeable outcrop of the land into the sea, especially when viewed from a ship, was given its English name well before this, probably in 1846, by surveyor George Smythe in honour of the Portuguese-born George Grey, Governor of South Australia from 1841 to 1845.

Nicolas Baudin, French explorer and cartographer, and leader of the Napoleonic expedition to map the coast of Australia, sailed past current-day Lorne in March 1802. In an onomastic fervour typical of hydrographers of the era, he bestowed French names on numerous features of the coast as he sailed past, some of which have been retained to the present day. Curiously, Baudin recorded no name for Lorne nor the *yet-to-be-a-place* that has come to be known as Point Grey, but he was inspired to call the headland just northeast of Lorne Pointe des Souffleurs, or 'Point of the Blowers'. These days that headland is known locally as 'Cinema Point' but I like to think that in choosing his name Baudin somehow presaged the kind of hubris contained in Village Well's 'Place Essence Report'. It's far more likely of course that Pointe des Souffleurs refers to whales seen blowing from their holes as he passed by.

———

Only a few months before our grandfather's arrival at the Pacific in his Standard Tourer, he had emerged alone one morning from the front door of his brick and weatherboard house in Wishart Street, East Kew, Melbourne. Between the door and the gate out onto the street was a narrow pathway. On either side of the pathway were a series of white standard rose bushes, which he had planted for his young rose-loving wife Rita not long after they married. Now our grandfather, a public servant of the Lands Department, a secretary of the Victorian Athletics Association, born at Hyanmi near the family farm at Mologa in 1884, bent down to pull out each of the white rose bushes one by one with his bare hands.

I have been told how quiet and gentlemanly he was, not inarticulate as such but not prone to gales of expressiveness either. I have inherited the notion that silence, rather than words, was his medium. The rests, or spaces in between. He has always existed for me in a quietude with its own very personal harmonic. His wife had died that morning. Her body lay still in the house. He had three children: two teenage daughters, and a younger son, Adrian, my father. Our grandfather was known to his friends as Bill Day, and pulling up the white roses was the only way Bill Day knew, on that well-mannered street in East Kew, to howl like the wind.

———

Our grandmother had been sick for about a year before she died. Our grandfather had looked after her at home and our father, who turned ten on the day she died, shared a bed with her during that final year. I'm not sure which of his friends recommended, a few weeks later, that Bill get away on his own for a few days down at Lorne. Their logic, as it was told to me by his second daughter, my Aunt Joan, was that he needed a spell, from work, and from the responsibilities of his new predicament as a single parent. He had had no time on his own to recover from what he had endured. So things were arranged: a room at the Pacific, a week's leave from the Lands Department, and his two older daughters to look after young Adrian.

Those anonymous friends who sent him to the coast, their names lost now, fallen through time's perforations in the pages of our family history, had no way of knowing what they were setting in train. But it was surely a good thing they had arranged, and it has always had a famous companion story in my mind. In 1910 Henry Lawson was also sent by a group of his friends for a break at Mallacoota when he had come out of Darlinghurst Gaol. The south coast was unfamiliar to him. The small amount he wrote about it, a few ballads and prose sketches, is full of Lawson melancholia but is also noteworthy for being ventilated by an occasional breeze of healing air:

> *Free from Fortune's slings and arrows,*
> *From all thoughts of rent or meal,*
> *Where the islets creeks and narrows*
> *Teem with fish and swarm with teal.*

You could not say that the funds raised to send Lawson away for a break significantly altered the course of his life, but as in the case of my grandfather Bill, the gesture was appreciated at the time and seemed to have the desired effect.

———

Sometimes the effects of such acts of kindness persist beyond the moment and for many years to come. From the top-storey sea-facing rooms of the Pacific the view is still beautiful in the present day. I take a room for the night to see it all over again for myself. The windows face east across blue water beyond the point and the pier towards Split Point Lighthouse, also to the north-east through the tops of the blue gums on Scotchmans Hill. Across the gentle arc and frith of Louttit Bay you look directly over to the timbered hills of what is nowadays known locally as North Lorne. This Grand Hotel, built in 1879, was an outpost of empire, a framing of natural wonders, a taming of a treacherous sea. Despite the many ships that had become wrecked on the coast, the cove of Lorne quite literally has its back to the wildest weather and a navigational light always in view. But being out on the southern edge of the point, the Grand Pacific is less protected. It is closer to the experience of the sublime so sought after by the exponents of early tourism. It catches the full brunt of the southerlies and the glancing edge of the south-westerlies whilst the centre of the town can remain immune. And when the strong easterly hits, no one, either at the edge or in the centre, can escape the whirling grain of salt, foam and stipple that the sea brings to the air. As Burke says in his *Philosophic Enquiry into the Origin of Our Ideas of the Sublime and Beautiful*: 'a clear idea is another name for a little idea'.

Right there amongst the awesome scale of nature and the wild unpredictability of life, the hotel offers a viewing platform, an ornamented haven, a late Victorian parenthesis built out of Erskine River stone, Gadubanud clay bricks and colonial mortar.

It seems strange staying in the hotel on what essentially is my home turf. It feels in itself tautological, or like I'm an imposter. So, at dinnertime, rather than going downstairs and suffering the blandishments of the staff, I step outside and take a stroll down to the restaurant by the pier. I drink a coffee at the bar and enjoy some banter with its proprietor Sammy Gazis, who I know from my years spent working in the fisherman's co-op next door. Then I walk across town on the rocks and beach at low tide to eat with the godmother of my youngest son at her house in North Lorne. We have a pleasant time. Lindy leaves the front door open to the surf across the road as we talk. I listen as much to it as to her. Perhaps she does too. Around 9 pm I say goodbye.

On the walk back I am annoyed by the bright strip-lights they installed when they built the new promenade pier in 2007, around the time the GORCC was considering the commissioning of Village Well's 'Place Essence Report'. The pier is lit up like an airport runway except only flesh and blood birds want to land. The lights are good for catching squid, but not for much else. They detract from the night sky, the stars. The original Gadubanud inhabitants of this area described the stars as the campfires of the ancestors.

I walk the beach and savour the particular quiet of closed shops. When I arrive back at the Pacific, I go straight through the foyer and up to my room. I make myself a cup of tea and get into bed. I think about playing some Gigli on my iPad but read Raffaele La Capria's *Capri And No Longer Capri* instead. But only for a half an hour or so. And then the moment comes when I turn out the light and lay my head on the pillow.

———

gannet, myrtle beech, crayfish, bullant, bluegum, wattlebird, sheoak, bandicoot, leucopogon ...

Pull these words out by their roots and see how little soil is clinging to them here. Pull the very same words out by their roots in old England (gannet, myrtle and beech, wattle and bird, she and oak), in France (crayfish, bull and ant, blue and gum), in Andhra Pradesh (bandicoot), in Ancient Greece (leucopogon), and you could be sitting around the campfires of the ancestors for at least a thousand and one nights.

———

Perhaps what Irv Teibel had discovered in his *Psychologically Ultimate Seashore* was not so much the modern concept of ambient music but the ancient resonance of the amniotic grotto. Respected psychoacoustic research overlaps to some extent with the smarm of

New Age 'healing ocean' CDs in its correlation of the effects of sound with our somatic preconditioning. It shows that the chain of our psychoacoustic responses to life is predicated on the fact that hearing is not only a biological but a perceptual activity. It begins in the realm of nanophysics, with the fact that all atomic matter vibrates. The frequency of these vibrations produces sound, which, amongst other things, can ultimately be moulded into what we call music. In utero the human ear begins to form almost immediately after conception and is fully grown and functioning after only sixteen weeks' gestation inside the womb. It is during this formative period that we begin our life as *listeners* to the atomic frequencies of life, for at this early stage we are *listeners* more than we are seers, or sniffers, or touchers, speakers or thinkers. The sound we hear assists in the actual growth of our brain and nervous system. In utero all is fluid sound; we hear the rhythm of our mother, her voice as she speaks to us, and we vaguely perceive, *by listening*, the enigma of a wider world coming towards us through a thin membrane of flesh and blood. Encased in the maternal body we are immersed in the sonic energy of life. There are no plastics like there are in the anthropocenic sea, and no technology other than that which our mysteriously organic existence has made.

By simply re-presenting the sound of the sea in 1969, Teibel's *Environments 1* struck a fundamental chord, and not just with the hippies. By leaving out any form of human musicianship other than sound treatments in the studio, *Environments 1* placed us in proximity to an original mode of *entrainment*, which is a term psychoacousticians use to describe how sounds alter the speed and activity of our brains, our breaths and our heartbeats. If one is prepared to believe that the womb, or amniotic grotto, feels to the foetus like a natural and safe place, providing it with everything it needs as it grows towards the state of maturity required for it to encounter the wider world, then one must also credit that the resembling *sish sish* of the ocean at night quite possibly triggers within us some kind of elemental memory of that prior condition.

Issuing from this amniotic dream there is a road without a sign, a coast without a real estate agent, a place without a name. For one or maybe two days of the year, usually in February, there is also a sea without a wave. This is the moment of the seine net and the flounder spear, when the kiss of tide on sand drops to a whisper, when the ocean bed is visible, when the deeper shapes can be made out. This still weather of a lake-like ocean comes at the tapering end of a run of northerlies, and has always reminded me of Franz Marc's painting, *The Sleeping Bull*. For a moment the stereotypic mode of brute power is withdrawn. Even Polyphemus must dream.

The earth moves elliptically, it is neither flat nor round, and some integers of time have names dreamt in the memory only. Some have no names at all. In Greek the source word *elleiptikos* implies a defectiveness in all this, but *elleiptikos* in turn comes from *elleipein* which actually means to 'leave out', to 'fall short'. The implication is the truth of imperfection.

A stitch is missed. A space is created. Some things are beyond description. These spaces encourage human yearning. There is a yearning for explanation, which often results in science, or what is called mythology. But there is also a biophiliac yearning to some-how sensually match the feeling or physical *sensation* of the space. The space our grandmother's death left behind. The space in our grandfather's heart that the sound of the ocean filled. This leads us to singing.

True songs of this space exist firstly as caves, contours, passing gullies. We feel their magnetism and tumble towards them. But they come and go, they dip and rise, teasing the solidity of the canon. They are harmonics of the world's fundamental note, indispensable in the timbre of the music of our dreams.

Did you hear the ocean last night?

It took me a long time to work this out, the partially obscured signal that has come down through the bloodlines, the story that dwells like the sibilance of the ocean itself, under everything I have written. Perhaps precisely because it is a story that is positioned so subliminally in the family, just like the ocean at night, it has magnetised my imagination. Long before 1841, when James and Mary Day arrived off the ship in Geelong and settled at Moriac and then ultimately on the Barwon River at Inverleigh, the cove of Lorne had another name. The beach sat like a crescent moon carved into the steep edge of the forest, a foyer to Gadubanud country, or king parrot country. In the language of the Wadawurrung across the bay at Split Point, the word for king parrot was 'yukope'; in the Peek Whurrong or 'kelp lip' language further west of the Otways around Port Fairy, it is 'waetuurong'. But the ancient local word for the cove of Lorne itself has been lost. It has become a word more like a fallen star, mingling among the sound of the waves in my grandfather's ear ...

———

If the lost word feels like a falling star, it follows, in a conflation of the metaphor entirely consistent with biophilia, that the spirits of the campfire ancestors of the night sky are always descending and walking among us. These are the type of personages, the living, dying people of the deep amniotic past of this country, that it is natural for any human to have a hunger to meet. So I ask myself: is every song, every story, every poem and novel I write, a *cooee* into the darkness?

I cock my ear, I raise my antennae, I watch watch watch, listen listen listen ...

———

It was not the *sight* of the blue sea in Lorne's famously limpid light that had the biggest impact on the solitary widower in 1937. Rather it was the *sound* of the sea at night.

When our grandfather returned to East Kew after his week at the Pacific he said two things to his young boy Adrian about his trip away. The first thing that had struck him was the voice of an Italian tenor that he had heard playing in the hotel. He would listen almost religiously to that voice for the rest of his days. The second thing that had struck him, and a magical thing it must have been in the ears of a kid who like his Dad had never seen the ocean, was the sound of the sea under his pillow at night. My father was told it was the most beautiful sound on earth.

For a man who didn't usually express his innermost feelings and sensations, this testimony of our grandfather's seems to have left a deep emotional groove. In the house without its mother it immediately took on the quality of a myth. Yes, there was another world, a world transcending the pain and rupture of death, a world apart from the dry parsimonious paddocks of Mologa and the hard bustle of Melbourne. It was a natural world, a beautiful world, the world, as it happened, of our forebears. In that place the sound of the sea came each night like a mother's lullaby.

———

Our grandfather's anecdote about the sound of the sea under his pillow at night became an alternative harmonic to unspeakable grief in the eaves of my father's childhood home. They could all hear it now, his father, himself, and his sisters: the sound of the ocean at night in the midst of a city wedged between the deprivations of the Great Depression and the brutalities of the Second World War. Even just the idea of the sound became a soothing flageolet in the house-timbre, a high and consolatory correspondence produced from a fundamental note of sadness and pain.

In the years after 1937, everyday life in Wishart Street, East Kew, never became normalised. My grandfather and my father's elder sisters were loving towards the boy, but the mother he had slept with through that last year of her life, the mother who passed away on his tenth birthday, had entered her afterlife as an all-encompassing yet subliminal sensation. For my grandfather it was an assuaging memory. The surf under his pillow in the high front room of the Pacific at Lorne. For my father, a wonderful tale, a sonic lure, an acoustic myth. A fabulous antidote to the sharp fact of her smell still permeating his pyjamas and pillowslips.

As soon as he was old enough he himself would head straight for the coast. We have been here ever since.

The sound of the ocean at night. Her loss was its key. Everything was wrong, but it would also be all right because far from the city a beauty equivalent to hers existed in a peaceful cove at the end of a heavenly road. The stars shone at night above a Grand Hotel on the point, and you could fall asleep and dream to the sound of *sish sish, sish sish* ...

One True Note?

1.

In Ian D. Clark's *Aboriginal Languages and Clans: An Historical Atlas of Western and Central Victoria*, in the section entitled 'Wada wurrung language history and demographic decline', there is a list of variant spellings of the name of this country and its people. Wadawurrung country, or Wadawurrung tabayl, in south-western Victoria, is bordered by Werribee River in the east, Ballarat and Beaufort in the north, and the Painkalac Creek here at Aireys Inlet in the south-west. Removing mistranscriptions from the list, Clark has identified 133 different recorded spellings of the word:

> *Watowrong, Wartorong, Wotowrong, Watourong, Wat-r-*
> *ong, Waddow-row, Wad-thou-rong, Waddow ro, Waddow,*
> *Wattowrong, Wattouerong, Wadthowrong, Wadthourong,*
> *Wadourong, Watouring, Waturong, Witowrong, Wadawerang,*
> *Wad.dow.wer.rer, Wartowerang, Wartowerong, Wartow*
> *werang, War.tow.wer.rong, Waterwrong, Wortowerong,*
> *Watawerong, Woolowrong, Wor-tow.wer.ong, Wor.tow.*
> *erong, Wad-dow-wer-rer, Wad dow wer rong, Wod.dow.*
> *wer.rong, Watowerong, Waddowerong, Wad-dowerong,*
> *Waddowerang, Wadong, Wadoung, Wadouro, Wadowrong,*
> *Wot-tow-rong, Witourong, Wadower, Witswrong, Wadowio,*
> *Wodowro, Widowra, Widoura, Wadowro, Wadoora, Witaoro,*

Griffith Review (2019)

Waddorow, Wawtowerang, Wartowong, Wotowerong,
Watowerong, Woodowrow, Wodourow, Wodowo, Witowurrong,
Woddowrong, Witouro, Wiitya whuurong, Wot-tow-rong, Wod-
dow-ro, Watorrong, Witowro, Wuddyawurra, Wathaurung,
Wudthurung, Wudthau'rung, Wudthauwurung, Wadthawurung,
Watchaora, Wood-thau-rang, Wuddiau rung, Wudthawurung,
Witowurung, Wud tha wrung, Wuddyawea, Wuddyawurru,
Woddowro, Wudthaurung, Wodowrong, Wito-wu-rrong,
Witoura, Wudjawurung, Waitowrung, Wataurun, Wudja:wuru,
Wudjawuru, Woodowro, Wudja wuru, Wothowurong,
Wataurung, Woddowerong, Wathaurung, Wadthaurung,
Wadourer, Wollowurong, Wadjawuru, Wadhawurung, Widouro,
Watha wurrung, Wudtharung, Waltaurun, Wudjawurong,
Witowurong, Wuddjawurro, Wudthaurun, Woltrowurong,
Watdjurang, Wathourung, Wadiwid, Wadawrang, Wateran,
Water-ang, Watowerang, Wadthaurang, Wadawio, Woddoro,
Wotherwurong, Wittowurrung, Witaioro, Wad-ja-wurru,
Wud-ja-warra, Wadja-wurrung, Witherwerong, Wittoro, Wad-
dow-er-er, Witoura, Wit-ya-whaurung, Wada wurung.

A single word. 133 versions. That the European colonists privileged a written Roman alphabet over oral communication, and that the Wadawurrung language at the time of first contact in the early 1800s was exclusively oral, are of course key reasons for this polyphony of misnomers. Perhaps, though, as a tool for understanding how complex the realities of colonial dispossession are, this list amounts to a compelling metaphor. It denotes both the pitfalls and the possibilities of trying to interpret this place in the exogenous language of written English.

I can read this list as both tragic *and* musical. It is also inherently farcical, or tragicomical. Also, as a pure coincidence of the number of words – 133 – the list has taken on an association for me with Wallace Stevens' prismatic poem 'Thirteen Ways of Looking at a Blackbird'. Try, just for starters, '133 Ways of Looking at a Heartland', or '133 Ways of Misunderstanding Tabayl'. In its permutative nature, the list feels like a programming code of what some academics call our 'anglo-Indigenous' landscape. Full of such close orthographic modulations, it requires the most intensely ironic concentration to transcribe the 133 spellings precisely.

———

Halldór Laxness, the Icelandic novelist who broke with modern tradition by writing in his own native Icelandic language rather than colonial Danish, won the Nobel Prize in 1955 two years before the publication of his novel *The Fish Can Sing*. In the novel an opera singer named Gardar Holm, a local boy made good in the opera houses of Europe, intermittently returns to his native soil with the promise that he will honour his countrymen by singing for them. As the singer repeatedly fails to fulfil this promise, the myth of his artistry burgeons to fill the space left by the absence of his song. The myth is further encouraged by Gardar Holm's philosophy, which he bestows on the novel's young narrator Alfgrimur, that life is the quest to attain the 'one true note'. The catch is that whoever attains this note will thereafter cease to sing. Thus Laxness, who with inspired and seemingly superhuman effort, returned his island's literature back to the autochthonous tongue of its ancient sagas, knew both the vast energy that such a quest for authenticity requires as well as the illusory, even impossible, nature of the task.

Language, like the wind, is hard to pin down. It relies on movement for its existence, as we rely on breath for life. The sound of language also often reminds me of water. It *forms, runs, braids, pools, knocks, rustles, rushes, flows* … Like a river it is always moving, even when it appears to be still. Its currents are endlessly various but the river itself remains the sum total and singular shape of those currents. The river is *cadence*.

Is the language I write in – *English* – a second language on this littoral where we live?

Or a third?

John Berger, in a small essay called 'Self-Portrait', which he published just before his death in early 2017, writes that, 'Mother Tongue is our first language, first heard as infants from the mouths of our mothers'. But what if 'Mother Tongue' was not to be attributed to the individual mother but more ambiently to what the Greeks called Gaia, or 'Mother Earth'? In this way, through the membrane of the womb, the words and sounds spoken by the human mother are recognised as part of a wider array of environmental sounds. Thus we can understand the womb as our first auditory learning space, and the sounds coming to us from the as yet unseen realm outside the womb as our first metaphysics.

If, as otolaryngologist Dr Alfred Tomatis maintains, the human ear is fully grown and functioning after only sixteen weeks' gestation and 'the ear's first function in utero is to govern the growth of the rest of the physical organism', then it follows that from such beginnings we learn to connect the close rhythms of our own blood with the mirror rhythms of a vast world. We begin too to decipher the repeating sonic agreements by which the first humans around us chose to communicate information within that vast biophonic sphere.

Always underneath though, before and surrounding these agreed upon phonemes and words, is the music we are made of, the first symphony of sound, or language, of our first *place*.

Perhaps Berger's sentence could therefore be recomposed:

> Mother ~~Tongue~~ Earth is our first language, first heard as infants ~~from the mouths of our mothers~~ conceived afresh into this new environment or life-world.

Noam Chomsky qualifies his notion that 'a human being or any complex organism has a system of cognitive structures that develop much in the way the physical organs of the body develop' by agreeing that 'they grow under particular environmental conditions, assuming a specific form that admits of some variation'.

To what extent the variations determined by environment can be embodied in written language is a key concern of mine here. David Abram, in a foundational text for the still emerging discipline of ecolinguistics, describes how, in the ancient Semitic cultures in which the first alphabets were developed, vowels were left out of written texts in order to avoid desacralising the world they described. The twenty-two letters of the Hebrew *aleph-beth*, for instance, were all consonants. This was some kind of early negotiated compromise between oral and written culture, whereby the air, or breath of life, intrinsic to the production of vowel sounds (as opposed to the sculptural physicality of consonants relying on the palate, lips, teeth, tongue, etc.) was excluded from texts to avoid the dangers of abstraction from the very life-world they were attempting to transpose into script. The reader of these ancient texts was forced then to creatively engage with the strictly consonantal content by choosing which vowel sound went where in each word. In this way, Abram believes,

> *a Hebrew text could not be experienced as a double – a stand-in or substitute – for the sensuous corporeal world. The Hebrew letters and texts were not sufficient unto themselves; in order to be read, they had to be added to, enspirited by the reader's breath. The invisible air, the same mystery that animates the visible terrain, was also needed to animate the visible letters, to make them come alive and to speak.*

By the reader having to insert the vowel sounds into the exclusively consonantal architecture of each written word, the text required an active, even performative participation for it to attain complete cogency, thereby admitting, and in part circumventing, the increased distancing from the psychoacoustic life-world that can be built in to written texts as compared to oral speech. The refusal to print the vowel sounds, which rely for their manufacture on the wider ubiquity of a more-than-human environment, ensured not only that the reader was 'enlisted as an agent of the writing' but also that written texts did not atomise or 'cool' into mere annotations of creation. Rather, they were always coming into being, in the mind and on the tongue of the reader, or *wreader*. In this way, to transpose Robert Lowell's classic definition of poetry to the wider question of language itself, the text maintained its status as an 'event, not the record of an event'.

The telling scene in the English writer Alan Garner's uncanny William Buckley novel *Strandloper*, which I have already recounted in this book, relates specifically to this point. Garner's books are very much driven by his topophilia, or powerful attachment to place. His work is famously saturated with a mythic swirl of endemic rocks, meres, trees and meteorological phenomena, and also with the vernacular palimpsest of the historical and pre-historical cultural landscape of his native Cheshire. The story of William Buckley, who famously escaped the putative Australian colonial settlement at present-day Sorrento in Port Phillip Bay in 1803 and lived for thirty-two years with the Wadawurrung before rejoining the Anglosphere not long after the first settlement of Melbourne, only found its place in Garner's creative orbit because Buckley was originally from his part of the world. What Garner brings to Buckley's story – which has always been claimed as an exclusively Australian story – is the idea that there was potentially deep sylvan dreaming on both sides of the cultural divide.

To replay the scene from *Strandloper*, Buckley is on the beach at Beangala, a place on the Bellarine Peninsula in south-west Victoria these days known as Indented Head. He is terribly homesick. To assuage his longing he writes the name of his childhood sweetheart back in England in the sand. *Het*, he writes, a nickname for Esther. A Wadawurrung elder entirely of Garner's imagining, who he calls Nullamboin, asks Buckley: 'Why do you cut sand?' Buckley explains that this writing or 'cutting sand' is a form of naming, a type of dreaming that can also be an expression of knowledge. Nullamboin is sceptical but wants to know more. He gets Buckley to write other words, the words of Wadawurrung deities, including Bundjil the eagle, in the sand. Verifying that these words can also be cut into rock or wood, Nullamboin reacts dramatically as the future ramifications of this new and superficial way of transmitting culture dawns on him.

Nullamboin rubs the sand and strides off: 'Then all will see without knowledge', he cries, 'without teaching, without dying into life! Weak men will sing! Boys will have eagles! All shall be mad!'

After reading *Strandloper*, and also some of the history around the desacralising Enclosure Acts of England that took place in Buckley's time, it seems logical that in many ways the pre-invasion Wadawurrung customs and beliefs would have been more familiar to this Cheshire bricklayer, who had grown up with many traditional and pantheistic customs of his region still extant, than they would be to us Moolacenes today.

There is a consistency here too between Nullamboin's fear and Abram's idea that the air, breath, or wind-mind, the medium through which our consciousness, and therefore our cognitive functioning, operates, is being obscured by the written word. In this way it might be said that the truncation that inevitably takes place between the world-in-itself and the language that describes it, is less pronounced in fully embodied oral cultures whose language has evolved biophonically within its specifically contoured region. It follows therefore that the onomatopeia often evident in Wadawurrung descriptors – 'parrwang' (magpie), 'go-im' (kangaroo), even 'yern' (moon) – is evidence of that lessening of truncation. It also follows that a writer attempting to write, or sing, a home landscape in grammatical units of agreed meaning, would be drawn towards words that reduce the truncation effect of language by actually *sounding* the world around them. In this way the very atmosphere we breath becomes the singing ingredients of our cultural expression. Story is given birth to, as if it is flesh itself. As Maurice Merleau-Ponty maintains in his *Phenomenology of Perception* – first published in 1962, the same year the Commonwealth Electoral Act was amended to provide that 'Indigenous people could enrol to vote in federal elections if they wished' – a word is not the 'mere sign of objects and meanings' but 'inhabits things and is the vehicle of meanings'. It is in fact 'the essence of the thing it describes' and 'resides in it on the same footing as its colour or form'.

In other words the descriptor and the object of description in any given phrase, lyric or sentence, enact a two-way exchange, as in the umbilical bond between mother and child, or the sensory communion between landscape and the dweller within it.

———

When Charles Taylor cites Wilhelm von Humboldt's expression of 'a feeling that there is something which the language does not directly contain, but which the (mind/soul), spurred on by language, must supply and the (drive), in turn, to couple everything felt by the soul with a sound', he seems to point us in the direction of the inherent mystery of the source of language. Taylor also contends that 'it is not only poets, novelists and artists who feel this, although it is the very stuff of their existence, but also just about everyone at some point in their lives'. Chomsky too, in regard to what he terms 'creative use' of language, maintains that it remains 'as much of a mystery now as it did centuries ago, and may turn out to be one of those ultimate secrets that ever will remain in obscurity, impenetrable to human intelligence.'

The idea of an impenetrable or mysterious source of language has an affinity with many ancient–ongoing Indigenous cultures, which privilege the unseen over the seen. When we hear David Prosser, a Yaegl man from the lower reaches of the Clarence River on the north coast of New South Wales, citing Gamilaroi elder Aunty Rose Fernando's declaration that 'language is our soul', we begin to enter again the realm of the unseen. Prosser says that when he first heard that phrase, 'it instantly entered the deepest part of my heart. And as I continued to think about what she had said I realised that that part of my heart was my soul.'

Of course Prosser's words are not meant to be understood physio-logically, but they nevertheless speak anatomically of unseen sources, thereby implying the embodied nature of our linguistic acquisition in lived environments. As such they also ask us to think in different ways about our 133 written misnomers. It is as if the colonial and postcolonial language collectors of Victoria, who in this context we might ironically call *stenographers of country*, were attempting to perform a task with the wrong instruments. Instead of listening within the context of unseen sources, or the 'deepest part of the heart', they were attempting to *capture* merely linguistic *material*. Instead of understanding the words in their full bio-etymological context, they were reducing them from a pollen-like existence amidst the living air to a ham-fisted afterlife on the static page. Whatever their many and various cultural, religious and economic motivations, they were indeed attempting to *pen* Indigenous culture, in both senses of that word. This penning impulse led in turn to the inscription of inadequate imitations, to the writing down of brittle dictations with tragic limitations.

Even allowing for the fluid situation-dependent semantics of languages such as Wadawurrung, where the sound or meaning of a word can change depending on time, place and other culturally significant factors or events, Merleau-Ponty's 'essence of the thing' when applied to our 133 transcribed misnomers becomes an essence of attenuation and misunderstanding rather than of the object, action, feeling, place or language it is intending to signify. We are left with a new series of meanings, a lexicon of glitches that desynchronises human culture with place. It is literally a tragic collision of the vehicles of meaning.

For instance, the list of 133 spellings of Wadawurrung is full of unintentional puns. Such as *Wadawio*. As in: 'What do we owe?' Or the constant repetition of the suffix 'wrong', in words like *Waterwrong*, *Woolowrong*, or *Witswrong*.

Another way of looking at the list is as a great ironic sounding-out of the difficulties of writing from, and about, a particular place within 'anglo-Indigenous country'. As I do.

———

Aireys Inlet, or Mangowak (supposedly meaning 'good place to hunt swans'), is the south-western border of the Turaltja clan of the Wadawurrung, also the border of Wadawurrung country and Gadubanud country, also the border of the wider Kulin nation and the Maar nation. Mangowak is within the boundaries of the Surf Coast Shire, also the cadastral county of Grant, the state electorate of Polwarth, the federal electorate of Wannon, the state of Victoria and the federated nation of Australia. It was when I was a teenager, growing up on the banks of the Painkalac in Aireys Inlet that reception of the ocean landscape and the flash of inspiration Elaine Scarry has called 'radiant ignition', began to feel indivisible for me.

> *Benganak goopmala-ilk talk-getyaweel Nganyakee ba deerda-beel laa-getyaweel*
> *Benganak beetyarra-ik waeema woorr-woorr werreeyt-ik*

> *The sky split open, showing the beauty of the first sunrise. They were so overjoyed to see the light and feel the warmth of the sun's heat, they burst into song.*

> *from 'Magpie' – told and translated by Uncle David Tournier*

Looking along the sepiatone of the Painkalac and down the line of the coast into the south-west, past Grassy Creek and Lorne to the towering headlands, or Taenarea, of the Otways, I felt both a freedom and an agitation, a filling-up and an emptying-out, a thrilling impetus and a terrible lack. This was different from an experience of the sublime in the Burkean sense, yet as the landscape entered me I was simultaneously filled with a recursive desire to respond, to somehow match it, and, in a quasi-Pindaric mood I was unconscious of at the time, to pay tribute to it.

Just a few years later, when I was in my early twenties, I wrote a poem that could be construed as an attempt to begin to tackle a crucial aspect of the difficulty of writing about this place in a language forcibly imposed upon it. By doing so I was beginning to attend to my feelings of confusion and unreadiness for the task.

'Those are not Tuscan hills ...'

the land takes away the g
Adds the b
Leaves you wanting to show
By the way you say
That you're in it, with its
Soil in your ears & shoes
In your hair & tears
It takes away the uni, the g,
The colonization so you're saying
I'm lovin' you, I'm headin' there
It'll be ok and such is life
And the bird's real name is not
That compliant import you've given it
This is sound this is sense
Those are not Tuscan hills.

It is unremarkable that in reaching for a mode of expression to match the historical context of dispossession, the continuing land grab, and the grand sonic atmosphere of the coastline, I ended up having to turn to Europe, and specifically the Mediterranean, as a negative catalyst. I knew already that the particular numinosity I was experiencing in the landscape could not simply be matched with received ideas, borrowed melody or Tuscan *terza rima*. At that time, the late 1980s, there was a fashion for all things Tuscan, not only amongst suburban property developers but also amongst the literary circles of Australia. David Malouf was living in Tuscany, Germaine Greer had a house in

Tuscany, Kate Grenville had just set a novel, *Dreamhouse*, in Tuscany. I was already beginning to draw on the Mediterranean as part of my genetic and cultural inheritance. (As I've already made clear, my ancestor Antonio Denerio arrived in Geelong in the 1840s from Riposto in Sicily at around the same time that my other ancestors James and Mary Day arrived in Geelong from Ireland.) But on a trip to France, Italy, Sicily, Greece and Crete in 1987, I also felt how worn the paths had become over there, how exhausted and even trivialised the Mediterranean landscape had become through an economic reliance on the tropes of Romanticism hyped to industrial levels. I had an inkling of an equivalent but fresher dream here at home, albeit with its own mythological antiquity, if only I could begin to listen and to comprehend. It may have seemed right for the older generations of Australian writers and artists to head to England, Europe and America, but I felt that for my own generation, or at least for myself, the time had come to stay put. To stay meant to grapple not only with the possibilities of new melodic dreams but with a dramatic inheritance of expropriation and absence, and a largely unframed contemporary response to the metaphysical landscape. It also meant a technical wrestling with an often atonal and caustic vernacular, and an attempt to find an accurate language for a post-volcanic yet atavistic environment of sulphur-crested screeching, bull-ant bites and tempestuous Bass Strait winters. All this had to be conjoined with the loyalty and affinity I felt for my family's own linguistic inheritance, from Ireland, from Sicily, and since 1841, from colonial Australia.

The silence in the landscape could be eerie, but the ocean was a radio, transmitting along the riverflat and into the heath and bush. It spoke to me of unseen things, of wondrous feasts, of battles fought in the past, feasts and battles we weren't taught about at school. On the ridgelines of wattle, messmate and xanthorrhoea above the cursive shoreline, or down amongst the enveloping frequencies of the tide on the beach, I cupped a hand to my ear and asked the question: *What actually happened? How did we get here and where the hell are those who were here before?*

Where, for instance, were the creation myths, the songs, the *arias* of word and image that must exist as a response to this very particular atmosphere?

Due to the repression at the time of Indigenous voices in the landscape, what I heard back in response was the sound of the place. It was a wonderful sound, *awesome*, but it was also disorienting, for it spoke of violence and dishonour.

———

In his 'Self-Portrait', John Berger warns that 'words, terms, phrases can be separated from the creature of their language and used as mere labels. They can become inert and empty'. He says that the 'repetitive use of acronyms is a simple example of this'.

By recomposing Berger's words – *Mother ~~Tongue~~ Earth is our first language, first heard as infants ~~from the mouths of our mothers~~ conceived afresh into this new environment or life-world* – I am implying that 'words, terms, phrases' 'become inert and empty' if their speakers cease listening to the language creature of Gaia, *place*, or Mother Earth. This has particular implications for someone like me, who writes in English from the once exclusively oral language-place that is Wadawurrung tabayl.

Continuing along the thread of Berger's thought, the following sentence from his 'Self-Portrait' becomes a deadly one indeed: 'Such dead "word-mongering" wipes out memory and breeds a ruthless complacency.'

This is the 'ruthless complacency' that is at the heart of the European colonial project in Australia. It is important that we don't speak of that project as existing only in the past. It is this very complacency that is still the first aesthetic challenge for the contemporary writer trying to be faithful, or to correspond to the complex language-creature, or *topos*, he or she is born into.

Largely due to my studies in the Wadawurrung language, which with the permission of now deceased Wadawurrung elder and language teacher Uncle David Tournier I began teaching at my children's primary school here in Mangowak in 2015, I have come to believe not only that fish can sing, as Halldór Laxness did, but that words come not only from our mother but like rain from the sky. Time and again the Wadawurrung words the children are learning are explicitly onomatopoeic. They sound like the things, and the environments of the things, they describe. 'Parrwang' (magpie), 'go-im' (kangaroo), 'yern' (moon).

So when nearly all our social contracts and agreements in Australia take place in imported English, do we have a problem? The more we fall in love with our country, the more we yearn to understand it, the more we experience the disorientation of the perpetual misnomer in our senses. Ours is a psychogeography of anxiety. A place of weakened literacy. We try 133 different remedies but remain uncertain about them all. And if in the end we revert to ironic forms of shorthand such as bullet lists (Village Well's 5Ps of Place Making) or acronyms that produce contrary puns (GORCC – Great Ocean Road Coast Committee, as in 'Gawk') we do so not only as efficiency measures and time-saving devices but as expressions of a future in which our Mother Earth may have to shout to be heard. And no matter what word you use for it, we all know what that means.

Otway Taenarum

1.

1988. It is five years after the Ash Wednesday bushfires, which devastated many parts of Victoria, including the coastline of the Eastern Otways. It is also Australia's Bicentennial year. A young man in his early twenties sits on the step of a small fibro bungalow in the Aireys Inlet riverflat, in the thick shade of two towering old radiata pines. Catching the light at his feet is a loamy brocade of russet pine needles, stretching across the yard to the sunroom of his family's house, one of the few buildings in the town to survive the fires.

In this yard there are vegetables growing, a lemon tree, a boat and outboard motor, chopped firewood, surfboards, fishing buoys, a bicycle, a car. Behind him on the step the door of the bungalow is open. Inside the bungalow there is a single bed and a desk with books and cassettes on it. There is music playing, a melody full of tremulous, wistful mandolins. The sound of the music blends with the ocean waves falling into the river mouth less than half a kilometre to the south of where he sits.

The music stops and a voice begins to speak.

Meanjin (2019)

The voice the young man hears from the bungalow cassette player is Italian; the words are Italian too. He listens as they are translated and spoken again in plummy English in the foreground of the music, and over the sound of the sea:

> *This house was inhabited by the sea, by the smell of the sea, the light of the sea, the voice of the sea. The sea was omnipresent.*

The voice pauses now, so that only the sound of the ocean can be heard, which importantly, the young man on the step now realises, is coming both from the recording and from the river mouth.

A woman's voice is heard next, once again speaking English but in a strong Neapolitan accent:

> *At times I have a very beautiful dream and there is always Palazzo Donn'Anna, and the very clear water. It is a part of my life that I wouldn't change with anybody else. I think it was a privilege to live in such an old, majestic, magic place.*

———

When I was in my early twenties and sitting on that bungalow step, a correspondence began to form between the depth of feeling I experienced in the bush and oceanscape around Aireys Inlet, or Mangowak, and the emotional and visual response I was beginning to have to certain works of fiction and poetry. Reading poets and novelists from many countries, including Australia, was to be ushered through a series of unique portals to a mental landscape of sensuous insight and numinous reflection. The experience, because of both its intensity and its liminal quality, converged with my sense of place on the coast. A responsive, cyclical, perpetual interaction was set up that spilt beyond the delineations of conscious thoughts or physical body into the 'response-ability' of literary forms.

Looking first at the landscape, then at the page I was reading, then back at the landscape while still sensing the page, then returning to the text with the life-world of landscape still in my nostrils, a desire was seeded for another page, a new page, on which I could write fresh words, lines, sentences, paragraphs, poems, fables, novels.

In defining the term *wreading*, that is, the simultaneous and recursive synthesis of the acts of reading and writing, the poet and critic Jed Rasula says: '"Wreading" is my neologism for the collaborative momentum initiated by certain texts.' This definition approximates my youthful experience. I noticed even at the time, while *wreading* the works of historical periods and from distant geographies, that this experience amounted to a magnification process which enlarged certain texts of fiction or poetry by placing them mentally in my own physical landscape. Therein I reanimated the narrative and characters within the optics, acoustics and olfactory parameters of my own ground. While reading literary works from other parts of Australia, but also from pre-Soviet Russia, from Second Empire France, from Victorian England, from the American Roaring Twenties or from Ancient Greece, I positioned the action of the work, the narrative events and settings, within my own regional topography. Thus, I pictured Count Vronsky from Tolstoy's *Anna Karenina* on a shooting expedition in the Allen Noble Bird Sanctuary in Aireys Inlet. I imagined Flaubert's characters Bouvard and Pécuchet inhabiting a country house not in Normandy, but on Lardner's Track near Gellibrand, in the heart of the Otway forest. The action of my *wread* version of Charles Dickens' *Bleak House* took place on the seam between forest and plain, in the grounds of the Western District property near Birregurra that borrowed its name. The arc of Jay Gatsby's gaze across the water to the green light on Daisy Buchanan's East Egg dock lay on the south-westerly diagonal from Split Point across Louttit Bay to the pier below the Grand Pacific Hotel in Lorne. Polyphemus's legendary hostages escaped not from a Cyclopean cave on the shores of Homeric Sicily, but from one of the two caves positioned just underneath the Split Point Lighthouse.

With this in mind it was perhaps a logical next step to seek the thrill provided by these non-endemic works of art in imaginative texts *intentionally* set in my hyper-local geography. But what I found when I went looking for such local equivalents was, apart from one or two exceptions, silence ... absence.

There *were* two books though. In the early 1950s the English-born detective writer Arthur Upfield had rented a house in Aireys Inlet in order to write a crime novel there. *The Clue of the New Shoe*, set in a fictional town called Split Point, featured Upfield's Aboriginal detective, Boney. When I first read it in my early twenties, the novel struck me as being atmospherically accurate but disappointingly generic in both a cultural and literary sense. (I nevertheless reprised another character from *The Clue of the New Shoe*, Fred Ayling, in my Mangowak novels. Also, the town of the narrator in my novel, *A Sand Archive*, is likewise called Split Point, which is of course the non-fictional name of the headland that the lighthouse sits on in Aireys Inlet.)

In 1980 Craig Robertson had written a novelised account of the life of escaped convict William Buckley, which dramatised Buckley's time in Mangowak and his life with the Wadawurrung in the surrounding area. By simply acknowledging alternative versions and possibilities of place by dramatising life before official white settlement, *Buckley's Hope* was compelling. Its ultimate significance to me, however, lay as much in the inclusion of a word list of Wadawurrung language at the back as it did in the body of the text. This glossary was my first encounter in a book of a language resembling that which was spoken in Mangowak for thousands of years, and led to me forming the band Barroworn, the name of which came from the spelling used for the Wadawurrung word for magpie in Robertson's list. After two years of extensive touring through both urban and remote regions of Victoria and Tasmania, Barroworn's only recorded album, *Mangowak Days*, was released in 1995.

Unlike other landscapes already famous for their literary histories such as the New England coast of North America, Dantean Tuscany, or the Lakes District of England, and even unlike less delineated but equally productive literary regions such as the Essex palimpsest documented by British chorographer James Canton in his *Out of Essex: Re-Imagining a Literary Landscape*, there was a distinct and resonating lack of literary forebears in my immediate midst. The two books of Upfield and Robertson were what came to hand, and from subsequent research I have found that there was not much more to discover. It is also worth noting that these two books were far from well known amongst the coastal community when I was growing up.

Thus there was an eerie lack of correspondence between a landscape that seemed so aesthetically generative, indeed so epic, and the silence of written responses to it. This gap between the ground I lived on and its imaginative written representations seemed significant. I began to reflect on the source landscapes of the books I'd been reading, the wread nature of my own landscape as I experienced it, and what had *not* been described. I became aware that my cultural landscape appeared not like the succulent creative and regenerative ground I was walking on, but like a dried-up riverbed bearing little resemblance to it.

> *The riverbed, dried-up, half-full of leaves.*
> *Us, listening to a river in the trees.*
>
> Seamus Heaney

The inheritance of a landscape almost entirely divested of its native peoples can too easily become inflected with the linear concept, also inherited, of the prior existence of a mythical lost paradise. This lost paradise, with its implication of humanity's Fall from grace into sin, is of course a key trope of Christianity, but as James Boyce has documented in his *Born Bad: Original Sin and the Making of the Western World*, it has also been thoroughly buttressed by Western philosophical culture from St Augustine to Richard Dawkins. Historian and museum ethnographer Philip Jones has also shown in his essay

'Beyond Songlines' how this strain of nostalgia has been reinforced in more recent years by European reductions of the 'history-collapsing' Aboriginal metaphysics of the Dreaming, or Dreamtime.

The Neapolitan novelist and thinker Raffaele La Capria characterises the concept of a lost idyll, or a lost harmony, in his own way, with the conceptual phrase *la bella giornata*, or 'the beautiful day'. He uses the term to help characterise his grief at the brutal commodification of his own root-landscapes of Capri and Naples, brutal in so many respects but essentially because of the way shrill tourism ignores *la bella giornata*, insofar as it refers, like the Dreaming, to an inner, or metaphysical existence, both intensely personal and entirely communal, that connects to the deep past but remains eternally present, and is therefore continually shaping the future.

At the same time as discovering the work of La Capria back in my twenties, I had also been reading non-fiction texts dealing with the dispossession and genocide that had taken place in the wider Victorian landscape around me. One of these books, *A Distant Field of Murder* by Jan Critchett, dealt with the historical situation in the Western District of Victoria by charting the violent disruption of Gunditjmara, Gadubanud, Gulidjan, Wadawurrung and other homelands by white settlement. Though far from identical, both La Capria's *la bella giornata* and the daily lived realities of Indigenous family and cultural life in Wadawurrung tabayl denoted a continuity of culture that was slipping from focus, that was marred and occluded, perhaps even ruined, by modern industrial society.

So increasingly now I was feeling the reality of what it was like to stand on a map among lost coordinates. Bad cultural weather had arrived in Wadawurrung country – my family had arrived with it – and the sound of the ocean filling the area of this map began to sound to me like a tear in a fabric I was not privy to understand.

———

Each summer morning my father would rise in the riverflat to go fishing, but before leaving the house he would invariably ask in an enthusiastic tone: 'Did you hear the ocean last night?' My presumption at this time was that to him this sound denoted a simple happiness, a breezy freedom. Not yet knowing about his own father's grief-stricken trip to Lorne in 1937, I was only half right.

Like *La Bella Giornata*, my grandfather's wondrous discovery at the Grand Pacific Hotel in Lorne was of both an intensely personal and an entirely communal nature – it was, as I described in 'The Ocean Last Night', the discovery of the 'sound of the ocean under his pillow at night'. Each evening during his visit, as he lay his head down to sleep, he would let the sound envelop him. When the week was over and he returned home to his young son, he described the most beautiful sound in the world.

It was at that point that the sound of the ocean at night established itself in our family as a maternal harmonic, a kind of sonic rosary beads, an acoustic medicine for grief. For me, however, born 'very young in a very old world' – to borrow Erik Satie's phrase – and unaware therefore of the way the bluewater landscape was resonating within our family's emotional history, the sound of the ocean did not yet contain the loss of my grandmother, the grief of my grandfather and my father, nor was it fully described by the enthusiasm of Dad's question as he readied his Evinrude outboard, his rods and nets. On the contrary, the sound of the ocean seemed as atavistic as the moon.

It did, however, form a question mark in my mind. Or multiple question marks. With every crash and breath of wave on the shore at night and with every recollection of that sound in the light of day, another equally perpetual quandary came.

What next? What now? How to write, to sing, to say?

———

Magnetised by a sense of all that had been lost, by the feeling of a vacuum (nature abhors a vacuum, in this case a vacuum of story and song), by *la bella giornata* and the broken song of the Wadawurrung, I immersed myself in what I considered at the time to be the only ethical resources at my disposal. Whatever sympathies or affinities I felt I had with what some academics erroneously call the anglo-Indigenous landscape, I would not, I *could* not, speak, or sing, for the people who had been dispossessed. Although I began at that time to make my first foray into Wadawurrung language, a simultaneous aspect of my realisation of the violent past of my country was that I was unmistakably, even as late as the 1980s, a European agent within it.

In short, my creative impulses certainly afforded me no exemption. As has been said of poet Judith Wright, I had both 'a deeply etched knowledge of being from a conquering people' *and* a simultaneous desire for a *'fertile* invoking of place'.

So, how, what, to write, to sing, to say?

By the time I was in my twenties an initial response had begun to form. I made the decision to start educating myself in the voices, music, literature, history and mythology of my two genetic bloodlines, Irish and Sicilian. I realised, for better or worse, that only within my own literal blood-zones of cultural inheritance did I feel comfortable to speak or sing. Only in Irish and Italian examples could I seek a correspondence with the luminosity I was experiencing; only in those traditions could I learn, or even borrow, a method, a tone, a cadence, the *techniques of a voice* that, when inevitably inflected by my own experience of the colonial geography, could approximate my *wreadings* of book, ocean and land.

I embarked on two simultaneous projects, the writing of my first novel *The Patron Saint of Eels* (2005), which narrates the metaphysical migration of an eighteenth-century southern Italian Franciscan monk into the landscape of twenty-first-century Mangowak, and the setting of poems by the Irish poet W.B. Yeats to music on a pump organ, or harmonium, a project that resulted in the album *The Black Tower: Songs from the Poetry of W.B. Yeats*, subsequently praised by the Yeats Society of Ireland, to my great surprise, as 'equal to, if not surpassing the finest musical interpretations of Yeats ever made'.

During these intensely hybridistic compositional days I would look down at the skin of my arm and remind myself that despite the fact that I was born here in Australia, like so many of the poems and stories I had been reading, thinking about, and singing, that skin, in evolutionary terms, had largely been made elsewhere. It was Irish skin, Sicilian skin, Atlantic skin, Mediterranean skin. More than 120 years before I was born, James and Mary Day were living only eighteen miles from Aireys Inlet, but what did that matter? I had their genes, their Irish freckles on my shoulders. Likewise, my great-great-grandfather Antonio Denerio from Riposto in Sicily arrived in Wadawurrung tabayl in those same 1840s. Because of my physiognomy and colouring, I had been embraced as Italian all my life, but what did that say? What, after all, is one hundred years in an 'old, majestic, magic place' like this? Is it a long time, a short time, a long enough time to shed a skin, to lose sight of where you came from?

By hunting amongst the creative quarry of Ireland and Italy, despite their geographic remove as landscapes, I hoped to discover the source materials of a relevant prelude, some pre-existing mythological and lyrical strata that could help me answer my own impulse to somehow expressively *match* the grandeur, sorrow and mystery of the world. To sing the land.

I hoped to discover something that had been left behind as well as taken away ...

2.

The Patron Saint of Eels was the first of three Mangowak novels, throughout the writing of which (and also during the writing of my novel of World War II Crete and King Island, *Archipelago of Souls*) I worked at Lorne Fisheries at the pier head on Point Grey in Lorne.

This fishery started as a fishermen's cooperative in the 1960s, when barracouta (*Thyrsites atun*) were being caught in quantities as large as 1000 to 2500 tonnes a year. At its peak there were twenty-four 'couta' boats on the Lorne pier, but when the stocks of *Thyrsites atun* began to dwindle due to a strengthening of the warm East Australian Current, the Lorne model transferred from a cooperative arrangement to a private business owned by local partners and run by a young Greek-Macedonian migrant, Christos Raskatos, and his family.

Despite this change of modus operandi, the cultural seeds of the cooperative fishery remained. To the local fishermen who now brought their crayfish (Southern Rock Lobster) and sharks up onto the patinated landing to be weighed and processed, the ocean had become over time not only a worksite and source of income but also a repository of story, mystery, mishap, humour and myth. It also became clear under the new arrangement that for Christos Raskatos, who had come to work in Lorne in the days of the co-op, and who was now the chief proprietor and driving force behind Lorne Fisheries, the ocean was an imaginative field with the potential to link and light up the two key realities of his life: his prior existence as a working-class child of Greek migrants in Geelong, and the metaphysical call of his family's cultural lineage back in the Mediterranean.

On two blackboards fixed to the front wall of the co-op building beside the pier on Point Grey, ostensibly there to announce the range and price of the daily catch, Christos Raskatos began to publish poetry. He continued doing so through four decades until the closure of Lorne Fisheries in 2016.

During these years the local residents, holiday-makers and tourists to whom Christos Raskatos sold seafood found themselves enmeshed in a universal story dissolving time and space. They were not only contemporary participants in a postcolonial fishery and tourism economy, but players in a continuous human drama for which the ocean of Bass Strait, and specifically Louttit Bay, provided a compelling and renewing analogue. Raskatos' co-op poems, which were written predominantly in English but occasionally in Greek, made reference to local events and people. They cast the deeds and postures of these people and events, however, in the context of the metaphysical paradigm of the myths of Ancient Greece. Over time, as the poems on the co-op blackboards began to function as a chronicle of the vicissitudes of the poet's own life and the life of the town, they began also to serve as a Homeric celebration of human continuities. In doing so the co-op poems served to re-equip Lorne with something that had largely been absent from the site since the expropriation of Gadubanud and Wadawurrung lands in the nineteenth century: a metaphysics of place.

Despite Philip Jones's explication in 'Beyond Songlines' of the acknowledged difficulties of precisely defining the concept of 'the Dreaming' or 'Dreamtime' in written English, the anthropologist W.E.H. Stanner in his 1953 essay 'The Dreaming' defined what he called 'the metaphysical gift' of traditional Aboriginal society as 'the ability to transcend oneself, to make acts of imagination so that one can stand "outside" or "away from" oneself, and turn the universe, oneself and one's fellows into objects of contemplation'. This definition shares at least some common ground with the perspective of Cheshire novelist and chorographer Alan Garner when he says: 'creativity is not an occupation. It is service to something beyond the self. In this broad sense, it partakes of the religious.'

As is evident in the topographical nomenclature of this coast where I write, where towns such as Anglesea, Torquay and Lorne were named after pre-existing British places or people in the manner of colonial selfies, since first white settlement 'locals' had looked to the ways in which the place reminded them of already extant cultural sites in the United Kingdom. Likewise, they had imported the Christian beliefs of Europe and built churches in order to permanently overlay these beliefs upon the place. While it is perhaps perfectly understandable that a European settler society should initially hearken back to its source culture in order to structure its new social arrangements, there is nevertheless an inherent disjuncture that takes place when the stories used by that society to explain the mysteries of human and animal life and the structure of the cosmos become, as it were, generic. A cultural distance is installed between the physical features of life and death as they are experienced in the sensual realm of the place itself and the way they are interpreted metaphysically.

To some extent, Christos Raskatos's co-op poems went part of the way towards lessening that distance. Through his combining of the demotic, local and often iconoclastic vernacular with a demonstrative use of a Homeric mythological inheritance, the poet was able to 'make acts of imagination', in Stanner's words, that turned 'the universe, oneself and one's fellows into objects of contemplation'. The co-op poems did this by imaginatively redefining the Lorne community as existing within what Stanner might call the 'everywhen'. Stanner's 1953 neologism may perhaps have its roots in the phrase 'ogne quando' from the 29th canto of Dante's Paradiso, which famously is set in a polytemporal realm outside the linear paradigm of European time. Stanner's 'everywhen' also resembles La Capria's Neapolitan *la bella giornata* in the way it folds the past, and geographically distant locations, into the historical and topographic present.

Thus, in Christos Raskatos's world, the application of originally place-specific Greek myths such as Mount Olympus, the Cretan labyrinth at Knossos, or the Taenarum (the Peloponnese entrance to Hades, located at Cape Taenarum), became viable. An Otway Taenarum became a mythographic reality. Indeed, his poems often referenced Hades, a mythological region which, as Julie Baleriaux has shown in her study of how meaning was given to subterranean rivers in ancient Mediterranean landscapes, 'may have been inspired by the widespread karstic landscapes in Greece' and, in particular, the Peloponnese around Cape Taenarum. It is interesting to note how the Otway basin too is predominantly a karst landscape, a characteristic feature of which is a porousness resulting from the dissolution of soluble rocks such as limestone, creating networks of underground streams, caves and sinkholes. Such features were described – a 'group of orifices', 'extraordinary caverns' – by the superintendent of the Port Phillip District and future Governor of Victoria, Charles Latrobe, in 1846, when his party rode through the forest to investigate the building of a lighthouse on Cape Otway to alleviate the incidence of shipwrecks in Bass Strait. In karst landscapes the same stream can run for miles on the surface before diving through swallets under the land and reappearing somewhere else. Baleriaux believes this feature of topographic porousness seeded Greek notions of the parallel unseen underworld of Hades. In Christos Raskatos's hands, this allegorical 'unseen' became once again a spoken everyday force in Lorne.

In this way the community was at least in part redefined, not by ethnicity or religion but by the way each moment of daily experience is given meaning by the journey through time and space that has preceded it. Thus, in Raskatos's poems the European neocolonial community was endowed with a human continuity stretching at least back to the heroic age of Homer's day. The community members of Lorne were presented back to themselves not merely as citizens of Australia but as agents in a metaphysical drama, whereby they were assigned their roles as ironic amphibians – half shore-dwellers, half in the waves – and preternaturalists, identities capable of dwelling in and thinking about a liminal space between spirit and body, between life and whatever precedes, succeeds or surrounds it. Ultimately the co-op poems claimed the common daily survival of life's high and low weathers, of all that the unpredictable ocean of existence can dish up, as a significant, even heroic, achievement in itself. The most 'ordinary' and uncelebrated Lorne people could therefore be represented as everyday locals with intrinsic relations not only to sea and land, but to other worlds of miracle, wonder and metaphysical power.

One function of the Lorne co-op poems then was to reinvest a sense of the sacred in a place that had almost been desacralised by invasion and colonised by the generic tropes of the British empire and its dominions. Another function was to decolonise the idea of heroism by wresting back the metaphysical realm from the humourless strictures of church and state. The working poet was quite literally taking the gods outside again, up into the beech and mountain ash forests of the Otways overlooking Bass Strait and the Southern Ocean, back into the realm of the hunts and humours of everyday life. On chalkboards streaked with saltspray, seaweed, pollen and wind, Christos reinserted a strata of pre-Christian mythology into the ancient east-facing cove of Lorne. In flamboyant style he re-personified the place, attributing to the physical environment the qualities and power of a Homeric goddess, or a dear but formidable old friend, therefore restoring the site as a place of worship *in itself*. In the co-op poems the topography of the Gadubanud littoral and the sea-light were once again the objects of transformational power and devotion, not the cloistered iconography inside the colonial church. On the salt-streaked co-op blackboards Christos cunningly improvised a voice that summoned pre-Christian deities in an attempt to match his surroundings, to reacknowledge and narrate not only the epic drama of the coastline, but the wonders of what we can't see and can never know, as well as the often unnoticed mysteries of everyday deeply felt emotion.

Unlike the novels I wrote while working alongside him in the fishery, Raskatos's co-op poems were never published in a book but only in the ephemeral and performative chalk of the striated, streaked and mottled workaday space that was the fishery on Point Grey. In their impermanence the co-op poems bore similarities to the nightly live music played through the summers of the 1970s and 80s by bands such as AC/DC and Cold Chisel in the Grand Pacific Hotel, which hovered in late Victorian grandeur above the pier and fishery, and where once the arias of Beniamino Gigli had been played on a gramophone in the foyer. The co-op poems sat in fact in an interstice between the oral and written traditions, not only insofar as the weather co-opted them by determining their legibility, but also due to the fact that the poet was often on hand to perform the written poem for the reader. These factors helped define the co-op poems as work by a poet living in between realms, one of which was halfway between manual labour and imaginative composition, another between the written and the spoken text, and yet another between the seen and unseen. As written on the blackboards, the poems could be read only for as long as the weather allowed, and by that fact alone they were symbiotic with the place. They were not separated from the environment they emerged from and thus one had to physically be *in the place* to encounter them. And if while reading them the reader got wet, whether from sea spray or rain, the texts themselves got wet as well.

3.

As is evident in his own place-based fiction, Alan Garner believes that 'what we call "creativity" is the bringing together of pre-existing entities that have not been seen to connect before'.

Here then, excluding the Australian texts I was also reading at the time of composing my Mangowak novels, is a list of components for my own psycho-geographic creative instrument, a list of some key inflectors, or companion species, from the literary traditions of my two migratory bloodlines:

W.B. Yeats, Lady Augusta Gregory, John McGahern, James Joyce, Seamus Heaney, Giuseppe di Lampedusa, Leonardo Sciascia, Luigi Pirandello, Anna Maria Ortese, Giovanni Verga, Raffaele La Capria, Norman Douglas, Marisa Fazio, Eugenio Montale, Salvatore Satta, Italo Calvino, Roberto Calasso . . .

Besieged by the seeming infinitude of contemporary analogies for the concepts of 'network' and 'community', I am tempted to describe this as a list not only of companion species, but as a textual neighbourhood, an epigenetic milieu, a mycelial library. My preferred way of looking at the ingredients of this list, however, is as the stops of a pump organ or harmonium, like the one my recurring character Ron McCoy plays in the second Mangowak novel, *Ron McCoy's Sea of Diamonds* (2007).

The list then can be seen as a set of readymade stops that I arranged in various combinations in order to respond to:

- what my grandfather heard under his pillow in the Grand Pacific Hotel at Lorne
- what my father heard when he went to sleep every night in his house in Aireys Inlet (Mangowak), and
- what I heard when as a younger man I cupped my ear on the sound of the ocean within the cultural absence in the landscape around me.

For instance, to extemporise: with the W.B. Yeats stop pulled, the harmonium is capable of intoning radical innocence, an innocence attained through maturation, through hard labour at the craft of writing, through a fascination with ancestral customs and beliefs. With the Lady Augusta Gregory stop activated, there is a relevant personal redemption at hand, in creative and ethnographic form, given that it was her husband, Robert Gregory, who was responsible for the land laws that contributed so specifically to the cultural devastation of the Irish potato famine. With the John McGahern stop open, the harmonium sounds reed-clear and unsentimental, and yet somehow full of love. It plays with an unwavering fidelity to regionality, with an emphasis on dark irony in the received opinions of the landscape. The Seamus Heaney stop, with its assiduous linguistic retrievals and ability to synthesise them with modern existence, re-inherits pastoral yet percussive sounds, which create tactile, luminous sensations of the timeless–everyday. By opening the Italianate stop of Giuseppe di Lampedusa we become aware, in the story of the late demise of the Salina family in his 1963 novel *Il Gattopardo*, or *The Leopard*, of a landscape tragically imbued with the past, a demesne of fallen grandeur. Adding Leonardo Sciascia's more contemporary Sicilian stop to this, we incorporate the unflinching cultural logic of Mafia brutality and fear. The harmonium begins to filter the events of small communities through a deeply moral lens. With the Marisa Fazio and Anna Maria Ortese stops open, we find the picaresque and Commedia Dell'Arte traditions reticulated through the natural thrill of magic realism, reintegrating materialism with fabulistic leaps of the mythic imagination. Through the Giovanni Verga stop, we sound the keys to provide working trials of the human figure in the heat-drugged landscape, and by opening the Roberto Calasso stop we intone a new trance-like music of multi-storied lands, a revisited acceptance of the inevitable mythological network in soil and place.

This harmonium is an imaginative foundry in which writer-forebears are filtered, inevitably, through a mysteriously alchemical and largely intuitive auditing process. Through the framework of the harmonium I seek both the fundamental note and the harmonics it issues, the voices of correspondence, in order to describe the sound of the ocean and the people living within its range, and to augment it for readers and listeners. The search for psychoacoustic accuracy, for the right sound or arrangement of sounds, for the right word or combination of words, the right character or combination of characters to animate upon a string of narrative, is both a truffling and a composting process, a trial and error *on the wallaby* process of the emotional imagination, as well as an exercise in autoethnographic tuning. I cock an ear, I comb an archive, I sniff the ground, I proffer a chord.

In attempting to document honestly the unsequestered everyday process of *making* that has resulted in the publication of my novels, I am seeking to deal in what Nicholas Jose has called 'the personal imperatives of history'. By this method, beauty without transgression is disqualified. Tragedy without humour likewise. Possession without dispossession has no purchase here. The imported, constantly mutating English language itself is intrinsically vernacularised, hybridised, rendered both demotic and high, tending towards sonic and sociological accuracy but remaining eternally tangential.

Inevitably then, I found myself beginning to pedal a dialectical instrument, a Celtic-Italian instrument, a breathing, literary, pollen-filled harmonium, exuding the floral wafts as well as the funereal tones of Wadawurrung country, producing synaesthetic texts born from the heaths and shores of the landscape with its botanical, zoological and sensory, as well as cultural, and *soulful*, diversity of stops.

Just as there is no stone without stipple, no lichen without basis, no ironstone headland without telluric rift and heat, I felt little stereotypic anxiety of influence as my Mangowak novels got underway, despite my resorting to traditional, literary, Irish and Mediterranean models. No doubt this unabashedness came partly from my own naiveté, but it also came from working alongside Christos Raskatos and the knowledge implied by his own embrace of the fact that by its very nature the littoral garden of words can never be devoid of flotsam and jetsam, things that have washed up, wild sonic frequencies, so-called invasive species, contravening rasp or song. Likewise, the arrangement of mimetic organ stops that we call the written sentence, proceeding as it does in a literary lineage, needs always to be stabilised by the geology of silence.

There is a sonic prose of a shore that teems with the presence and absence of past voices, as well as the serial mathematics of stem, petal, stamen, sun and moon. Every tide, like every day, is the same but somehow different.

Did you hear the ocean last night?

4.

Now, on the bungalow step, the young man hears the voice beginning to speak, over the sound of recorded fishermen's songs, and the recorded sea in the background:

> *Naples is nearly 3000 years old and for most, if not all of that time, fishermen have worked here at their nets and their boats. At least until just a few years ago.*

The melodies of the fishermen go on, but for periods the voice that accompanies them stops speaking.

Our young man sits in an undoubtedly *old, majestic, magic* place ... in a cultural landscape where, according to Buckley's account of his time in Wadawurrung tabayl, a local site once existed, and therefore might exist still, that was the source of all the world's songs. Perhaps this was an opening in the porous karst limestone of our area, a stony rift that led from under the overhanging branches of a drooping she-oak into a Wadawurrung Taenarum, or underworld. These days I wonder, admittedly with a degree of satiric scorn in my thoughts, what such a site would sell for on some glossy muzaky Surf Coast real estate sign.

Yes, according to what Buckley recounted of his thirty-two years among the lifesaving hospitality of the Wadawurrung, this is also a cultural landscape in which one very special person had the role of maintaining the local sticks that keep the sky up off the earth. This person was the keeper of the light and breath in the world, and I'm often speculating as I walk about which species of tree would best serve the function of holding the sky up like that – perhaps the ironbark or 'ngangahook', the hazel pomaderris, or maybe the tea-tree or 'boono', chosen for the same strength and flexibility that made it so good for fashioning into craypots before the days of plastic and steel. Only months before the arrival of the land-grabbing English boats in Corio Bay in 1835 – just six years before my family members also disembarked – in a most fabulistic but nevertheless gravely coded call to arms, the word went out across Wadawurrung country for everyone to bring whatever tools they had from every corner of the world to this special person. The call had gone out that the sky-supporting sticks were coming under grave threat, that the whole world was teetering and in danger of collapsing into darkness.

The young man sits on the step underneath the pines, dwelling in lost glimmers and recurring inklings of that actually unwritable thing, the *Dreaming*.

The light speaks to him, it has a voice, *voices* in fact, and so of course he dwells also in another mythological stratum of his inheritance: in Stanner's *everywhen*, in Dante's *'ogne quando'*. In *The Divine Comedy* the idea of *ogne quando* is uttered by Dante only when, having been guided by Virgil through the molten depths of the underworld, and having subsequently climbed the Purgatorial mountain positioned in his own imagined Southern Ocean, he listens to Beatrice's description of it with tears perpetually streaming from his eyes. His tears spring as if from the source of all the world's songs, as he begins to comprehend the overwhelming significance of what Beatrice is describing: the generative, fearless, fertile and *perpetual* nature of any authentic and genuinely imaginative moral code.

So the young man sits under the pines now, with the sound of the ocean both in the air and on tape, in a landscape drenched with such emotion, with *la bella giornata* melodies of Naples mixing with the sky-climbing Bass Strait sonics in his ears, the whiff of cooking fires coming to him across the inspired screen of Blake and Botticelli's visual renditions of Dante's three realms: Hell, Purgatory and Paradise; or to put it differently, the Taenarum, the mountain of expiation in the Southern Ocean, and the twinkling of ancestral campfires in the perpetually wheeling night sky.

In the shade on the bungalow step he smokes a cigarette. He listens to the protean melody of the sea. Only this song bears any resemblance to the deep but open-ended passion he feels at the centre of his world. The groundedness and groundlessness. The enigma of his forebears in the landscape, the upwellings of the oceanic heart, upwellings brought about by loss and migration. The 133 different spellings of the word Wadawurrung that are to be found in the historical record – 133 ways of looking at a heartland.

The sound of the ocean contains it all.

He sits on the step underneath the pines, one non-endemic species below another. There is a richness and a loss, laughter and a keening. Very old beginnings of a possible new way of being here.

Being Here

Back in 2015, when we were getting the local language work going here at the Aireys Inlet Primary School in Mangowak, every Monday morning I'd try to fire up the whole-school assembly about Wadawurrung language. Each week the students learned, and still do, new Wadawurrung words, and inevitably with those words came new ways of looking at the cultural history of their home landscape. On the first Monday of every month, and on other special occasions, they also sing the Mangowak Song, a boisterous yet melancholy and yearning piece written with some of the words they have learnt, the lyrics a mixture of English and Wadawurrung. This is the song's first verse:

> I'm from Mangowak where the murnong grows
> Where the garra blooms along the wintry roads
> I've got a smart tonton like the old ngoorang
> Where the boonea swim that's where I am

The murnong is the yam daisy; the garra, the wattle; the tonton, the brain; the ngoorang, the bull ant; and the boonea is the eel.

It is not lost on me, the fact that I, as a non-Indigenous, fifth-generation Australian, am sharing Wadawurrung language with non-Aboriginal students of what is these days an affluent coastal town. How could it be, after listening to aboriginal friends and after the years I have

Griffith Review (2022)

spent writing songs, novels, poems and essays that try to come to terms with the personally intimate and wider cultural background I inherited when I was, as Erik Satie once said, 'born very young in a very old world'? The broken song and awful absence along this western Victorian coast that always sits near the core of my work still exists – I feel it every time I stand up in front of the children – but it is by now an absence I have spent many years interrogating. Nowadays I see it as not only a necessity but an honour to speak of the ongoing presence in that absence, and to sing of all that in the guiding presence of local Elders, to the future adults of my area.

In December 2016 Tandop (Uncle) David Tournier told me the story of how he once caught a white eel in Corio Bay. As he told me the story he was eating a local black eel we'd caught in the Painkalac the night before. David hadn't eaten eel for a while and when he'd finished telling what was quite literally a hair-raising tale about the white eel getting tangled up in his hair, we both sat quietly watching a white cockatoo sauntering across the school deck where the assemblies are held. As we sat there I told Tandop David the story of the cockatoo called Sunshine I met a few years ago. Individual cockatoos often live for many decades and Sunshine had been born back in the 1930s, at which point she was taught a few English words. She still spoke with a Depression-era accent and lexicon. *Mother!* she would shriek when she wanted to be fed. David reminded me of the Wadawurrung word for the white cockie: 'Djernip'. Sunshine was a djernip. As opposed to a gherang, one of the Wadawurrung words for the local black cockatoo. We live in a world of delicately tuned balances, I thought. Night and day, djernip and gherang. Or imbalances: blackfella and coloniser, hooded plover and hungry fox, black eel and white eel. I wondered to myself: What on earth would be the word for a white eel? David and I talked about language then, the everyday magic it contains, and he told me how he was working on translating the Mangowak Song completely into Wadawurrung. I'm hopeful that one day one of the students from the school might grow up to help out with this task that Tandop David ran out of earthly time for. In my view these are the jobs that, with the blessing and guidance of local elders, we need to undertake to help in the long process of restoring balance to this land.

Before most of my role at the school was passed along to Amanda George, a tireless local parent, activist and community lawyer of Scots/Irish heritage, I'd include some kind of object in the Monday assemblies – it could be a ngangahook branch from the grove next to the school, which was ceremonially opened as the Mangowak Sanctuary by Tandop David on the day we cooked the eel. It could be a piece of nyooroo from the nearby ocean cliffs, a mobile phone (yarna larka), the picture of Narrandjerri Elder David Unaipon on the Australian $50 note, or a boonea caught in the Painkalac as it slithers through the middened terraces of the town on its way to meeting the sea under the Split Point lighthouse. One Monday, in the middle of autumn here in Mangowak, I took in a crab brittlegill mushroom. The crab brittlegill is one of some 750 varieties of mushroom gathered under the genus name russula. One local variety – *Russula xerampelina* – grows on the banks of the Painkalac just fifty or so metres from my front door. As I held up the mushroom in front of the school I explained to the kids how the crab brittlegills love pine trees, particularly non-indigenous pines such as *Pinus radiata*. They grow in the earth we live upon, in the soil we call home, but only in the right symbiotic mix of nutrients and sunlight created in grassy clearings near these introduced trees. I occasionally see russula fungi growing in the bush around here but being what the mycologists call 'ectomycorrhizal symbionts', the great likelihood is that *Russula xerampelina* would not be so prevalent in the town without the existence of the introduced pines. The interesting point though is that the crab brittlegills themselves, unlike the pines, were never intentionally introduced into Australia by colonisation. It is not a case of a spore being introduced by a colonial mycologist, or a seed being planted by a land-grabbing grazier. Rather, the crab brittlegills have spontaneously and symbiotically proliferated within the mycelial profile of what some might call the new 'Anglo-Indigenous' soil conditions.

It is in those very soil conditions that I tell the kids how when I walk around the place and see a crab brittlegill growing, I get optimistic.

This is for two reasons. The first reason is basic, the crab brittlegills are really yum, and I know that myself and my family will be eating well that night. The second reason is that the crab brittlegill has developed into a little symbol for me of the way that we could all learn from the monocultural horrors of our white-obsessed history to grow here instead in a properly symbiotic way, in this soil, without having to seem too out of place, or too dominant, and without spreading like invasive weeds or an invading power destroying its very host.

If I was talking to an audience of academic adults rather than a group of primary school-aged children, I might at this point cite Donna Haraway's symchthonic ideas of 'conjugal kin', 'ongoingness' and her theory that our survival depends increasingly on our ability to work together as 'companion species'. ('Symchthonic' is Haraway's coinage, sprung into being from the Greek derived prefix, 'sym', meaning 'together', and the equally Greek 'chthonic', meaning 'to dwell in the earth'.) Or I might cite Thomas Berry's coining of the term 'Ecozoic era', to name a future in which humans will overcome their current fate as a ridiculously self-isolated species and willingly re-enter the teeming symbiosis of earthly life forms. With the children, however, I simply point out how, despite the fact that I have been noticing the crab brittlegills all my life, it wasn't until I was an adult that I began to actually eat them, never having been told by my parents, and them not having been told by theirs, nor theirs by theirs, nor by anyone else, that they were edible and delicious. As with so much in my home landscape, my ignorance of the delights of the crab brittlegill is therefore multi-generational; and yet it was my own thirteen-year-old son who, through his own interest and research, informed me that it could be eaten and enjoyed.

The beaded glasswort (*Salicornia quinqueflora*) is a similar but even more telling case, I tell the kids. This salty native succulent grows in great abundance all over the Painkalac river flat here in Mangowak. In Korea it has long been viewed as a highly restorative and nutritious 'superfood', akin to ginseng, but here in 'Aireys Inlet', despite my family and friends' longstanding appetite for hunting and foraging, no one ever told me what a beautiful food it was. This was because, due directly to the dispossession of the Wadawurrung in our area, no one knew. 'The greatest song of the land is the food it produces,' I tell the kids, quoting that most Anglo-Indigenous of Australian writers, Eric Rolls. You are what you eat, I say to them, so don't miss out on the connection. Try to understand your place, listen to what it's telling you so you can be here properly and look after things well.

This listening out for balance and connection can often deliver unforeseen stories, like the one Tandop David told me about the white eel. So I also tell them about the international nature of the beaded glasswort and how it has, more likely than not, been spread through the marshes and wetlands of the East Asian-Australasian Flyway by migratory waterbirds such as the eastern curlew. Harry Saddler, in his book on the eastern curlew, describes the transplantation of glasswort seeds along the migratory path of the curlew as it flies each year from far eastern Russia to Australia, including southern Victoria and Tasmania. Loving the glasswort as they do, the eastern curlews digest them and excrete the seeds at different points of their landfall as they make their way along the flyway. So this, I say, is where yet another layer of wonder comes into the story. What the curlew loves to eat the most it also drops off as an intergenerational seed package as it goes, ensuring that the glasswort is distributed at the appropriate stopovers – Papua New Guinea, the Philippines, China, Japan, Korea – on its long, indeed epic, route along the flyway. The question I put to the kids then is: what exactly does it mean to be local to our place if the glasswort in the riverflat might have been dropped off by a bird that first developed a taste for it somewhere closer to modern day Russia? Is the glasswort stranger or kin? Can we live together as good companions? And aren't we all interconnected in ways that aren't obvious at the first, or even the thousandth glance?

You bet.

Writing the essays in this book over the period of time since we wrote the Mangowak Song at the school, a period of time in which all the school classrooms and house names have been changed to Wadawurrung, has involved what Ruth Blair, in her essay on the phenomena of the bioregional novel, calls 'a constant process of relationship and negotiation amongst phenomena'. In our local case it's often aspirational phenomena, as the real-estate prices along the Great Ocean Road hike up and the demographic changes. In her essay 'What Happens When You Tell Somebody Else's Story', Alexis Wright states that 'we are all collectively the inheritors and generators of the country's psyche' and it's inevitable that my process as a non-Aboriginal writer in the late twentieth and early twenty-first century must reflect that. In fact, the process of how I have come to *be here* as a writer is a key part of the ongoing challenge of how to *be here* as a human being. A challenge that never ends. As Ruth Behar wisely says in her work on the interplay between the written and spoken word: 'The experience is always larger than anything you can write about.'

That sense of something larger is represented for me best in a spatial sense by the sound of the ocean at night. In trying to notate the mystery and immensity of that sound I have become aware of the irony of the aim: to write about the presence of something so ongoingly big is only possible by writing about the absence it sings of. To nail it down would be like trying to nail down where the eastern curlew first developed a taste for what is now our local salty bean. I have no doubt that the urgency of the challenges of *being here* is compounded by the alarming meteorological, and therefore psychogeographical, conditions of our industrial and post-industrial epoch where, as Bruno Latour puts it, 'a huge operation has been going on...to deanimate materiality rather forcefully to obtain, in the end, something like a "material world"'. Latour's philosophical humour is always refreshing, and this is a good example of the subversive way he changes our view of 'taken-for-granted' terms. His criticism of the way our materialism wages a war on life, and his intelligent positivity about the importance of naming this war, is hopefully connected in an entirely inevitable way to the manner in which I have dramatised the cultural and demographic turbulence of the Mangowak biota and mise-en-scene in my fiction. That I make an attempt to write of an *emotional geography* – a phrase which in the time of Latour's philosophical forbears in France would have been viewed as a contradiction in terms – by listening to the land and seascape, as well as to its oldest inhabitants, importantly includes the process of being asked questions by them. Two-way questions, such as those I might ask the schoolkids about the ancient food drop-offs of the eastern curlew. Or curious quixotic questions such as those I am often asking myself in solitude. Like asking a cave how it came to be and then listening to the timbre of the question's echo. Or asking the eels where they go when they migrate, and then fully imagining the answer before I even begin to confer with Dr Google.

I think of this process as a ballad of sorts, a ballad of rigour and dreaming. Trying to strike a balance between these energies always seems the right way to go about it. In my novels the quixotic questions lead, like symbiotic hyphae in a mycelium, to generation and creation. In these essays the process is more geneological, interrogative, even confessional. But in all instances the answers are triggered in a conjoined way so as to find empathetic correspondence between our intimate selves and the world that nourishes us.

In my experience, when we fill the space with narratives that include the untold, the unseen, or, if you like, the material of the immaterial, the place begins to animate like a friend. Latour's 'material world' is restored to life. I begin to consider myself in the context of the white eel. Actually, it's a bit like the difference between playing a digital piano and a real one. The harmonics of the biota begin to connect us to a place of ancient-ongoing voices, personages, memories, echoes, sadness, possibilities, dreams and mythologies, and thus we hear it better and treat it better (not that there needs to be a moral outcome from responding to the ancient call to sing and tell).

Indeed, I agree with David Abram's contention that intelligence is not ours alone but rather

> a property of the earth; we are in it, of it, immersed in its depths. And indeed each terrain, each ecology, seems to have its own particular intelligence, its unique vernacular of soil and leaf and sky.

In the context of attempting, as an Australian of Irish-Sicilian blood, to write about my connection to Wadawurrung tabayl, it also feels important to point out how this idea of Abram's connects with what Maria Takolander has described as 'the creation of a parochial culture as a strategy of decolonisation…a distancing from the centre… and a means of self assertion'. Time and again my agent in London reports back that publishers over there find my work excellent but 'too Australian'. I am not the first Australian author to experience this attitude but Takolander's comment points to why I take such a 'rejection' as almost a badge of honour. Though I would never have the gall to compare myself with the following great writers, imagine, for instance, if Arundhati Roy was told her work was 'too Indian'. Or Janet Frame that her work was too Kiwi. Or if Chaucer was dismissed for being 'too English' and Homer for being 'too Mediterranean'. In fact, in the context of the currently teeming work going on to reconstruct, embrace and celebrate aboriginal languages right across this continent, all of these wonderful authors could equally be described as not being quite local enough. I believe the inherited emotional ingredients of the way the sound of a place enters our speech can circumvent any obvious need for local colour as a mark of authenticity. If you let it in, it will just be there anyway.

There is a universal human story of possession and dispossession, of migration and adhesion, grief and loss, in the very air. Our interpretations, or notations, of that air take on a local sensuousness which, within the context of our hope for a truly post-colonial Australia, is at the heart of what we're trying to figure out and feel. A recursive and perpetual motion is set up, akin to the wheel of the stars. We write and sing both high and low, from the universal to the local and back again, along the flyways of ancient hearts, from the personal arteries of inherited memory to the acoustic community of living voices, whether they be regional, international, real or imagined. Or perpetually implied by the sound of the waves and the song of the ground beneath our feet.

Three

Wreading in the Moolacene

Idling in Green Places

The proliferation goes on. The number of new words being coined to name the reality and effects of our current era of natural and cultural crisis seems at times to be itself some kind of teeming linguistic correction to species extinction on a heating planet. I've listed them before in previous essays and reviews – Anthropocene, Capitalocene, Ecocene, Symbiocene, Gynocene, Cthulucene, etc. I've also added Moolacene to the list, which employs the Wadawurrung word 'moola' from my local region, meaning 'shadow'. 'Moola' is of course also the US-derived slang word for money, which many people think is at the heart of the issue.

The hatching of such words abounds like thrip on one of those gusty heat-spiking days with which we are becoming increasingly familiar. All the various neologisms have their supporters and detractors, for there are as many questions about this era as there are names for it. No, more. None of these questions though is more pertinent to those with an empathetic turn of mind than the one Melbourne writer and naturalist Harry Saddler asks in the final pages of his book on that hardy, mud-interrogating, migratory bird the eastern curlew.

The Weekend Australian
McGregor, R 2019, *Idling in Green Places: A Life of Alec Chisholm*, Australian Scholarly Publishing, Melbourne;
Seddon, G 2019, *Selected Writings*, ed. A Gaynor, La Trobe University Press, Melbourne

Each year, with many other species of shorebirds, the eastern curlew flies the East Asian–Australasian migratory pathway from the mudflats of Australia to Siberia and back. Along the way they stop in Korea, China and Japan, three countries in which the spread of land development for human habitation and industry has rapidly swallowed the kind of nutrient-rich mudflats the birds need to survive. Reflecting then on the crisis the birds face, Saddler wonders whether an animal can sense the impending extinction of its species. 'Does an Eastern Curlew,' he asks, 'flying in ever-dwindling flocks, recall the great company that it once travelled in, and sense the loss? Before it migrates does it worry, in a deep and wordless place that we all share, about not leaving in time? Not finding enough to eat? Not returning? Does it feel lonely, on its migration, feeding in its patch of mud, in flocks but always in thrall to its own indivisible impulse to fly?'

Saddler's thinking about these questions leads him to a new perspective on a turn of mind that was once viewed by science as pure anathema, that of 'anthropomorphism'. He believes that anthropomorphism – the attribution of human traits to non-human entities – 'has things backwards' and that it is high time we stopped 'keeping animals at a distance from ourselves' and started 'recognising the animalness that underlies our very behaviour'.

This question of anthropomorphism is at the heart of three recently published books that, in their own way, trace a lineage of Australian nature writing over the last hundred years. Alec Chisholm was born in the central Victorian town of Maryborough in 1890, and, according to *Idling in Green Places*, a new biography of Chisholm by academic and 'keen birder' Russell McGregor, had left school by the age of twelve due to the fact that there was almost zero focus in the Victorian school curriculum at that time on what he was interested in: nature. The sound of birds as Chisholm heard them from inside the classroom, and his fascination with their behaviour and habitats, thus drew this rather rare egg away from the dry pedants and out into the ironbarks and big skies of his home town.

By the time he was only eighteen, Chisholm was back in the school at Maryborough, this time as a guest lecturer on the natural world. When he was asked in later life why he became a naturalist, he thought the question misconceived. The real question was not why he came to be enchanted by nature but why others ever came to lose that enchantment. Implied in this view of course is its own inbuilt form of enchantment, for it seemed beyond Chisholm's comprehension that any child would not be born completely enthralled by nature. But of course many are, and always have been.

This presumption of Chisholm's is loaded with something rather fey, indeed with an inheritance of the sentiment-laden 'charms of nature' as they were interpreted in the realms of the British empire and through the ornamental influence of Victorian-era poets. And it is this feyness, and his willingness to augment the precision and hard-won knowledge of his fieldwork with metaphor and analogy, that had a great deal to do with Chisholm's immense popularity as a pioneering nature writer of this country.

His attitude to bowerbirds is a case in point. Chisholm believed that the construction and decoration of bowers qualified these birds as 'the chief aesthetes of the universe next to mankind'. In books such as *Mateship With Birds* and *Bird Wonders of Australia* he wrote copiously of birds as lovers of sound, even as artists. As the twentieth century entered its final hyper-materialistic and anti-anthropomorphic decades, his work fell well out of fashion as a result.

It's perhaps timely then that Chisholm's contribution to the conservation and appreciation of our biota is celebrated in McGregor's work, just as many key thinkers around the globe are reconnecting to what Indigenous people have always known. Animals are neither our specimens nor only our tucker. They are our kin.

Like Alec Chisholm, George Seddon was born in an Australian country town. For the municipally minded Seddon, most projects began with the perspectives accessed by that early country life in Horsham, where the fundamentals of food production and environmental literacy were almost unavoidable, and forever formative. Like Chisholm, and a lot of other naturalists and bio-historians for whom a passion for the natural world fosters an awareness of the great connectedness inherent in both nature and culture, Seddon became something of a polymath, famously holding three separate professorships, in literature, geology and environmental science. Also like Chisholm, he was a great contributor to the public weal, working tirelessly over many decades to refine his prescient environmental perspectives via the art of the possible. Hence he worked with governments and corporate bodies at a high level, advising them on things such as the appropriate routes for those great steel giants that march electricity wires across our landscape in rural and suburban areas. Seddon was responsible for the discretion of so many of those routes, and a whole lot more, and this willingness of his to apply his knowledge, training and wisdom in the can-do avenues of power certainly distinguishes his life story.

His enormous capacities took him right around the world, and whether it was in Italy, England or America, he had little time for ideological hubris that eschewed practical objectives. Thus it was often the debates around anthropomorphic tendencies that Seddon had in the gun. Andrea Gaynor's editing of Seddon's *Selected Writings* makes for a stimulating and timely collection therefore, both in the way it highlights Seddon's passion for gardens and the cultural landscape, and in its analysis of epistemological issues. A brilliant example of this is Gaynor's inclusion of Seddon's 1972 essay, 'The Rhetoric and Ethics of the Environmental Protest Movement', which, as well as having a decidedly caustic relevance to our current era of urgent protest, also returns us to the Janus-faced logic of anthropomorphism for which, as Seddon says, 'there is no intelligible alternative'.

For Tim Flannery, Seddon's words have long been 'beacons', perhaps in the same manner that for someone of my generation, Flannery's own words have often shown the way. For decades Flannery's essays and books have offered crucial summaries and clarifying perspectives on global biodiversity, climate, Australian history, mammals, megafauna, and possibilities for alternative energy sources, be it geothermal or kelp. Like Seddon he is a scholar, an adviser to government, and a traveller who has been able to co-opt the often arthritic university apparatus for genuinely adventurous, useful and creative purposes. The publication of Flannery's *Life: Selected Writings*, is a testament to that independent brilliance, a testament also to his canny talent for combining the high pitch and the common touch. If his work is less explicitly philosophical than Seddon's or Chisholm's that is perhaps because they have laid the ground before him, but it is also because Flannery's writing is so affixed to his era, and thus always marked by a redemptive urgency. For the most part his writing really does show and explain rather than tell and instruct, and in this respect his style has an openness and a narrative momentum that improves on both Chisholm and Seddon.

There are many substantial standout essays in *Life*, which collects extracts from Flannery's own books, work commissioned by the *New York Review of Books*, personal reminiscences about acquaintances and colleagues such as Robert Hughes and Martin Copley, a chapter from his novel *The Mystery of the Venus Island Fetish*, and many of his forewords to other books. One of these forewords, 'The Passing of Birrarang', written for *The Birth of Melbourne* in 2004, shows Flannery's writing at its finest. Effortlessly merging natural and cultural history with beautifully drawn personal memories of growing up around Port Phillip Bay, 'The Passing of Birrarang' provides an exceptional genius loci set piece as well as a seminal portrait of an illegally founded modern city transitioning into the Moolacene.

As varied and intrepid as Flannery's working life has been, there is a sense in which his career has been hijacked, or at least continually repurposed, by the climate emergency of our era. The crisis that is currently hatching so many new words, ideas and perspectives, and that has caused us to readdress not only our energy sources but also such fundamental concepts of Western objectivity as anthropomorphism, has turned him into an activist, a political lobbyist, a philanthropic conservationist and a celebrity. That he has been able to maintain both the fascinating substance and personable readability of his written work – his recent book *Europe* is a case in point – marks him out as an even more exceptional multi-tasker than Seddon. In fact, if I had to think of one Australian who has best served to ameliorate at least some of the dents and chips taken off our national shine during this period of our worst denial, it would not be Shane Warne, Hugh Jackman or Nick Cave. It would be this less fashionable but nevertheless inspiring mammologist, who has devoted his talents and courageous energy to making the world a better place to live, and not just for us humans.

Betraying the Loch

In an early chapter of *Landmarks*, Robert Macfarlane recounts how, in Oliver Rackham's book *The History of the Countryside* (1986), the ways a 'landscape is lost' are divided into four categories:

1. loss of beauty
2. loss of freedom
3. loss of wildlife and vegetation
4. loss of meaning.

Macfarlane admires 'the way that aesthetics, human experience, ecology and semantics are given parity' in Rackham's list. That seems almost true, but the list is nonetheless interpretable as a pecking order, a scale of importance, which should perhaps, some thirty years later, be rearranged to demonstrate the increasing relevance of Macfarlane's own project as arguably the pre-eminent British nature writer in the climate change era.

In a landscape such as Great Britain's, where London had a population much larger than that of contemporary Melbourne or Sydney as far back as 1911, the very real 'loss of wildlife and vegetation' should surely head the list, followed by the attendant and less quantifiable loss of meaning, loss of freedom, loss of beauty. Although Macfarlane's

Sydney Review of Books
Macfarlane, R 2015, *Landmarks*, Penguin Random House, London

writing has, in the past, occasionally drawn attention to itself through an overabundance of grace notes, his concern in *Landmarks* is not so much with reprising any decorative or 'what-ho' tradition of intrepid literary adventurers, but rather with the urgent – as opposed to nostalgic – need to re-engage Britain's largely metropolitan population with the marvellously specific and intricate habitats that continue to be smashed by industrialisation, population growth and sprawl. But there is a downside to this, a downside of reception, which is worth analysing, especially given his style's compatibility with literary tourism.

Famously, Macfarlane prefers to filter, if not efface, his enjoyment of the outdoors through admiring portraits of other nature writers. *Landmarks* is no different from his earlier books in this respect, but crucially its chapters alternate between these biographical set pieces and the immensely purposeful stimulus of glossaries of place-specific words of the British Isles. To qualify for a place in what is, by this stage, looking like the Macfarlane canon, a writer must be not only an exemplar of intrepid solitude and a brilliant *littérateur* of nature, but also a little neglected or forgotten. Those familiar with Macfarlane's work might be surprised, therefore, to find him in *Landmarks* re-retrieving a writer such as Roger Deakin, whom he has already championed. But we also find new additions to his canon: the assiduous, arthritic, peregrine-obsessed J.A. Baker, for example; as well as that rather saint-like nineteenth-century hunter and author of *The Amateur Poacher* (1879), Richard Jefferies.

Macfarlane's portraiture is essentially romantic in nature, with even at times the hint of hagiography about it. But in his chapter on Baker's *The Peregrine* (1967), he forces us to confront what is a crucial underlying concept in the new self-reflexive resurgence of nature writing in the UK – 'species shame'. Baker observes of human beings: 'We stink of death. We carry it with us.' The intensity of this language of self-loathing inverts Macfarlane's even-temperedness, and it serves him well to include it in these pages. For the criticism of Macfarlane's work in the past has not only been directed at the rather ornamental style with which he has curated his and his heroes' 'lost landscapes'; he has also been knocked for lacking the kind of self-investigation he admires in others. He has a talent for comparing natural with synthetic phenomena, but one suspects that lines like 'Foam, the creamy colour of writing paper, gathered between shore stones', from *The Wild Places* (2007), have a de-wilding effect on his subject. When compounded by vanities such as the author folding a dead seagull's wings across its chest (in the same book), the effect is a kind of schmaltz, which encloses the subject in a mixture of the antique and the New Age.

It is a quandary of the currently abounding place-literature that by bringing such softening frames to so-called 'wild' places, and by writing so charmingly about them, authors are in fact robbing these places of the 'wildness' and the psycho-geographical freedom they purport to love. Or are they? When one considers that the great majority of Britain has long been domesticated anyway (the reader often suspects a Ballard-ish motorway is conveniently just out of the frame in many instances of contemporary nature writing in the UK), and that the so-called 'wild' landscapes of even a country as vast as Australia are often no such thing, as Bruce Pascoe, Bill Gammage and others have shown, then it is easy to conclude that any Wordsworthian impulse to leave these landscapes 'untouched' is an illusory one.

That is only the case, however, if we are not considering the chief inhabitants of such places: the animals, for whom the absence of humans must be a boon. In a recent essay in the *London Review of Books*, a prominent figure in the new wave of nature writing in the UK, Scottish poet Kathleen Jamie described her hopes for Lochmill, a secluded reservoir near where she lives. Lochmill is in the process of being taken out of private ownership by a community buy-back scheme. Jamie describes how when she and her husband visited the loch not long after ninety-five per cent of the community voted 'yes' to the buy-back idea, they did so with a new sense of 'ownership and responsibility'. But when she describes them chancing upon a narrow deer trail they had 'never noticed before' and flushing out a 'rare' woodcock from under the bracken, one cannot help but project forward to consider the effects Jamie's newly enthused and nature-loving community will have on the living creatures of Lochmill. Through a surfeit of good intentions, this quiet lacustrine habitat – 'you wouldn't know the loch existed unless you were looking for it' – may well be suddenly inundated with people. No doubt subcommittees will be formed to maintain the loch's 'wildness', but nevertheless a new battle will begin.

When a remarkably similar situation arose recently in my own area in south-west Victoria, community enthusiasm for the reclamation of our own bush-clad water catchment included dreams of waterskiing and mountain-bike trails. So perhaps Jamie presumes too much in her essay about the compatibility of a human 'community' with a formerly quiet landscape. Her piece triggers thoughts of celebrities who proudly reveal their favourite getaways in interviews, complete with google map links. No matter how sensitively it is 'managed', the discovery of each new destination potentially flushes another 'rare' species out of its home.

Orcadian poet George Mackay Brown understood this well when he published his poem 'Trout Fisher' back in 1965, which tells the story of Semphill, a fisherman who earns his money by showing city visitors the tricks of fishing his local island loch:

> 'Forgive me, every speckled trout,'
> Says Semphill then,
> 'And every swan and eider on these waters.
> Certain strange men
> Taking advantage of my poverty
> Have wheedled all my subtle loch-craft out
> So that their butchery
> Seem fine technique in the ear of wives and daughters.
> And I betray the loch for a white coin.'

This is what humans do, of course, and talented writers are no exception. Look at the novel form, for instance. It is an excellent vehicle for evoking place, and it has created whole industries of literary tourism that attract people to previously 'unregarded' space. Think of

Captain Corelli's Mandolin and the once quiet isle of Cephalonia; or think of the Romantic poets and the Lakes District. When Wordsworth bemoans the introduction of ornamental gardening into his local district in the 1820s, he is very persuasive. He prefers the slow and subtle gradation of wild tones to the quick installation of strict lines, and so do his fans.

One suspects that the relatively remote and wintry Scottish Cairngorms could never achieve the levels of tourism of the Lakes District or a sunny Mediterranean island, but with the popularity of 'cold tourism' in the global-warming era I can't help wondering what even the smaller effects of Macfarlane's championing of Nan Shepherd's beautiful Cairngorms book *The Living Mountain* (1977) will be on the fauna and flora of that region. When one considers how successful Macfarlane and other UK nature writers such as Helen Macdonald have been, and that the publishing phenomenon of new nature writing has been described in the pages of *The Guardian* as the current *Fifty Shades of Grey*, one must at least begin to think about it – especially in a century of environmental crises, population explosions and intense digitisations, in which we are sure to see the First World continuing to privilege and market the 'authentic', the 'wild' and the 'pure' in increasingly evangelical terms.

What is clear in all this is that, in an age of social media and hyper-connectivity, reception is bound to creation, just as tourism is bound to art. The more loved a work of art is, the more negative its effect on the landscape it describes may be. This is the bind that a charismatic writer like Macfarlane will always find himself in. His small and delicately crafted book on the holloways of England may well have already sparked its own subcategory of tourism. This kind of reception can work both ways, of course, and Macfarlane's impeccably produced homage to the holloways may be responsible for the preservation of some of these landscapes in the years ahead. Whatever the case, in a country with over 61 million people living in only 93,000 square miles of land, he has made certain that, as psycho-geographical phenomena, as sites of freedom and release, the holloways will remain neither 'wild' nor unregarded.

Twenty-first-century nature writers have a responsibility to acknowledge this conundrum they are in. To ignore reception is these days, in this of all fields, to be not only counterproductive but potentially acting in bad faith. Thankfully, it is clear by the self-reflexivity of *Landmarks* that Macfarlane is aware of this. As well as the chapters of literary homage, there are many passages in which he attends to such complexities. Most importantly, by the act of making regionally specific language the primary focus of his book, he shifts his lens from the fragility of particular locations, from the vicarious fiction of 'wild places', to the very real and salutary textures of the cultural landscape.

—

The trigger for *Landmarks* was Macfarlane's discovery of a unique linguistic solution to the problem of a proposed wind farm project on the outer Hebridean island of Lewis. The planned installation of 234 turbines, standing 140 metres tall (more than twice the height of Nelson's Column) and with a blade span of over eighty metres, was predicated upon the idea that the interior moorland of the island was a pejorative 'wilderness', a terra nullius, a 'vast dead place'. The islanders of Lewis set out to prove this wrong. In doing so, they created a Peat Glossary, a collection of words specifically originating in that very space, thereby proving that the so-called terra nullius was in fact a *verba terrae*, and therefore a cultural landscape. The wind farm proposal was defeated and the islanders were so invigorated by their success that they began to envisage the Peat Glossary as part of a larger, perhaps even global, Counter-Desecration Phrasebook.

When Macfarlane came across this concept on a visit there in 2007, he undoubtedly recognised a fertile confluence of his interests: landscape, language, the environmental crisis at hand. In essence, Macfarlane is attempting in *Landmarks* to do for the British Isles what the people of Lewis did for their little island. His tone, burnished with his genteel mannerliness, could hardly be said to be radical, but his urgent environmentalism is nevertheless there, behind the choice of every word in his chthonic glossaries, giving *Landmarks* that rarely successful texture of the polemical and the poetic.

Both these qualities are at their most powerful in Macfarlane's assembled glossaries of nearly lost toponyms, topograms and earthy descriptors of the British landscape. He makes the point early on that 'language is always late for its subject'. In doing so, he perhaps signals his desire to counter any possible dangers of reception by cupping an attentive ear not to a wild destination vulnerable to human pressures, but to the phenomenological space between creation and naming, the sensorium landscape independent of the colonising 'word' of Genesis, or any other frame-heavy religious, lifestyle, or lifestyle-as-religion depiction.

Just as language 'produces experience', so too does nature name itself. The scale of the human figure in the landscape means that the impulse towards utterance often springs from the need to find expressions that correspond to the network of our senses. Thus the specific qualities of a landform or the recurring motif of the weather will demand and generate an equally specific terminology. In the pages of *Landmarks*, we find the proof of this to be sonic as much as philological. The evidence is ever present in the glossaries, which owe something to Seamus Heaney's lifelong assimilation of the Gaelic and Nordic word-hoard into poetry, and also to John Stilgoe's revelatory *Shallow Water Dictionary* of 1990. Stilgoe was intent on retrieving long-buried linguistic objects from the guzzles of America's New England estuaries. In Macfarlane's list of words for 'watery ground', in his wider glossary of Flatlands language, we find such dug-up items as the Scots word *slunk*, meaning a 'muddy or marshy place, a miry hollow'. In his Waterlands glossary, in the subcategory of 'moving water', we find, from East Anglia, the onomatopoeic *drindle* – 'diminutive run of water, smaller than a currel'. From Lancashire, in the list for 'pools, ponds and lakes', we have *flosh* – a 'stagnant pool overgrown with reeds'. And from North Lancashire, in the Coastlands glossary, there is *skeer* – a 'stone patch on the sea floor in shallow water'.

Skeer is an interesting one. Can the sound of what is essentially a regional geological term be expressive of an emotion it triggers, which is at the same time a physical sensation? For anyone whose foot has suddenly touched a hard flat stone on the sea bed it would seem so. The initial sibilance leading into the hard thud of 'k' provides a percussive yet sensuous prelude to the micro-panic of the word's mercurial tail, with its echoes of 'veer' and 'sheer'. The sudden elemental change on our skin, in an archetypal realm – the sea – that holds so much mystery and fear for us, is captured and felt. The poetic concision of *skeer* is exemplary.

Slunk also. Though reminiscent of words such as *sludge, gunk, slump,* even *slop* or *slippery,* its terminal landing on the telluric 'k' introduces, indeed telescopes, the precise geological moment in which the land fell into the shape worthy of the description. Like so many other words in *Landmarks*' glossaries, *slunk* qualifies as a kind of dreamtime word, referring to its subject both as once-upon-a-time and still coming-into-being.

As it was for Heaney and so many other English-language poets of Britain and Ireland, *Beowulf* is a foundation text in all of this. Naturally, there are many Celtic words in the lists – ur-sounding nouns such as *sgoinn,* meaning a 'small pool in the rocky bed of a stream in which salmon get imprisoned when the tide is low', or *gurracag,* a 'heap of hay or corn not yet made into stacks'. But equally there is much regional diversity evident in words such as *plim,* which in the Cotswolds means 'to swell with moisture', and *êtchièrviéthe,* which is a Jèrriais, or Jersey Norman term, meaning a 'rock frequented by cormorants'.

When encountering picture-words such as these, of common elements in the landscape, one cannot help but think of the loss of language that has occurred here in Australia since 1788. This is an example of the subtle efficacy of Macfarlane's politics in *Landmarks*. The pleasure I take as a reader in the glottal and sibilant music of his glossaries does not have me combing the net for cheap fares to Britain, but instead has me reaching for my local Wadawurrung words for the things that coexist with me every day, for birds such as the 'tulum' (black duck) or 'peret-peret' (spur-winged plover); for rainbow, 'brinbeal', and mullet, 'dorla'.

The rub is that I also reach for the lost precision of whatever the word must have been here in south-west Victoria for the cormorant-shat rock opposite my house – our lost *êtchièrviéthe* – or the Aboriginal tidal fish trap two miles down the road, the now vanished local version of a *sgoinn*. The native language reanimates the littoral before me, bringing the shore and sky to life in a way that superimposed English never could. One only has to wander down the main street of my nearest regional centre, Geelong, to realise that knowing what the street name actually means – 'moorabool': mussel – can transform one's sense of even a regional city, leading the eye through desultory malls and gentrified woolstores to the ancient water-glitter at the bottom of the CBD slope. One can taste the word *moorabool* on the tongue – it is quite literally the tang of the place – whereas Swanston Street in Melbourne makes me think only of the Tasmanian land-grabber it was named after, and Oxford Street in Sydney, when compared with the languages of the Eora, is just a sad simulacrum.

Macfarlane's point is that language has the power to situate us, to ground us wherever we are and get us noticing the organic world. We need not emit carbon to experience beauty; the journey is on our tongue. He points to the Sussex dialect noun *smeuse* as a case in point. Meaning 'the gap in the base of a hedge made by the regular passage of a small animal', *smeuse* is an example of how a word can usher us into a life lived at a different scale. As Macfarlane says, 'now I know the word *smeuse*, I will notice these signs of creaturely movement more often'. Noticing is in this case the first and indispensable step towards creaturely cohabitation with a mutual sense of respect and obligation.

So does landscape writing, as Macfarlane suggests in *Landmarks*, begin in the aesthetic and end in the ethical? Certainly, in the case of

Australia it must, as violent dispossessions push hard on the heels as soon as one begins even to think of writing about its landscape. But also, at a more general level, the better you come to know a thing, the more you want to care for it. And that caring might just mean leaving it alone. In a chapter entitled 'Bastard Countryside', Macfarlane leads us into a less narcissistic and more evolved connection to place, where aesthetic disjuncture, the surprise and poetry of the visual glitch, the rhythms of the broken down and the torn up, even the poisoned pastoral, can be the sustenance that is found. These are the Edgelands, the post-industrial and suburban landscapes written about by Richard Mabey, Iain Sinclair and Will Self: the scrappy, remnant city-edge, rather than the pristine romantic tor. Appreciation of these landscapes requires the kind of decentred and realistic eye W.H. Auden employed in his 'Ode to Gaea':

> ... what, to Her, the real one, can our good landscapes be but lies,
> those words where tigers chum with deer and no root dies,
> that tideless bay where children
> play Bishop on a golden shore?

Macfarlane includes within his glossary of 'Edgelands', terms such as *soft estate* – 'natural habitats that have evolved along the borders and verges of motorways and trunk roads' – and *bukli tan*, a Anglo Romani term that defines 'waste-ground by the roadside'. There is also *swedeland* – 'countryside as perceived by someone from a town or city', and *browings* – 'cleared areas that were formerly brambled'. Importantly, he reminds us that the clear-eyed Richard Jefferies documented these Edgelands as far back as the late 1800s, most noticeably in his book *Nature Near London* (1883).

Jefferies' book is truly a wonder of close observation and particularity, but as Macfarlane puts it, the landscape in his work 'refuses to act as a flat frieze that yields its content stably to the viewer'. Like Nan Shepherd five decades later, Jefferies evolved an independent yet intersubjective way of being with nature, an approach that pre-dated the work of ethologists such as Konrad Lorenz, as well as the influential phenomenology of Maurice Merleau-Ponty and Edmund Husserl. For

Jefferies, the landscape was 'volatile and unruly' – not a place of sighs and sentiment where the tiger and the deer cohabit, let alone the lion and the lamb, but a centreless site of knowledge and experience often 'dynamically disobedient to the eye'. When we learn that as early as 1850 more people in England lived in cities than in rural areas (a point the planet as a whole is said to have reached in 2010), the cultural palimpsest of the Edgelands grows in fascination. Even back then, Jefferies saw his *Nature Near London* as fulfilling an archival function, and he was not so much prescient in this as intensely realistic. Nan Shepherd's statement from *The Living Mountain* that 'the focal point is everywhere. Nothing has reference to me, the looker' would fit easily into his sensibility, as it would with a painter like Cézanne, who was conducting his own parallel experiments in landscape at the same time as Jefferies was writing.

Ultimately, then, what Macfarlane leads us towards in *Landmarks* is a focus on environmental literacy, a honing of our ability to see and understand what is still there but always vanishing. To make his point, he describes how in the 2007 updated *Oxford Junior Dictionary*, words deemed irrelevant to a twenty-first-century childhood were removed by the editors, while other new coinages gained admission in their place. When forced to release a list of removed words, Oxford University Press revealed that among them were: *ash, beech, bluebell, buttercup, cowslip, cygnet, dandelion, fern, heather, heron, kingfisher, lark, nectar, pasture* and *willow*. New words coming into the dictionary included: *attachment, blog, broadband, bullet-point, celebrity, chatroom, cut-and-paste, MP3 player* and *voice-mail*.

There is an unavoidably tragic note to the excision of willows and herons from the linguistic landscape of future generations. One even wonders whether the cygnet is somehow having its very future removed by being cut from the dictionary's pages. Or like the *smeuse*, will its flying under the philological radar mean it will go unnoticed and therefore be left alone? Macfarlane thinks not. For him, noticing is everything, and language functions as its greatest enabler. In the final chapter of *Landmarks*, he deals with the language of children, 'Childish', in which fresh tropes of the imagination and the self-generating instinct for inventing new language is celebrated as a living continuation of the old word-hoard. Ending his book like this is a refreshing way of reiterating his central tenet, which is that if there is no room for a cygnet in the lexicon of new generations, there may not be any swans around by the time they are old. He leaves the pages of the final glossary following the Childish chapter blank, 'for future place-words and the reader's own terms'.

The Dehydrated Homeland:
the Poetry of John Kinsella

John Kinsella grew up in Noongar country in Western Australia, in a landscape now labelled as one of the earth's 'biodiversity hotspots'. Settled on the ancient rock platform of the Yilgarn Craton, the slow accumulation of flora and fauna over millennia on the landscape from Geraldton through to Esperance is so vast that it is difficult to contain in the human mind. Certainly it is impossible to understand it properly without the insights that come with deep cultural feeling, the reality of personal experience, and the sense that it exists not only as the subject of a flowcharted purview but as a polytemporal and metaphysical heartland.

What is almost equally astounding as the biodiversity of this landscape is the eco-cultural misreading it has suffered since white settlement, most particularly by physiocrats addicted to European modes of sheep and wheat farming. Clearly the label of 'hotspot' not only celebrates the remnant biological complexity of the region but also serves as a warning, a term of alarm designed to pre-empt disaster, in the manner of an 'accident hotspot' on our roads. It is estimated, for instance, that in the wheatbelt area where Kinsella lives and writes, 24,500 jam wattles were once cleared to fence a single farm. In this manner ninety per cent of the ancient vegetation of the wheatbelt has

The Weekend Australian
Kinsella, J 2016, *Drowning in Wheat: Selected Poems 1980–2015*,
Picador, London

been cleared to create an agricultural landscape that is doomed to fail its own utilitarian aspirations.

In Kinsella's hands this landscape becomes an aesthetic and tragic site, indeed a place emblematic of the whole earth's clanging cauldron. That he is undoubtedly a key laureate of this destruction, particularly of its apparatus and attitudes, its creatures and pain, is made abundantly clear by both the consistency and extent of *Drowning in Wheat: Selected Poems*.

From the beginning, Kinsella's poetic arc has been profuse, intense, urgent with rebellious energy. He has been accused of publishing too much, and therefore of somehow lacking composure, but the great service of this overview is that it shows for the first time the cogency of Kinsella's long-term project. What becomes clear in these pages is that Kinsella's commitment has been quite simple all along. He does what Australians once prided themselves on doing best: he calls a spade a spade.

This may seem a surprising description of a poet who has a reputation for being intellectually difficult, even obtuse. Yet from his first poems in the early 1980s, to his most recent poems, Kinsella has deployed an eclectic arsenal of traditional and invented poetic methods in order to notate the phenomenological complexity of our mistreatment of the earth. Undoubtedly Kinsella is an academic of note – he is a fellow of Churchill College in Cambridge amongst other roles – but even so, his poetry has always blended high theory with a demotic, or down-to-earth voice. This is due perhaps to his art being fuelled by a kind of Damascene realisation, not that he is somehow personally gifted or anointed, but simply that he has been born into a spiritually divested place, a once teeming but currently salt-leached landscape perfectly indicative of what is now accepted as perhaps the biggest challenge ever to have faced humankind.

As such there is a Blakean as well as a cerebral pleasure in Kinsella's poems. 'The point is to redeem the text as glory & joy', he writes in the poem 'Polytype'. But this 'glory & joy' comes not with magisterial pomp intact but via a verification of the rural landscape he experiences: the voices and language of the people in it and of it, the brutality of it's mega-mechanisation, and the deadset cadences of its colonisation.

> *Death was a fantasy*
> *made real*
> *in the bush enclaves*
> *of my uncle's farm*
> *Vermin!*
> *was the password*
> *before touching*
> *a gun.*

From the very earliest poems to the current crop we read lines intentionally dispossessed of mellifluity and pared back to a consonantal meanness. Thus the poet rejects any notion of bucolic romance, notating a dehydrated homeland in honest terms and intuiting early that the whole thing, the mess he loves so much, is, more importantly, a glaring travesty.

There is another kind of pleasure here too, increasingly hard to find these days, of witnessing a writer's unabashed sincerity for his subject. Yet Kinsella's sincerity never comes through sacrificing the intricacies of his mind. In 'Echidna', a brilliant and moving poem dedicated to Jacques Derrida, Kinsella writes:

> *Down where*
> *the highway is sensed in the movement of sand-particles, the*
> *hérisson – istrice in Italian,*
> *in English, hedgehog – excavates*
> *determinedly. At risk, this bristling heart*
> *litters the road with dedication,*
> *symbols of the national psyche*
> *left to bloat in the sun's blistering*
> *prosody*

In lines like this, and by challenging formal play with caustic quantum leaps via vernacular image and metaphor, Kinsella's technical range is made to serve his purpose. At times, in a narrative poem like 'The Wild West', from his mid-1990s book *Silo: A Pastoral Symphony*, he even coopts the bush yarn tropes of yore, peopling his lines with character, chat and incident. Yet in the poems from *Doppler Effect* (2004) he deals more in the discarded husks of such modes, travelling past calcified traditions into the nourishment of more recent trends in eco-linguistic philosophy.

Along with those of other innovative Australian poets like Patrick Jones or Michael Farrell, this facet of Kinsella's stylistic project has at times been dismissed as 'experimental'. But a full century after Dada, 'experimental' surely constitutes a nothing-term, better replaced by describing the ways in which the work advances, or reticulates, or composts the form. Implied also in such facile criticism is an assumption that language must never be fully released from its role as our grammatical drudge-currency, and that for poetry to be properly from rural Australia it needs to be made with the pentametric equivalent of a post-and-rail fence, or to include the kind of 'salt of the earth' minimalism you might find down the pub or around the CWA urn. But what can easily be missed in discussions of Kinsella's work is the way the collusion of oblique syntax and subject creates an allegorical vehicle – be it tercet, aquifer or ute – with which to document the expropriation of a formerly sacralised continent by nostalgic farming methods.

Likewise, a major sequence such as 'The Rust Eclogues':

> *the reddish brown surface*
> *discolouration*
> *is the racism of words*
> *as the weather hums*
> *a few bars of a heritage*
> *listing*

does much more than describe the tragedy of intensified weather and salination. The very groundwater of these eclogues, their lineage in Virgil, for instance, has been evaporated into a terse form appropriate to the now anti-pastoral subject. Experimentation in this case is no such thing. Rather, it is an artful explication of historical crimes and contemporary emergencies.

That said, a certain amount of environmental literacy will help in understanding the subtleties of Kinsella's art. Freo probably won't give you the lexicon you need here, nor will Northcote or Newtown. From these politically green enclaves you could miss much, and read Kinsella a little like you might read John Ashbery. But whereas Ashbery has a genius for slow-mo obliquities and grinning disjunctures, Kinsella's work is fired with a more specific psychogeography and a directly anarchic personality. Perhaps therein lies his 'Australianness'. Whatever the case, context does affect our reception, and read by the Darling River *Drowning in Wheat* might remind you more of Phillip Hodgins than Ashbery. To a greater degree than either Ashbery or Hodgins however, Kinsella is intent on reiterating the same theme, almost entirely excluding the expected poetic territory of his own inner life in favour of expressing a more porous ecological self, which, despite much global bureaucratese, is still the elephant in the room.

> *I keep*
> *rewriting the same poem. But there were*
> *many occasions I witnessed – the word's*
> *appropriate – and a book entirely composed*
> *of poems about sheep killing would not*
> *be enough. Maybe a line for each organ?*
> *A page for each carcass? A section of the skins*
> *laid out over the fence …*
> *there was no random*
> *gesture in the killing, and the prejudice*
> *was lost as good people grew used to it*
> *Forgive them Lord, they know not what they do?*

In that telling last question mark is the poet's despair at not having an easy salve, let alone the consolation of right words. Perhaps Kinsella writes copiously as a result, becoming the vegan eco-exhaust of the nation. One wonders, for instance, whether he would have been a caustic archetype even in the pre-1788 Australia of storied night skies and deep taproots. But no, he is not just blue smoke. More a magpie scouting for shapes with which to mirror the reality of present and future eco-horror. He keeps finding these shapes too, strewn around his crystallised wheatbelt landscape. He locates them in the same way Rumi found wisdoms, so that we must adjust our expectations of poetry in his presence, from a vertical to a horizontal view.

Like his eastern-states counterpart at Bunyah, Kinsella is in this way a genuinely continental poet. Multifarious yet unified. Teeming yet singular. Macro in scope yet on the level of the insects. We don't have to scan for the tectonics but we are shown them nevertheless, and to read these nearly 400 pages is not so much to drown in wheat (the title seems a little weak) as to endure the tears of our own species-shame being eviscerated from their very ducts. In the same way as the river beside my house has become increasingly parched and algal these last twelve months. In the same way as Kinsella describes the salt rising through the land as our *coo-ee* refractor, our comeuppance.

Cartography of Loss:
Five Novels of Patrick Modiano

At the beginning of the Nazi Occupation of France in May 1940, with Western Europe in Hitler's grip and the invasion of England seemingly a fait accompli, large sections of the demoralised French population took not only a pragmatic approach to the likelihood of a colonised future, but sought out scapegoats among their own local population for ignominious humiliation. The typical victims were communists and Jews. Despite much revisionism in postwar years, fuelled in part by Charles de Gaulle's deliberate policy of repackaging his nation's maligned moral identity as steadfast and heroic, the fact remains that after the initial emergence of a resistance movement in underground pamphlets, flyers and journalism, it wasn't until fourteen months after the invasion that the first German soldier was killed in Occupied Paris, when a young subaltern named Alphonse Moser was shot at the Barbès-Rochechouart metro station.

Patrick Modiano was born in 1945, twelve months after the eventual liberation of Paris and only weeks before the official end of the war. By the time he published his first novel *La Place de l'Etoile*, in April 1968 at the age of twenty-two, the official packaging of the French

The Weekend Australian
Modiano, P 2015, *The Occupation Trilogy*, trans. C Hillier, P Wolf,
F Wynne, Bloomsbury, London; Modiano, P 2015, *Little Jewel*,
trans. P Hueston, Text Publishing, Melbourne; Modiano, P 2015,
Paris Nocturne, trans. P Weston-Evans, Text Publishing, Melbourne

Resistance as a triumph of innate Gallic integrity was beginning to unravel. Within just a few weeks of the release of *La Place de l'Etoile*, Paris was famously thrust into chaos, shut down by student riots and worker strikes brought on by years of denial on this and many other issues, culminating in the first ever police invasion of the Sorbonne.

The publication of *La Place de l'Etoile* resonated then, and with its bristling iconoclastic intensity it does so today. The title of the novel refers to the broad square around the iconic Arc de Triomphe, into which twelve avenues, including the Champs-Elysées, converge to form a star. Originally this square, now called Place Charles de Gaulle but still known locally as Place de l'Etoile, or just Etoile, meaning 'Star', was a rise of ground where a number of feudal hunting routes converged. By calling his novel *La Place de l'Etoile*, with its pointed reference to the Star of David that French Jews were made to wear during the German Occupation, Modiano not only adds to the layers but provocatively challenges the simplistic triumphalism of the site.

Modiano's Jewish father refused to wear the star and only avoided deportation to the death camps due to his black-market dealings with gangs linked to the French Gestapo. Crucially, therefore, his son's inheritance was a morally ambiguous one, a murky legacy obscured by his parents' reluctance to talk about what they did or didn't do in the oppressive years between 1940 and 1944. In keeping with this enigma, the Place de l'Etoile in Modiano's novel becomes something even more complex. In fact, it becomes not so much a star as an asterisk of ambiguity, symbolising the many and complex perspectives on Jewish identity in France, and the varying reactions therefore of the local population to German Occupation.

It has taken Modiano winning the Nobel Prize in 2014 for this first English translation of *La Place de l'Etoile* to appear, and it comes as something of a revelation. Unlike the spare, mesmeric and melancholic novels to which we have had access in English so far, *La Place de l'Etoile* is a superabundant and sparring work of shards and fizzing fragments, in which the mnemonic narrator adopts a succession of masks displaying varying degrees of Jewish assimilation, ranging from a conservative student at the Ecole Normale Supérieure to a trader of middle-class French girls as whores to Brazil. His is a vile persona but a Promethean voice, as he casts himself as both Jewish and a collaborator, a Nazi and an individualist, a 'militarist Jew like Capitaine Dreyfus-Stroheim', a 'self-loathing Jew like Simone Weil-Céline', an 'eminent Jew in the mould of Proust-Daniel Halévy-Maurois', a 'collaborationist Jew, a bookish Jew, a bucolic Jewish…a snobbish Jew'. He is all these things, and in sentences teeming with precocious aesthetic energy Modiano creates an incendiary mash-up that combines the chameleonic refuges of the European Jew with the neurotic tyranny of anti-Semites.

It is a pyrotechnic display, pent-up, mercurial, and no doubt influenced by his early mentor and Oulipo co-founder Raymond Queneau. But the book is not just virtuosic, it detonates a whole era. Like the cobblestones hurled by the students of 1968 around the Sorbonne, *La Place de l'Etoile* smashes through the respectable defences and composed edifices of the postwar cultural rebuild. Such is the luminous blaze it sheds on an officially curated past that the rest of Modiano's work – he has published nearly thirty novels since – now seems even more like a smoking ember than it already did.

The publication in English of *La Place de l'Etoile*, along with his following two novels, *The Night Watch* and *Ring Roads*, in a volume called *The Occupation Trilogy*, is part of the Modiano awakening that has taken place in the Anglosphere since the Nobel Prize. *The Night Watch* is a far more stolid affair than *La Place de l'Etoile*, a dense monologue narrated by a double agent of the Occupation, in a Paris portrayed as a morally submerged city, underwater, sinking, drowning. The narrator describes himself as an 'informant, looter, assassin, perhaps. But no worse than the next man. I followed the crowd, nothing more.' *The Night Watch* shows how someone prepared to just go with the flow can find themselves drowning in a surfeit of crime and guilt. The important point here is not that the narrator is amoral but that he is unconscious.

Ring Roads, however, published in 1972, was Modiano's first exploration of the father–son relationship so crucial to his work. By keeping his shady activities between 1940 and 1944 from his son, Modiano's father left not only a moral but a narrative vacuum. In doing so he unwittingly turned that son into a unique and alchemical archivist. In *Ring Roads*, Paris is converted again into a preternatural realm, this time 'a great dark forest filled with traps'. As with Modiano's later masterpiece *Dora Bruder*, the novel starts from an archival source, an old photograph of the narrator's father drinking with friends in a provincial bar outside Paris. We scan the photograph closely before Modiano sets it in motion, extrapolating a plot and *mise-en-scène* in order to investigate his inheritance of survivor shame. A small coterie publishes an anti-Semitic newspaper called *C'est la Vie*. The father of the young novelist–narrator is not only involved in the project but is simultaneously despised as a Jew within it. Immersed among these noirish eidolons of the past the action takes on the disjunctive logic of a dream. We are reeled through the viewfinder as if in search of the narrator's spine. But when we are returned at the end of the plot to the plasticity of the photograph, it comes with reality's sting. By way of contrast we are forced to confront the facile amnesia of official renditions, and of cultural tourism, where the image from provincial France of yesteryear is fetishised for its grainy retinal charm, commodified as a kind of historical porn disassociated from the labyrinthine truths of the war.

With formal reflexivity such as this, Modiano's novels focus the wider communal significance of his own personal archaeology. The more he narrows the view, the wider his lens becomes. The effect across his body of work is hypnotic, the novels being painstakingly braided together. He has said that he writes the same book over and over and so he does. So too does the sun shine a subtly different light each day on the same old world. In Modiano's case this repetition becomes musical in its effect. He limits the stops of his instrument in order to strike a slightly different chord each time, the hints and strains overlapping and resounding, first from the inside, then from the outside, first from the obliquities of memory, then from the necessities of the heart. If, for instance, *La Place de l'Etoile* is brilliant anger blaring from the experimental era of the 1960s, by the time we get to *Little Jewel* in 2001 we find ourselves soulfully embedded amongst quieter and deeper reeds. By this stage Modiano's narrator has come full circle; she is unassuming, her language clear and sparse, yet she is at sea in the same old drowning city of Paris, the same city full of claustrophobic traps, ghost-arrondissements and sudden pastoral breaches.

A trick of Modiano's lasting popularity in France is that his books are often built on structures reminiscent of the detective novel, most specifically of Georges Simenon. In *Little Jewel* the narrator, many years after being abandoned as a child, catches sight of her mother in a yellow coat on the metro and sets out to track her. We travel from Chatelet across to the streets of Vincennes, we search the Bois de Boulogne and through the shadows around the Moulin Rouge. Each encounter, each neon sign and garage becomes a node of significance in the author's cartography of loss. By this we are made to feel the awful emotional vulnerability of a small girl's abandonment, almost as if we are reading Madame Bovary from the perspective of her child. Of the Gare d'Austerlitz, where the child was dropped off by the mother so long ago, she recalls wearing a name tag around her neck for those who would collect her down the line. 'Many years later,' she says, 'I noticed that if I happened to be near the Gare d'Austerlitz I experienced an odd sensation. Everything suddenly felt colder and darker.'

Psycho-geographical sensitivities such as this are Modiano's speciality. In his hands the place that is Paris becomes a sensory field, a somatic city in which memory is located on the street and in the body. In this way *Little Jewel* brings us right up close to the legacy of lovelessness at the heart of Modiano's long retrieval process.

In *Paris Nocturne*, published a year later in 2002, the eternal return at the core of the novels is made explicit. Here the triggering event is not a photograph or the sighting of his mother in a yellow coat but a minor yet eerie car accident on the Place des Pyramides. As the narrator begins an obsessive investigation into the circumstances and people involved in the accident, we find ourselves bound again into the

Modiano echo chamber. Specific ingredients recur from *Little Jewel* and other novels: a lost dog, the smell of ether, a phrase: the 'murmur of wind through leaves'. A seemingly innocuous event has occurred, but like a pebble in a pool the ripples begin to radiate across what, in the aftermath of the war, de Gaulle and others chose to portray as the smooth surface of things. The ripples of Modiano's pool, however, refuse such narcissistic reflections; instead they overlap and interfere with each other in a way that the facile clarity of official national histories would never allow. The natural intervals between the arcs buckle and warp with sorrowful intimacy. The past and the present become the one painful but somehow beautiful contusion. Ultimately we become aware that these novels are not just a collection of marks on a further collection of pages but a metaphysical archive of a complex personal and collective trauma. In Modiano place is a mirror, each of the streets of his home city a palimpsest. We gain access to an inner life that otherwise goes undetected.

Mislaid Books of the Sea

1. Sarah Orne Jewett's *The Country of the Pointed Firs*

Beauty attracts both lovers and pornographers, and beautiful coastlines are just the same. As a case in point, F. Scott Fitzgerald penned *The Great Gatsby* in 1922, whilst living in the village of Kings Point on Great Neck, Long Island, a tiny farm village that had over the previous thirty years been slowly transforming into a dormitory town for NYC commuters. Like a lot of Fitzgerald's writings, *Gatsby* is subtly augmented with potent descriptions of the beautiful North American littoral, which he sets against the insatiable dramas of New World capitalism and industrialisation. This is from the book's last page:

> *Most of the big shore places were closed now and there were hardly any lights except the shadowy, moving glow of a ferryboat across the Sound. And as the moon rose higher the inessential houses began to melt away until gradually I became aware of the old island here that flowered once for Dutch sailors'*

Great Ocean Quarterly
Jewett, SO 2000, *The Country of the Pointed Firs and Other Stories*, Signet Classic, New York; Jansson, T 1966, *Moominpappa at Sea*, Ernest Benn, London; Steinbeck, J 1958, *The Log from the Sea of Cortez: The Narrative Portion of the Book, Sea of Cortez with a Profile 'About Ed Ricketts'*, Heineman, London; Brown, GM, 2005, *The Collected Poems of George Mackay Brown*, John Murray, London

eyes – a fresh, green breast of the new world. Its vanished trees, the trees that had made way for Gatsby's house, had once pandered in whispers to the last and greatest of all human dreams; for a transitory enchanted moment man must have held his breath in the presence of this continent, compelled into an aesthetic contemplation he neither understood nor desired, face to face for the last time in history with something commensurate to his capacity for wonder.

Of course we know in Australia that those Dutch sailors were not experiencing that feeling for 'the last time in history', but nevertheless Fitzgerald manages to smuggle into *Gatsby* a much overlooked sense of the dignity and magic of the oyster-laden Mattinecock tribal lands that were being sacrificed for all those 'inessential houses'.

In 1896, some three decades before Fitzgerald wrote *Gatsby*, a little further up that same eastern seaboard on the southern coast of Maine, the lesser-known novelist, short-story writer and poet Sarah Orne Jewett was writing not so much of the materialism about to descend but of the gentler European prehistory that existed in the fragrant little coastal villages she had grown up amongst.

Jewett was Maine-born in 1849, a granddaughter of shipwrights, daughter of doctors, and destined for a life outdoors. Suffering from infant rheumatoid arthritis, she was prescribed long walks and encouraged by her father to lead 'a healthy, open-air life rather than set to the tasks and lessons of the school-room'. Like so many writers before and since it was through this walking that she established an open ear for landscape history, a nose and eye for the rich wist and allegories of nature, and a desire to capture the palette and melody of the sea and shore.

The Harvard landscape historian John Stilgoe has brilliantly docu-mented the cultural history of the New England shoreline, including the influx of tens of thousands of New England holidaymakers onto the southern Maine coast during Sarah Orne Jewett's lifetime. But back in the day, Jewett wrote not so much about the changes: the aggravations of noise, the coming of conning signage, the crowding of the haddock grounds; but of 'that vast obscurity beyond the city' where the sweet charm of alongshore life and the hard-won epigrammatic humours of fish houses and offshore hermitage islands were still hanging on.

Henry James described Jewett's novella *The Country of the Pointed Firs* as a 'beautiful little quantum of achievement', and it is surely a minor masterpiece, which is often the best kind. It is a short but sweet book, full of craft, precision and kindness, and has for me come to represent the ideal of a quietist novel perfectly suited to the gentle pathos often found in tiny sea-gazing towns.

The narrator of *The Country of the Pointed Firs* is an unattached young lady writer who takes a room in the house of Mrs Almiry Todd, a feisty older woman whose expertise as an amateur naturopath and herb gardener has led her into an unofficial partnership with the village doctor in attending to the ailments of the town. In the opening pages the wafting perfumes of Mrs Todd's garden, combined with the ever-present luff of the sea, suffuse events with an astringent good health and a seemingly timeless wisdom.

What follows from the narrator's lodging in Mrs Todd's house is a series of character portraits in which she comes to know and grow fond of the inhabitants of the town. These include a classic cast: the retired sea captain Littlepage, who has 'overset' his brain by reading too much Milton; the heartsore widower fisherman Elijah Tilley, who constructs painted buoys on his house field so as to avoid striking underground reefs with his plough; Miss Joanna the hermit, who takes herself off to live alone on Shell-heap Island after a broken love affair; and Mrs Todd's own mother, the bright-eyed and bird-like Mrs Blackett, who lives with her son William out on Green Island and whose sincere but sardonic relationship with everyone she meets has a quality that reminds me of people I knew here on the Victorian west coast as a child, some of whom still remain.

It is one of the powers of literature, as opposed to cinema, that we take signals from the tone and setting of a book to picture from our own experience the interiors and landscapes in which the action is set. Never having been to Maine myself, my *Country of the Pointed Firs* is therefore a blend of heath and limestone cliffs, fibro and weatherboard houses, correa, pelargonium and kikuyu front and back gardens, and muttonbirdy beach. The wit and detail of Sarah Orne Jewett's writing, her fidelity to vernacular and maritime speech, the botanical reverence of her characters, all conjure and correlate with memories and realities I value in my own realm.

The fact that Jewett wrote the novel as her home coast was first coming under the type of commodification we are still experiencing gives *The Country of the Pointed Firs* an added value. I've no doubt the book was always somehow redolent of a passing world, but it is now more than ever a valuable moral and aesthetic guide to what a rich littoral life should be. Not a life of aspirational wealth, obese architecture and over-regulation, but a life of slow knowledge, deep neighbourliness, and humility before the majesty of earth and sea.

Which brings me back to the eloquent last line of *The Great Gatsby*, written 'down south' of Maine just twenty-six years after Jewett composed her 'beautiful little quantum'. A lot had happened in those twenty-six years, not all of it good, and a lot more has happened since. But one thing hasn't changed. It takes writers of Jewett's and Fitzgerald's quality to properly tell the tale.

> *So we beat on, boats against the current, borne back ceaselessly into the past.*

2. Tove Jansson's *Moominpappa at Sea*

The Finnish writer and illustrator Tove Jansson was both a hopeless islomaniac and a terrible sufferer from pharosphilia. In other words she was mad for islands and a great lover of lighthouses. Of all the books on the sea I know, and of all the writers who have lived on islands, Jansson's *Moominpappa at Sea*, is perhaps the most enchanting and strange.

Removed from school by her artist parents at fifteen so that she could follow in their footsteps, Tove came of age as an artist during the Second World War in Finland where, to escape the terror of the Soviet bombardments, she found herself retreating into her own imaginary universe, a folkloric world of whimsical troll-like creatures she called Moomins. The Moomins lived in a sweet and preternatural valley where vivid cataclysms occurred but, unlike in wartime Helsinki, could always be overcome. Moominvalley was an alternative landscape unriven by human violence or military technology, a place where, as Jansson declared, she could create her first happy ending.

Combining an original and naive illustrative style with her gently adventuresome narratives Jansson soon found that the small pudgy white Moomins and their travails struck a chord with anyone who encountered them. At the end of the war her first Moomin book came out, *Småtrollen och den stora översvämningen*, or *The Moomins and the Great Flood*. Scandinavian readers immediately fell in love with it, and with the release of its follow-up, *Comet in Moominland*, Jansson set in motion a worldwide publishing phenomenon well beyond her wildest dreams.

As readers' passions for the Moomins spread across the postwar globe through the 1950s and 60s, the alternative and loving world the pacifist Tove had created to escape from the war began to feel encroached upon again, this time by fame. The demands on her time became intense, and as a result her girlhood desire to live on her own postage-stamp island in the Pellinge archipelago in the Gulf of Finland returned to the forefront of her mind. Her family had always holidayed on the Swedish island of Bredskär, from where, far out on the outermost skerries of the archipelago, she had been entranced as a child by a mysterious lighthouse and also by the quasi-mythological Kummelskär, a larger island further out into the open waters of the gulf. Continually besieged now by the ironies of her success, she felt the need to get away, particularly so because she had also found the love of her life in graphic artist Tuulikki Pietilä, or 'Tooti', as she was known. Tove often used the code words *rive gauche* or 'the spook side' to describe their relationship, in a Finland where homosexuality was a criminal offence. All these factors combined saw her enquiring about the possibility of purchasing remote Kummelskär.

As it turned out Kummelskär was deemed illegal for habitation because of the fragility of its herring habitats, but the island of Klovharun, itself well within the Pellinge conservation area, became a possibility. The idiosyncratic process by which the couple came to live on this island played itself out during the same period Jansson was composing *Moominpappa at Sea*. A notice was put up on the wall of the general store on a neighbouring island asking people to vote on whether Tove and Tooti should be allowed to live on Klovharun. The conditions stated were that they neither own Klovharun nor lease it out to others until Tove's death – when it would return to the community – and that as payment they make a donation to the Pellinge Fishing Association. No legal papers were to be involved. One can only sigh now at the lack of paperwork and bureaucratic interference, especially in light of the knowledge that the Pellinge community voted in the gay artists' favour. Finally Jansson had the island solitude she'd always dreamed about, and a real-life companion to her beautiful island book.

Moominpappa at Sea is a distinctive novel in Jansson's output because it marks the bridge between her Moomin books, which have always been lovingly deemed 'children's literature for adults', and her later work, which was for adults alone. By the time she settled with Tooti on Klovharun it was 1965 and she was returning to her youthful desires to be considered a 'serious' artist. So it was that in *Moominpappa at Sea* she set out to explore the different ways in which we use the sea and its islands to escape the psychological pressures of ordinary life.

The book starts with the Moomins deciding, like Tove and Tooti, to move from their familiar surroundings and to risk a great adventure on the sea. This makeshift adventure is led by Moominpappa, Jansson's hapless patriarch, a would-be meteorologist and scientist who needs to assert his manhood by inhabiting a wild place and taking charge of it. With him is his loyal wife Moominmamma, their timid but highly imaginative child Moomintroll, and the strangely acerbic adjunct Little My, who in her subversive scepticism is a bit like a Nordic forerunner to Lisa Simpson.

The island they set out for, which Moominpappa has long been aware of because of the beam of its light, turns out not to be an easy playground but an eerie and storm-harried enigma. When they arrive the lighthouse is on the blink. Moominpappa immediately sets out to establish some order, blustering around trying to set things to right. He documents the wind speeds in his journal as if that will somehow make them abate, tinkers unsuccessfully with the recalcitrant beacon, and declaims constantly his masculine superiority over the world they have found. Meanwhile, however, the pelagic mysteries and circadian patterns of the island and its weather continue.

As things grow more and more inhospitable the little nuclear family of forest trolls, now exiled on a great sea under an endless and inscrutable sky, each peel away into their own coping mechanisms. Little Moomintroll gets to know the island by night, encountering dancing phosphorescent seahorses on the beach and a dark shadowy creature called The Groke, who represents the anti-lyric within the story just as Little My represents the anti-romantic. Little My herself befriends the island's only human inhabitant, a mysteriously incommunicative fisherman whose position on the margins of 'civilised' life obviously attracts her.

But it is Moominmamma, with her recourse to creativity rather than science, who best captures the essence of Tove Jansson's consolatory genius. As her husband's island dream becomes increasingly unhinged, rather than trying to impose herself on a world with which she is not familiar, Moominmamma elects to simply paint the world as she would like it to be, on the interior walls of the lighthouse kitchen.

One can't help but read *Moominpappa at Sea*, in all its loving naivete and atmospheric brilliance, as Tove Jansson's mature allegory on the restlessness of human desire and our need to avoid life's difficulties by escaping to our own psycho-geographical havens. Through her invention of the symbolic world of the Moomins during the harrowing realities of the war in Helsinki, she herself had chosen to do exactly as Moominmamma does when she paints her dreams on the inner walls of the lighthouse. She neither tried to subdue the threats all around her nor give in to her own slough of despond. Instead, artistic creation became the real haven, for Moominmamma and for Tove, as they rendered their hopes for a better world with skill and enchantment, and with all the sea's moods and mysteries as their friend.

3. Ed Rickett's and John Steinbeck's *Sea of Cortez: A Leisurely Journal of Travel and Research*

> *We have a book to write about the Gulf of California. We could do one of several things about its design. But we have decided to let it form itself: its boundaries a boat and a sea; its duration a six weeks' charter time; its subject everything we could see and think and even imagine; its limits – our own, without reservation.*

There are many books that have grown to be loved and lauded but that started out derided or ignored. Take Herman Melville's *Moby Dick*, for instance, these days generally regarded as the Great American Novel but which in the life of its author lay sadly dormant and neglected. When the book was published in 1851, roughly 3000 copies were printed, a few hundred of which were lost not long after in a warehouse fire. Yet upon Melville's death some forty years later, the remaining copies had still not sold. The progenitor of the *Pequod*, Captain Ahab, Starbuck, Queequeg and the great symbolic white whale itself, died as a customs officer on the wharfs in New York with the total American earnings of *Moby Dick* coming to $556. It wasn't until thirty years after Melville's death that through the persistent championing of the well-connected but now little-known English writer Viola Meynell the book was included in the Oxford World Classics series and this greatest of all mislaid books of the sea was pointed in the direction of the vast readership it still enjoys today. Touché, Viola, I say!

Another classic American novel that started life in a far from an ideal way was John Steinbeck's *The Grapes of Wrath*. This radical fictional testimony of the Great Depression was received with such aggressiveness when it was first published in 1939, and the process of writing it had been so harrowing and arduous, that Steinbeck resolved to give up the bleeding art of fiction in favour of becoming a cool-blooded scientist.

In this Steinbeck was greatly influenced by the example of his old mate, the marine biologist Ed Ricketts. Doyen of the financially precarious and decidedly dipsomaniacal Pacific Biological Laboratories on Cannery Row in Monterey, Ed Ricketts was by nature actually the opposite of the cool head and objective materialist Steinbeck may have wished he could become. 'He forbade his mind to think of metaphysical or extra-physical matters, and his mind refused to obey him' was how the novelist came to describe Ricketts in the end. The two men sprang from very different professional disciplines, but in the manner of sine curves or great brimming poetic metaphors came to overlap and intersect each other through the expansive energy of their dreams and passions, and thus to become fast and firm friends.

At the end of 1939 Ricketts was, like Steinbeck, in recuperation mode, although in his case it was from a disastrous romance rather than a controversial novel. Together they conceived for themselves a marine escape valve, in the shape of a seventy-five-foot sardine boat called the *Western Flyer*, which they chartered for a six-week trip south to Mexico, into the Gulf of California to be precise, otherwise known as the Sea of Cortez. The purpose of the expedition would ostensibly be scientific – in rubber boots and with dip nets and specimen jars they would comb the low-tide pools of the sparsely populated gulf, collecting marine invertebrates to take back to the Pacific Laboratories in Monterey. In actual fact, as is well evident in their log of the trip, first published with co-authorship in 1941 as *Sea of Cortez: A Leisurely Journal of Travel and Research*, Steinbeck and Ricketts took a working holiday to ruminate at length not only on the biogeographical diversities of the sea Jacques Cousteau later described as 'the aquarium of the world', but also on the problematic way in which the human scientific community likes to masquerade as its clear-sighted and objective-minded lord.

Sea of Cortez: A Leisurely Journal of Travel and Research, as well as being a daily proto-blog of an expedition in which over fifty new species of tidal fauna were documented, is most entertainingly a discussion concerning the sea of mankind's hubris and the rocky shores of its existential doubt. Alongside the list of the creatures collected on the littoral – sea hares, holothurians, chitons, heart urchins, sand dollars, stalk-eyed conchs, 'sloppy-guts' anemones, heliasters and Sally Lightfoot crabs, to name but a few – the two men, in a collaboration resembling at times the left and right brains of one unified organism and at others the alternating flashes of contradictory navigational lights, expound on the faulty ego of science while humorously playing up the idiosyncrasies of both their knockabout crew and the Hansen Sea-Cow, the unreliable outboard engine of their shore-going skiff.

From this most loquacious of sea logs one could quote a list of insights almost as long as the inventory of molluscs, corals and sponges they collected. Indeed, it is a book by two very likeable minds, both of whom are at the top of their game and obviously enjoying the escape from life's troubles. Hence their writing is fearless and flexible, humorous and free. They enjoy a beer on the deck of the *Western Flyer* whilst railing against the absurdity of both the European War (Germany had invaded Denmark as they sailed), and the wasteful bycatch of Japanese trawlers (which they encountered near Guaymas and commented on presciently). Always, however, they remain warmly democratic and unjudgemental towards the individuals such systemic barbarisms employ. In this way Steinbeck and Rickett's sceptical digressions never dull the joy they take in moving as slowly as possible around a teeming piece of life's water.

After six weeks, with the *Western Flyer* packed to its gills with creatures preserved in formaldehyde and anaesthetised in Epsom salts, the voyage of scientific self-interrogation and personal recovery finally drew to its close. Slowly, regretfully, the old purse-seiner crept down the eastern waters of the gulf, its crew now properly sardonic about the recalcitrant Hansen Sea-Cow, its pair of gifted naturalists reluctantly returning to the maelstrom of their normal daily lives. The following year the book of their expedition was published only a week before the Japanese attack on Pearl Harbor and consequently sunk from trace.

Seventy-five years later, with the once myriad species of the Sea of Cortez vanishing at a desolating rate, both the bare data of the original log and the philosophic aperçus that accompanied it have ecological, intellectual, and life-affirming value. For this is that rare type of book whose purpose is both scientific and spiritual. By carefully documenting the former diversity to which the present day Gulf of California could, with wise regulation and care, return, and by writing up their journey with such wit, brio and common sense, Steinbeck and Ricketts have given us not only a wonderful read but also a model of accessible science writing we'd do well not to ignore in this era of diminishing returns.

4. George Mackay Brown's *Collected Poems*

When winter comes and the moon-drawn sea cracks its whip in the river mouth of sleepless nights, it is then that you want the poems of George Mackay Brown from the Orkney Islands on your bedside table. A postman's son born in 1921 in the old Viking town of Stromness, Brown is a poet whose imaginative instinct in the face of the ocean's amoral power is both beautiful and true. His poems teem with compassion for characters trying to measure up to the waves, others burrowing themselves away, some trying to mirror the enigmas of the sea in music, still others attempting to package it up for visitors. All of them of course end up in the same place.

> The old go, one by one, like guttered flames.
>   This past winter
>   Tammag the bee-man has taken his cold blank mask
>   To the honeycomb under the hill,
>   Corston who ploughed out the moor

Unyoked and gone; and I ask,
Is Heddle lame, that in youth could dance and saunter
A way to the chastest bed?
The kirkyard is full of their names
Chiselled in stone. Only myself and Yule
In the ale-house now, speak of the great whale year.

Reading Brown's poems here amongst the relatively new white settlements of coastal Victoria, it can seem at times as if he lived for a thousand years. In truth, however, this was an illusion of his art. He had explored and absorbed the Scandinavian aspects of his home islands, saturating himself in the ancient Norse, Icelandic and Orkneyinga sagas, until each line of his poems began to feel itself like something etched into the stone of a cold sea-cave. While Allen Ginsberg and co. howled from the tumultuous postwar cities of the west, Brown, through illness and shyness, stayed put in an independent, northern and arcane world. His work became a freakish reticulation of nature's voices. It could not be read as sentimental, nostalgic, decorative or cute, but rather as poetry from a deeply lived local life, full of the failure and injustice of reality as well as the incorrigibility and social exposure of the coastal village.

To his great benefit, and to the benefit of his poetry, and therefore to us, Brown suffered not only from tuberculosis but also from what W.H. Auden called topophilia – or *place-love*. In GMB's case it was truly an obsession and an addiction. The Orkney Islands were his cradle, his word-foundry, his tabernacle, his pub and poet's creel. It was there that he grew up in poverty and it was there as a man that he concentrated hard, peering into the blades of ocean glare for the right shapes of his vision, inscribing the foibles and fates of his people and their history in a body of work that seems more relevant than ever in our hyper-connective yet disconnected world.

Well conversant with the currents of twentieth-century poetic movements through his early but brief foray into the big academic smoke of Edinburgh, Brown forged his own unique style of modernism from local and littoral sources, chiefly the image-based runes of Ancient

Norse that were carved into the stone cliffs of the Orkney shores. He took on the aesthetic lessons of these runes, absorbing them into his poetic bloodstream, and thus it is that his work feels so genuinely new and old. This art beyond time was no accident – 'Language, open the sacred quarry', he cries in 'The Image in the Hills' – and his creative loyalty was not to any ideological or progressive concept but to the more elemental and imperfect truth of the islands. 'Poor bright places' as he called them, where ordinary working people eked out their days amongst the tragic scale and marvellous wonders of the sea.

Charmingly antiquated as it can feel to read of stone and skerry, of firth-craft, and holm-sight, of slow wells and homing rudders, it requires a sophisticated poetic intelligence to travel beyond the ornamental spin that often passes for coastal culture these days. To put it simply, it is Brown's uncompromising fidelity to place that makes his poems so powerful, nor can we forget the passion of his artistic commitment, which he declared early when he wrote:

> In the fire of images
> Gladly I put my hand.

He valued the ancestral lineage in both his own work and that of the fishing and farming community around him. Thus he developed powers of observation and paratactic expression unsurpassed by any other twentieth-century poet. He watched, he read, he listened in the pubs, he 'interrogated the silence', he saw the way things were changing on the Orkneys, and how nothing had changed in the human heart at all. In response he crafted poems that reanimate the old sea-magic of the centuries of St Magnus and Thorfinn, also the violence on the islands during the Scottish Reformation, weaving it all in a long slow tapestry, right in amongst the tawdry muzak of modern tourism.

Brown himself became something of a target for this tourism near the end of his life. Visitors would knock on the door of his pebbledashed cottage so frequently that he took to hanging a sign out that said, 'No callers before 2pm' or 'WORKING ALL DAY'. Indebted to the natural world but observant of contemporary culture he tells in the poem

'Trout Fisher', published in 1965, of the sad dilemma of Semphill, a fisherman whose money is made by helping city visitors fish the island lochs:

> 'Forgive me, every speckled trout,'
> Says Semphill then,
> 'And every swan and eider on these waters.
> Certain strange men
> Taking advantage of my poverty
> Have wheedled all my subtle loch-craft out
> So that their butchery
> Seem fine technique in the ear of wives and daughters.
> And I betray the loch for a white coin.'

Brown wrote volumes of short stories as well as poetry, novels too, one of which, *Beside the Ocean of Time*, was shortlisted for the Booker Prize in 1994. Such splashes of fame, however, caused him great anxiety, living as he did on his own often precarious psychological fault line. But he could not avoid the respect and adulation. Though he only travelled to England once in his life, other poets began to make the pilgrimage to visit him in Stromness: Seamus Heaney, Ted Hughes, Robert Lowell, people who knew a thing or two about stringing words together to form gale-shapes or to scale the rocky strata of the human heart. When they left to go back to their own poems, and their own numinous landscapes, Brown would carry on witnessing the creelers' fingers burning in the dawn. And yes, even through the years of his celebrity on the island the poems kept coming, like the 'purple samurai' in the craypots, or the spuming pods sighted from the headlands back in the great whale year. The Orcadian poet would relaunch his boat of word and rhythm, his inner soundscape would flash and stream again with salt water. After hard toil and in solitude his prey would be caught, the page would be printed. Another poem would go out from the islands, witness to the people he was from, the gull-gaunt tide and shore, the ocean of time that surrounds us all.

The Submerged Moon:
Nora Webster by Colm Tóibín

It is amusing to think of Colm Tóibín and Jeffrey Eugenides being ticked off over dinner with art historians at Princeton University for, on the one hand, regurgitating social realist novels for middle-class consumers, while on the other daring to speak the 'holy' avant-garde name of Samuel Beckett. Tóibín has told this anecdote with a degree of relish, convinced as he is, through his exhaustive reading and, in particular, his study of the exquisite dissections of Henry James, that an outwardly provocative style is not his thing. Though his novel *Nora Webster*, seen through the lens of nineteenth- and twentieth-century 'isms', undoubtedly exhibits the generic traits of social realism, its plain style and its eponymous character are powerful and expertly brandished weapons. Tóibín's friend and guide John McGahern used to laugh at what the avant-garde missed in Beckett – namely, that many of his linguistic inventions were based on idioms of Irish speech. Tóibín also knows that when it comes to expxressing 'the within of things' – to borrow a phrase from Pierre Teilhard de Chardin, the Catholic palaeontologist whose influence in the Vatican II era is evident in the milieu of this book – social realism can be as sharp and as subtle a mode as there is.

After nine books of fiction and a plethora of stimulating and often personal essays on reading and writing, we know that everything in

Sydney Review of Books
Tóibín, C 2014, *Nora Webster*, Picador, London

Tóibín has a lineage in his own accessible brand of literary scholarship. The title of *Nora Webster* rings out like an in-joke of the Irish middle class at the expense of the lacquered and iconic *Anna Karenina* by the socially utopian Tolstoy, and the tragically frou-frou *Madame Bovary* by the aesthetically utopian Flaubert. What Tóibín specialises in, most particularly in his Wexford novels – of which *Nora Webster* could be called the fifth, but is more properly the third, after *The Heather Blazing* (1992) and *The Blackwater Lightship* (1999) – is a stylistic faithfulness to the largely undramatic middle-class landscape of south-eastern Ireland.

Tóibín has been aghast at being mislabelled a 'storyteller' rather than a novelist. But the key to his rejection of the term lies not in his raised eyebrow at its folksy imprecision and New Age connotations; nor is it due to any lack of interest in the kind of oral archaeology that W.B. Yeats and Lady Gregory undertook on the west coast of Ireland in the late 1800s. Rather, it lies in Tóibín's particular emphasis on the pact of solitude between the main protagonist and the reader of a novel. This solitude involves the kind of escapism that the Princeton art historians were looking down their nose at. Nowhere in Tóibín is there any arch repudiation of the kind of vicariousness long associated with the reading of novels. This is one of the readerly zones he has explored in his essays, in which he has reflected on the ingredients of his own sensibility, picking up the quieter, less dipsomaniacal strands of the Irish tradition – McGahern, John Synge, Mary Lavin – in order to clarify the thorough fidelity required of work in the wake of modernism's split atom. Tóibín's quest, in surveying the literary gods, has been to re-haunt his fictional county of hushed, anti-touristic landscapes, with its vulnerable women who nevertheless suffer no fools, and its men who are benevolent and intelligent, yet often attenuated. In doing so, he has reoriented the Irish canon towards these 'quiet' writers, an act as rebellious and historically necessary as the noisier experiments of the avant-garde.

Nora Webster is a case in point. In fact, it may well be Tóibín's most effective case yet. For one, the major event of the novel – the death of Nora's husband Maurice – happens before the novel begins, precluding any easy cinematic tropes and allowing us, in a narrative simulation of 'big bang' cosmologies, to begin after the beginning, as it were. In this sense, but in this sense only, *Nora Webster* is a naturalistic novel.

It is the late 1960s. Nora is in her house, in an ordinary Enniscorthy street, with the two youngest of her four children, Donal and Conor, who, unlike their two older sisters, are still heavily reliant on their 'mammy'. People are disingenuous in Enniscorthy, as they are everywhere, but this is not to be held against them. In the opening pages, two people come to the door who are not seen for the rest of the novel. The first is Nora's immediate neighbour Tom O'Connor, who is there to sympathise. It is clear that Tom is keeping a close watch on every well-meaning step that approaches Nora's house, but as he consoles her – not about Maurice's death, but about the glut of maudlin condolences it has triggered – he lays on his superiority just a little too thick. She can't wait to get back into the house and away from him.

The second knock on the door comes from someone we have met before: the widowed mother of Eilis Lacey, the heroine of Tóibín's *Brooklyn* (2009). May Lacey – 'the little woman who lives in Court Street', whispers young Conor – has come in the sympathetic mode but on a pragmatic mission. She wants to know if Nora is planning to sell the holiday house on the coast at Cush now that Maurice has died. The implication is that with the loss of income it may be a necessity. May's son-in-exile, Jack, whose repressed nostalgia for Ireland is also familiar to us from *Brooklyn*, wants to know.

As it turns out, the selling of the house at Cush, not far along the strand from the Redmonds' house in *The Heather Blazing*, and just along the coast from the house where the Devereauxs came to nurse Declan in *The Blackwater Lightship*, is exactly what Nora decides she must do. And so we are introduced to the widow as a pragmatist, with the burden of solitary decisions to make and surrounded by cloying propinquity at every step.

Like their mother, the boys Donal and Conor are terribly afflicted by their father's death, but in different ways. Donal has developed a stammer. Conor, the youngest, with 'his sweet loyalty, his open need to be taken care of', is a lightning rod for the love and affection grief stirs up. He is extroverted, but he is not blithe; he is too conscientious for that. Despite his chattiness, he too is shouldering a heavy load.

———

Like Maurice in the novel, Tóibín's father Michael was an Enniscorthy schoolteacher, an active member of Fianna Fáil, and a local historian. Michael Tóibín died young, in 1967, when Colm was twelve, about the same age as Donal. The young Colm also had a stammer. This goes part of the way to explaining the unnerving accuracy of Tóibín's habitation of Nora's parenting mind, but not all the way. Only some of us, after all, can remember the precise and often quite unmusical manner in which the anxious family dialogue of childhood breathed, the way the whole fate of the world seemed to, and did, hinge upon an empty hallway, an emptier back room, or a front porch of anxiety. But even fewer are able to represent it in a way that is not excessively dramatised but has the incremental anguish of a genuinely autochthonous novel. Robert Lowell's remark on poetry is transferable here to Tóibín's prose: 'A poem is an event,' Lowell wrote, 'not the record of an event.'

There is a sense in which *The Master* (2004), Tóibín's novel about Henry James, and *The Testament of Mary* (2012), his novella about the mother of Jesus, both of which are remarkable achievements in themselves, have been ideal preparations for *Nora Webster* inhabiting the house where the formative loss of his life occurred. Tóibín's immersion in James has helped him accumulate the tools of a fastidious yet empathetic craft, while his depiction of a loving but caustic and telluric Mary has prepared him for this novel, in which

Tóibín witnesses his own grief as a teenage boy through the inner workings of a bereaved mother's mind.

We are privy to no one's thoughts but Nora's. The effect is excruciating. We worry along with her about just how broken and fragile Donal and Conor might be, particularly Donal. This anxiety about the wellbeing of the fatherless boys is the book's narrative engine. Tóibín repeatedly withholds the consequences of Donal's vulnerability while sounding a note of impending doom. Nora's imperfect yet instinctive empathy will be broken into pieces; as it is, she is straining, oscillating between strength and passivity, holding things together, barely managing to interpret the silences, the boys' bewilderment, the girls' burgeoning adulthood and their desire for a frank and mature flow of information.

Through the patronage of his aunt and uncle, Margaret and Jim, Donal is encouraged in his interest in photography. He finds his distance from the traumatised household in the darkroom Margaret has built for him under her stairs. But have his affections been hijacked by his aunt? Will he come to some harm there, as he did when his stammer developed, while he was staying with Aunt Josie as his father was dying? Will he remain forever distant now, from both his mother and his own grief? Will he twist and distort in all that developing darkness? Nora feels his distance and we feel it too. When, through the neighbourly orchestrations of Enniscorthy, Nora is offered a job in the office of a local family business, Gibney's, where she had worked before she was married, the problems and anxieties are compounded. The boys come home after school each day to an empty house. We are not only led to worry about what will happen to them in those intervening hours, but crucially, we intuit how formative these days and weeks may eventually become. Their father is dead, but still everywhere present in the house; their mother is alive, but too often absent.

It was while revisiting the work of Thom Gunn, not long after the poet's death in 2004, that Tóibín experienced a breakthrough in his approach to such personal material. He had previously ascribed the rapport he had always felt with Gunn's work, particularly the intensity with which he read him as a teenager, to the fact that they were both gay. In his book of essays on gay writers, *Love in a Dark Time* (2002), Tóibín reports that he had come to the same conclusion about the affinity he had felt as a teenager with the work of Elizabeth Bishop, Thomas Mann and James Baldwin. But in a lecture he gave in Key West in early 2013, he described how, as he stood among his books comparing certain disclosures Gunn had made about his mother's death in an interview with certain lines of Bishop's, the penny finally dropped. All of them – Tóibín, Gunn, Bishop, Mann and Baldwin – had lost a parent in their childhood or early adulthood. In the case of Gunn and Bishop, they, like Tóibín, had never explicitly written about the event or the pain it had caused. Instead, they had chosen to carry the grief under their work like a submerged moon, always at a distance and in shadow, but present in every beam, every burst and caesura of their style. As Tóibín stood by the shelves, book in hand, he understood that it was on the battlefield of grief versus reason, rather than that of marginalised sexuality, that he related to these writers.

It is in light of this realisation that *Nora Webster* should be viewed as an apotheosis. With this novel, we can no longer avoid the clarity of Tóibín's project, in which the parabolae of self and art, the workings of the ordering mind, the tragic spirit, and the always enigmatic engines of invention and remembrance are in perpetual and *conscious* interplay. As a craftsman, Tóibín is able to cross the divide, to turn himself inside out, to surrender his own terrible experience to a delicately registered historical narrative about the Irish middle class. He has fictionalised his home landscape many times before, but always with the undertow of that submerged moon. As with Bishop and Gunn, this withholding has given him power as a writer. With *Nora Webster*, he has gone 'out to the hazel wood', as it were, to sing up this key source of his power and place it squarely onto the page.

When Nora takes the office job at Gibney's, she enters into what is essentially a provincial fiefdom. The Gibneys' family business is rigged with lineage and generational obligation. It is overseen by obsessive mercantile men, but underpinned by dynamic, even shamanic women.

Nora's quietly patrician social persona emerges in a way that recalls a sentence from Tóibín's memoir, *A Guest at the Feast* (2011), in which he describes his mother as having performed 'a lifelong imitation of an ordinary woman'.

As the novel moves out of the house and into the town, the action becomes weighted, not with only a personal past, but with a collective or tribal history. These collective layers are both explicit and implied, real and imagined. In the same way that, in *Brooklyn*, Enniscorthy is depicted as a foundry of accent and lore on the old side of the Atlantic, the pre-Christian matriarchy of the Sidhe makes itself felt in *Nora Webster* through the power of nuns and aunts. Tóibín has thought a lot about the role of aunts in the literature he loves, and he is famously good at female characters. Nora's and Maurice's sisters play a potent role in the novel. But when Nora's trouble at Gibney's ignites, it is not an aunt but a nun who has the freedom and, crucially, the knowledge to help her. This nun, Sister Thomas, wields a decidedly practical yet almost thaumaturgical power.

At the peak of the conflict with her immediate boss, Francie Kavanagh, Nora storms out of the office with a pair of scissors in her hands. She finds herself out at the coast near the old holiday house at Cush. A thick sea-fog has descended. As she parks her car, she thinks of the day long ago, almost in another lifetime, when she and her friend Greta had mocked Francie for her rustic rough edges. As Nora steps across the stones near the river and onto the strand, she also remembers the shocking pain Maurice experienced in the days before he died: his moans could be heard through the hospital. Sister Thomas was there saying prayers, Jim and Margaret too, and 'old Father Quaid'. As 'the luminous grey-whiteness was moved down the strand by the mild wind towards Curracloe', she sees through the fog a nun on the beach. As she draws closer, she sees that it is Sister Thomas. The nun commands Nora to return to town. She tells her that the Lord has been watching her, and that 'the boys will be home from school waiting for you'.

'He has not been watching over me!' Nora declares. 'No one has been watching over me!' The defiance is loaded with modernity, independence and awful pain, but the nun and the fog translate the conversation into the dialect of the sacred. 'We walk among them sometimes,' Sister Thomas tells Nora, 'the ones who have left us. They are filled with something that none of us knows yet. It is a mystery.'

Crucially, the preternatural atmosphere of this meeting has a corresponding ground in reality. There are old debts to be repaid in the town, and Sister Thomas has leverage with the Gibney's. She will see to it that Nora has what she requires to continue working in the office, including the reining-in of Francie Kavanagh. The omniscience of Sister Thomas, with its Mafia-like implications, is in fact the product of the nun's role as a consecrated counsellor for a community of women deeply invested in the social architecture of the Catholic faith. Sister Thomas indeed works on another plane. For decades she has been privy to the secret motivations of the town, not so much because she is holy, but because she was long ago ordained in the role of being so. In Tóibín, the reality of this socio-religious contract is not employed as a denigration or cancellation of faith's possibilities. Rather, it has a matrilineal feel and, as such, is presented as a psycho-geographical fact of his home county.

Not long after the meeting in the sea-fog, the nun turns up at Nora's door to explain the mechanics of what she has arranged and how it all will work. Nora is caught out. 'I don't like people knowing my business,' she tells Sister Thomas. 'Your mother was the same,' the nun tells her:

> *I knew her when she sang. She was a wonderful singer, but it was the pride, or the not liking people knowing her business, that made her difficult. And that did her no good. Now, you are more practical. And we should be grateful for that.*

If the novel has a turning point, this is it. Like most tribal Catholics, Nora is neither pious nor atheistic, but she does, through her cultural inheritance, have knowledge of a metaphysical landscape. After her exchange with Sister Thomas, her life begins to find its bearings in exactly that terrain. There is no evidence in the novel of her having any personal conversation with a deity, but through the nun the consolation of the vernacular church surrounds her, as much through its practical applications as its broader spiritual implications.

———

Well over a hundred years ago, W.B. Yeats envisaged a future for Ireland in which writers such as Tóibín and John McGahern, William Trevor and Claire Keegan, would come to the fore. Famously ambivalent towards the rising middle classes, Yeats wrote in an overview of Irish writing in 1891 that, despite a willingness to 'cloak all unpleasant matters' and to 'moralise with ease', the new middle class voice, represented at the time by Gerald Griffin, nevertheless possessed a 'sense of order and comeliness that may sometime give Ireland a new literature'.

In *Nora Webster*, it is as if Colm Tóibín has set to the task of resolving Yeats' caveats and perfecting this 'new literature'. He is undoubtedly fascinated by the 'order' of which the poet spoke, and the 'comeliness' we can rescue from redundancy by replacing it with 'quiet'. But to understand and appreciate the importance of Tóibín's work, it is necessary to consider the final technical achievement of the novel. Having immersed us in the solitary run of Nora's mind, having led us out of this privacy into the challenges of her exposure in the small circle of Gibney's, the novel extends its circumference to the wider nation and the dramatic and violent events in Derry on Bloody Sunday, 1972.

As reports come through of the slaughter of innocent people by British soldiers during the civil rights march, Donal photographs the events as they appear on the television screen. This penchant for photographing significant events on television, Nora suspects, is an obsessive transference of his grief – or is he merely 'bright', as the Irish Catholic middle class like to say of their children? The following day in Dublin the British Embassy is burned down by protesters. Donal and Conor's elder sister Aine is confirmed as having been on the picket. She goes missing for days afterwards. The hesitant beginnings of Nora's personal recovery are suddenly at risk.

The novel captures the national mood, its real-time anxiety, its live immediacy. The burned embassy was on Merrion Square, where Maurice and Nora had their honeymoon. She points this out to the boys as images flash up on the screen, and the detail brings the drama home to them even more. The public and private worlds are intertwined. There has been enough loss in this house in the normal course of life and death without this. As the days unfold, concern about Aine's disappearance converts infamous events into a closely felt crisis. Through an expertly honed intimism Tóibín has anchored us in the heart and mind of one woman, transforming a distant historical event into the lived experience of brutality, disturbed sleep and gut-twisting worry it was for those involved.

Intrinsic to Tóibín's work, from *The South* (1990) and *The Sign of the Cross: Travels in Catholic Europe* (1994) through to *Nora Webster*, is a social realist reformulation of what were known in Catholic circles, once upon a time, as 'holy mysteries'. You will find no cheap irony in Tóibín about this. He has made himself a conduit for the concept, with its rootedness in ordinary human failure, loss and vulnerability. In his renderings of modest regional lives, he delineates the psychological and generational processes by which the numinous seeps in, how the ghosts come, and how it is the ghosts' right to come, whether you believe in them or not. These are the players and this is the stage; these are the cadences, not of anything as immaterial as the spirits themselves, but of a culture in which the spirits have been given a voice and shape, on an island where visions and beliefs beyond rationality have always crept in.

When Aine is discovered safe and sound, Nora is released. The ghosts of her own mother and her marriage begin to take up their positions in her mind. These final pages are both haunting and realistic. As with grief, this is never just a matter for the individual in isolation. There are afternotes ringing in the eaves, qualifying chambers under our feet. The same can be said of the novel form itself when in Tóibín's hands.

Colm Tóibín is doing the work that the often rowdy history of his people has made most necessary: the close, quiet and realistic work for which even the heraldic, aristocratic-minded Yeats had such hope. In the wake of centuries of dispossession and violence, the value of this project is not to be found in recidivist reflections on the peculiarly Irish nature of Tóibín's genius. Rather, it lies in understanding how indispensable to his fiction is the prolonged and faithful study he is making of his native culture. In this, he is both a universal and a superbly grounded writer who understands how modern psychologies morph and conform in the context of local and metaphysical traditions. As such, he will always be looking back, even as he writes us into the future.

The Sea's Curation: Felicity Plunkett's *A Kinder Sea*

Felicity Plunkett's poetry is immersive, luxuriant, but with an underlying Anglo-Celtic beat and thud. It is personal poetry, not exactly direct but not excessively abstract either. There is no set polemic or ideological position here, rather an inquiring pleasure taken in the sensuality of sound in language, and an investigation of how one might go about constructing an authentic bridge between world and word, between the emotional life we live and its second life in utterance.

We might call this a poetry about poetics, but for the fact that Plunkett's well-fashioned work turns out to have unusually wide appeal. In a fractious culture whose perception of poetry typically encourages either the glib doggerels of overwrought performance or the idea that verse is somehow as arcane as philately, that might just be an achievement in itself.

A key to this wide appeal is the poet's ear and the precedence she gives to it, the sense that there is something listening as well as thinking and playing – some seabed – under the current of words on the page. This undersong is talent, in the Latin and Greek sense of the word, a currency of lyric aptitude that many poets, and many interesting poets, work without. Suffice to say, we live in largely post-lyrical times

The Weekend Australian
Plunkett, F 2020, *A Kinder Sea*, UQP, Brisbane

but Plunkett's is not an art achieved via deconstructed aspiration. Notwithstanding her erudite lexical range, she strings poems together in a live and percussive way.

She gets carried away, too, buoyed, *inspired*, like any singer. Thus after her striking first book, *Vanishing Point*, her second collection, *A Kinder Sea*, sees her arguing with her own voice and form as she goes. This argument, one could even call it a battle, is not just about modes of expression but very much about the self and its impact on the world. The coupling of intelligence and spontaneity is always present here, not as an entirely harmonious totality but rather as the expressive torque created when a poet's aesthetic sophistication wrangles with the way words come to her via sonority and melodic facility, giving her access to insight and wisdom.

Of course the library of the sea is vast but if *A Kinder Sea* brings any poet to mind it is Eugène Guillevic, the twentieth-century Breton who, like Plunkett, was also obsessed with the sea. Guillevic worked assiduously to dissolve the modern conceit of the individual poetic voice through submerging it in the wider marine and lithic elements of his home coast in Brittany. This involved a persistent acknowledgement of the kind of phenomenological corrections – 'the sea was not a mask/no more was she' – we find in Wallace Steven's 'The Idea of Order at Key West', which in turn led Guillevic to an extreme austerity of language, a refusal, for instance, to employ the charisma of metaphor. Indeed, by the time of his great poem of place, 'Carnac', Guillevic's art had assumed its own elemental status as something indisputably solid and real, like granite, a menhir, or, in Plunkett's phrase, 'the sea which mutes my words'.

In *A Kinder Sea*, Plunkett can be seen interrogating her very desire to speak. Her writing then, despite its visual power, is decidedly anti-selfie. It is as much in fact about effacing the self, the self that stakes a claim, as it is about defining or presenting it. In poems like 'Becoming the Sea' and 'Confetti by Dada', she speaks therefore with tragic relevance to a time where the species of which she is a member wants, no, *needs*, to ameliorate its impact on earth. A key question of *A Kinder Sea* is therefore both a deeply personal one and also one of resounding collective relevance. How do we live, love, suffer and speak, and leave a mark that has little or no trace at all?

> *I want you to find me. I want my disappearance to be*
> *Untranslatable. Feeding prayers into the sea's throat*
>
> *I run as fast as ink but we are both dissolving:*

One strategy Plunkett employs is to fashion herself as someone handing words over to 'the sea's curation'. That she is nonetheless vigilant about her poetic habitat is evident in her repeated self-caution to avoid excessive or spurious 'embroidery'. Indeed, in the poem 'Volta do Mar', she narrates a quest to get to the kind of *thingness* Guillevic sought, at the same time as it is perfectly clear how much she naturally loves to adorn, to stitch, to pretty-up and sing.

> *Unbraid the plait of chord*
> *and breath. Slide each phrase from the library*
>
> *of connections. Words are sand, strand: grit*
> *and brine, silent, beyond harrows.*

As a collection *A Kinder Sea* is held together by two beautifully made sequences, 'Glass Letters' and 'In Search of the Miraculous'. The latter reveals a tendency that was noticeable in Plunkett's first collection, a documentary, even novelistic, edge to her style, as she fills her lens with characterful mariners otherwise lost to the blue fathoms of history. 'Glass Letters', on the other hand, is a twelve-poem run of muscular solitude. It fulfils the consoling role of prayer while answering the poet's own doubts by speaking in tactile yet unrhymed couplets that balance decoration with fierce intent. It also does the classical job of romantic petition.

In fact, many of the poems in *A Kinder Sea* include the 'you' of love songs. But this 'you' is constantly shifting, like sand under the tide, moving into and out of new and old shapes, micro to macro, aperture to barrier, from unsentimentality to passion for the physical lover or compassion for the wounded self or friend.

Occasionally the excesses of which the poet suspects herself do rise, and imagery, even word selections, become mere grace notes or double up in a deflating way, as when we are returned in the poem 'Anomiidae' to the curation metaphor mentioned above, this time via the shoreline rather than the sea. Unsurprisingly, painful autobiographical material is more carefully weighed, particularly in 'On Carrying: Seven Cledons', where raw loss has us leaning in, and feeling as a reader should, which in itself is proof of Plunkett's sensitivity to process, the way art needs to wait sometimes until the right note is heard.

An interesting, and in some ways adjacent, aspect of *A Kinder Sea* is the sense we get that part of the difficulty Plunkett has in achieving the honestly unadorned line comes not only from her sonic gifts but that she writes in a culture addicted to beauty as commodity rather than as aesthetic truth. None of us is immune to this, either in reaction or resistance. 'Omission courts commission', as she writes in 'Confetti by Dada'. Nevertheless this predicament has Plunkett yearning, as so many do in these times, 'to remake the world'.

It is ironic then that poets have always known that a good way to begin remaking the world is by cultivating the type of listening-in and singing-out that Plunkett manages in *A Kinder Sea*. It's a tenuous and recursive activity though, and one that requires a kind of effacement that isn't often taught in creative writing departments, though it should be. It follows too that this type of courage, when properly embodied in an accessible technique, is evidence that a culture which marginalises the type of deep attention poetry requires is actually practising a version of self-harm. For as *A Kinder Sea* demonstrates, poetry, like the sea, is always over and above, ahead of, deeper than, beneath, and far beyond the game. As an ancient art it has always been a survival tool and a diagnostic for the future, a necessary luxury for its readers more than its practitioners, for whom it is often simply the breath of life.

Colonial Haunts: Save As by A. Frances Johnson

'The flag's taking off for that filthy place, and our jargon's drowning out the drums.' A. Frances Johnson's 2021 collection *Save As* begins with this quote from Rimbaud, which immediately betrays her appreciation for both the European avant-garde and the viral nature of the context from which it emerged. Johnson is a poet, painter, novelist and academic acutely sensitive to such colonial haunts, perhaps largely due to the delight she takes in the other-tones offered up by historical subject matter. She has displayed this previously in *Eugene's Falls* (2007), an expansive novel about Eugene von Guerard, and in exhibitions dealing with the ambiguous textures of botanical empire building. Interestingly, though, her layers of historical literacy have led to a skilful inspection of her own aesthetic fetishes, writing as she does in a time when ever more bilge water seems to be issuing from the half-drowned ship of Western culture.

Because Johnson is both a loquacious imaginer and a hands-on maker of images, her range demands that her art must be self-reflexive, must see itself in others, and in what we are all part of. Poetry, with its licence for the slow burn of oblique remonstration, often does this best. That 'Nature is a scene by Caspar David Friedrich' is not lost on Johnson, nor that we have become lethal precisely because of our fantasias, our Victorian kit-edifices, our flying machines and

Australian Book Review
Johnson, AF 2021, *Save As*, Puncher & Wattmann, Newcastle, NSW

omnivorous sequestration of landscape. Thus the need, in this era of cool-bent redemption, the era not of the coal scuttle but of the scuttle from coal, to fess up. Indeed, this is becoming our signature in part, the ratifying of artistic worth via its appetite for correction, and Johnson, as a professor in creative writing specialising in eco-fictions, is inevitably well positioned to know the score.

So it is that in *Save As* her creative and critical impulses are well and truly mashed up, the moral audit here being thoroughly threaded through the artefact. The book is divided into two halves: 'Save Us' and 'Save As'. The former includes the perfect pitch of 'My Father's Thesaurus', a genuinely heart-rending blend of portraiture, wit and crisp lineation that won the Peter Porter Poetry Prize in 2020. The tone of family elegies defines this first section, including 'Ring-in', where the poet's grief aligns with her eye for motif on a road trip to collect her mother's wedding rings. The tenderness of daggy memorial quests is inescapable here as the poet paints the moments – '*My friend drives, lamblike behind the wheel, gentle with speed limits, / a processional reprise*' – then scarifies the images she makes – '*We find the place, a plain Besser-brick parlour / framed in doric grief, the short drive massed with orphaned / icebergs that can never know life as a true rose*'. The skill of these elegies lies in their unpretentious avoidance of the pitfalls best defined by Wilde's dictum: 'all bad poetry springs from genuine feeling'.

In 'Bypass Town', Johnson observes how '*Like us, hills are stumped / by buzz-saws we can't see*'. This is perhaps another key to her viewfinder style. One even senses that, as with Picasso, her challenge is not to muster up ideas but to come to grips with her own inborn facility. Objects, concepts, tableaux, and ironic idioms arrive with a copiousness that must make the poet particularly aware of our human temptation to plunder. So poise becomes a quest for equidistance, *le mot juste*, and the balance between collection and dispersal. As in:

> *Love, I have come back*
> *for a blue wren teapot, six crocheted*
> *antimacassars, a daphne planter*

and the ventricular rictus of a death
certificate, a paper chest.

This is how Johnson walks the line in this first section of the book, the line of her own need to celebrate and memorialise in forms that also guard and protect the souls departed, all of whom inhabit the living poet. That she is successful is the magic of her book, marshalling an abundant repertoire and a dark self-effacement to connect the reader to what is often highly personal material.

In the second section, 'Save As', poems of the lurid Anthropocene investigate the cusp of pointlessness and self-indulgence. Once again, the prismatic faculties of the poet monitor the space by assessing our inability to escape or transcend a highly mediated predicament even as we describe it. *'Retire "I"', she writes, 'let it hang its head / and not conspire with / mea culpa's last egotism'*. It's a bind we're in, and so the poems are too. These poems of the second half are reaching for ways to depict the glare of climate and screen when sometimes perhaps only kitsch will do. They wrangle, revise and deplore – *'River gods self-harm as the privatised aquifer hoards'* – and at times the outrage at the neoliberal bomb on ecology is itself acerbic to the point of a too-obvious heat. We get the anger and frustration at ScoMo et al., but in diluting some of her artistry here Johnson risks simulating the issue. The fact that it took blokes a 240,000-mile trip to the moon to look back and realise our blue planet was perfect is nevertheless a point well made.

Stay home, boil the bathwater, was Patrick White's advice. That's if you've got a home. Whatever the case, *Save As* reminds us that surrealism now seems not so much an art movement as a geophysical portent. Bioluminescent, garish, and at times unable to escape the automatic brief of posthuman cadence, we fail, and admit to it. That's the point of course.

Hepworthish: Eleanor Clayton's *Barbara Hepworth: Art and Life*

Brancusi famously said that making a work of art is not in itself a difficult thing, the hard part is putting oneself in the state of mind in which a work of art is made. Eleanor Clayton's new biography of English sculptor Barbara Hepworth is in its own way a celebration of just how devoted Hepworth was to maintaining that elusive state of mind to which Brancusi referred. Unlike Sally Festing's 1995 Hepworth biography, *Barbara Hepworth: A Life of Forms*, Clayton eschews any attempt to narrate or analyse Hepworth's private feelings or emotional make-up. Instead she narrows her focus most austerely to the practice of the working sculptor, her aesthetic philosophies, and the compelling yet subtle variations of her output.

Born in 1903, Hepworth belongs, with the likes of Scriabin, the later Yeats and Mondrian, to that school of metaphysical modernism shaped as much by the spiritual experimentalism of the era as by political or technological concerns. Brought up by Christian Scientist parents in Yorkshire, where her father was a county surveyor, she valued thought over materiality, even as she spent her life wrestling with the expressive possibilities of the ultimate materials of wood and stone. For Mondrian, who became friends with Hepworth in the early 1930s, an immersion in theosophy triggered the dramatic shift

Australian Book Review
Clayton, E 2021 *Barbara Hepworth: Art & Life*,
Thames & Hudson, London

from his figurative and rather ultra-Dutch early work to the primary colour grids that ultimately became a signature of modernist art and design. In Hepworth's case, however, her extreme sensitivity to the given iconographies of the geological landscape consumed her early, resulting in a lifelong absorption in the dialogue between spirit and matter, and a body of work that continually inhabited the liminal zone between abstraction and the figure.

It is a strength of Clayton's book that the progression of Hepworth's sculpture through the decades comes across as an extended metaphor for this acute sense she had of always living in poetic relation to geophysical elements. Well before her celebrated move to St Ives on the Cornish coast in the late 1930s, Hepworth was already grappling with the possibilities of shaping these material elements into three-dimensional similes for human existence. Wood and stone, and more often than not white marble, became her diagnostic milieu, as well as her aesthetic guides. It was out of this sense that she shaped a version of the human being as a part of, rather than as an adjunct to, life on earth.

Hepworth's rate of production is legendary, and it is remarkable to think of all the decades she spent grappling with tonnage and heft in her various coastal studios. There is no doubt the physical demands of her work required a ruthless and relentless mode of application, as well as strong forearms. Indeed it was only in those initial days at St Ives, when she was looking after the triplets she had with her second husband, the painter Ben Nicholson, that she took anything that might have resembled a pause from her art. With Nicholson always nicking off to London, Hepworth most certainly had her hands full with 'running a nursery school, double-cropping a tiny garden for food, and trying to feed and protect the children'. She managed some brief drawings at night but momentarily the chisel, the lathe and the hammers lay still. Even so, she described the coming of the babies as a great boon to her creative life, marvelling at how 'all the forms flew quickly into their right places in the first carving I did after SRS were born'. SRS was her acronym for the triplets Simon, Rachel and Sarah, a shorthand that in its own way reflects the pressures she was under.

It is implied in the mode of Clayton's account that Hepworth's reputation for emotional austerity was, in the epic scheme of her achievement, a surface issue only. That she channelled into her work a passionate love of nature, and a fascination with the gravitational realities of existence, is self-evident here. As such Clayton's decision to demonstrate how the art *was* the life does the Hepworth oeuvre a great service, decluttering it from preoccupations with personality and second-hand gossip. The carefully calibrated interplay between text and image throughout the volume also serves this cause; the rhythm of text and illustration is wonderfully managed, enabling superbly printed visual examples on sturdy paper stock to clarify much of what is philosophically and aesthetically engaging in the text. For instance, the sculptor's phenomenological use of multiple tautly strung fishing lines in her sculptures is augmented by Hepworth's own description of how 'the strings were the tension I felt between myself and the sea, the wind or the hills'. Perfectly positioned reproductions of works such as Sculpture with Colour (Deep Blue and Red) as well as Hepworth's crystalline Drawings for Sculpture also clarify how her remarkable technical facility was all in the service of a strikingly biomorphic imagination.

Hepworth's signature mid-century work distilled a blend of the Cornish sea climate and an intuited inheritance of Mediterranean conditions of geology and light. Back in the 1920s she had been part of the turn away from casting in bronze in favour of direct carving into wood or stone, a shift pioneered by Brancusi and perfectly in step with Western art's spiritual and technological crises. But equally, as the years went by and Hepworth pursued the creation of more exact material equivalences for her intuitive sense of organic scale, she created many large monumental sculptures in bronze, such as the famous 'Winged Figure' of 1963, commissioned for the John Lewis Department Store on Oxford Street in London.

Hepworth died in dramatic fashion in 1975, alone in a fire in her studio in St Ives at the age of seventy-two. The welcome reinvestigations of modernism that have occurred in this century, particularly in terms of how abstraction and experimentalism can help elucidate the cultural causes and implications of the ecological crisis, has seen her relevance increase after the interregnum of neglect she suffered in the years after her death. Of course this new 'Hepworthish' modernism retains the experimentalism necessary to match the prisms and layers of our complex human experience, without subscribing to the depersonalised mechanisation that, in futurist and other pompous coteries, was once upon a time considered key to our projected transcendence of nature in a shining future. Nothing of course shines so deeply, so replete with the precious ephemerality, indeed the *mortality*, of gloss, as water on wood or stone.

Added to these neo-modernist layers of the Moolacene comes the remarkable sense of Hepworth as a feminine hero of unsentimental discipline and profound insight. Naturally enough she resisted categorisation of any kind, once stating that although she hoped her work would always be constructive, 'I don't want to be called "Contructivist", any more than "Nicholson".' Likewise, and in keeping with her self-effacing style, Hepworth made light of what she was up against as a woman in the male hegemony of twentieth-century British art. A salient point to be taken from this is that she saw her art in a more genuinely transcendent light, a perspective perhaps best exemplified in a letter she wrote to the art critic E.H. Ramsden in 1943. 'I think there's only one standard of sculpture, painting, writing, music. I hate female or male work. The only equilibrium seems to be the fusion of strength and tenderness.'

Pilfered Albion

The concept of 'trespass' first entered English law records in the thirteenth century. That this appearance fell between the arrival of William the Conqueror in 1066 and the reformation of the English church by Henry VIII in 1534 is no accident. The manner in which the English commons were enclosed by the statutes of the wealthy landowning class involved a slow but resolute process that had everything to do with, on the one hand, the arrival of Norman delineations of property, and, on the other, the disbanding of the monasteries that had worked in a bartering symbiosis with the people of the common landscapes of England.

During those long centuries, and forever since, the once permeable membranes of England's countryside have been stopped and barred into an impenetrable grid of privatised demesnes wherein some ninety-two per cent of the land and ninety-seven per cent of the waterways are currently locked away from public use. These estates are off limits where once, as our own James Boyce has shown in *Imperial Mud* (2020), his study of the Fens, the indigenous population lived with a concept of *property* related not to the material ownership of land but solely to communal rights of use and reciprocal cultural duties.

Australian Book Review
Hayes, N 2020, *The Book of Trespass*, Bloomsbury, London

Nick Hayes' *The Book of Trespass* chronicles the criminalisation of the landscape via a thorough interrogation of the apparatus and nomenclature of class. Hayes grounds his litany of exhaustive research with tales of his own trespasses, by foot and kayak, onto the major aristocratic estates of England. Each chapter, in fact, is framed by the author venturing into one or another forbidden zone of exclusionary power, where, as he writes, 'the woods felt like an empty marquee, hushed, the party long gone'.

This sense of a vanished festivity permeates this book. Through Hayes' lens, English culture was once not so different from pre-1788 Australia, a thesis specifically addressed by Boyce's *Imperial Mud*. In their own ways, both books show how, through a series of land grabs facilitated by parliamentary cliques in their own favour, the cultural heartlands of old Albion were systematically stolen from its people.

That's not to say that the population didn't fight back. One of the strengths of Hayes' account is his celebration of the various uprisings, protests and rebellions that resisted and campaigned against the demise of England into its currently class-riven and sequestered state. These fightbacks were the forerunners to the Occupy Movement, Grow Heathrow, Extinction Rebellion, and other protests of trespass in our current day. By performing the useful function of accounting for this ongoing spirit of reclamation Hayes' book points the way towards an unstitching of the expropriative corset that has tightened over his island.

He is brilliant at using the language of power to illustrate the dubiousness of its own stolen prerogatives. His explorations into the etymology of various relevant words, including *trespass* itself, shows the layering of presumption that has obscured the island's formerly intervolved regional cultures. When he fails to elicit any real dramatic spice through his own illegal escapades, he bites the bullet and arranges a meeting with the largest private landowner in his own home region of West Berkshire, the former MP, Richard Benyon. Hayes finds this good-looking scion – controller of 12,332 acres – entirely charming until he begins to unravel some of this history for him. A stereotypic storm cloud passes over the formerly beneficent face and Hayes is left standing alone as the inheritor of the enclosed commons stomps off in umbrage at being told his own story and the story of his forbears.

As well as being a thorough, if at times sermonising, historian, Hayes is also an accomplished illustrator. Each chapter is adorned with visual representations of the scenes of his own trespasses. Interestingly, the faceted style of these linocuts is in itself highly structured, thereby proving that the natural desire for the right to roam – so often decried by the horses-and-hounds set as the anarchic yearning of something akin to Kenneth Grahame's weasels – does not in any way have to destroy a refined cultural aesthetic perfectly in step with the analogue contours and retinal harmonies of the land. Indeed, Hayes rightly points to countries such as Sweden, Iceland, Finland and the Czech Republic, in which reciprocal use of the landscape is an intrinsic feature of nationhood. Just over the English border in Scotland are a set of roaming rules by which Hayes abides in every one of his trespasses in the book, thus proving poet John Clare's view that the abstract delineations of maps, and the rules that go with them, can turn a poet into a criminal at the stroke of a pen.

In fact, it is interesting to wonder whether what is often taken to be a natural inclination towards the pastoral and lyric in the history of English literature has in fact been seeded all along by the millions of acres of English natural space that have been lost or, as Hayes might say, *pilfered*, since the Norman invasion. With only eight per cent of England remaining accessible to the general population, the ancestral memory of these once common lands lies limestone deep in the cultural psyche. It's probable then that the sense of othering implied by the Romantic fetishisation of landscape has most likely been intensified in compensation. Indeed, the ornamental mythology of hedgerow and skylark that still persists to the delight of many may well be even more nostalgic than we thought. Is it some kind of epigenetic manifestation inflected with a literary version of PTSD? The fact that the very best of England's nature poets were seldom from the landowner families only adds weight to the theory.

This Unknown Island: the Poetry of Michael Farrell, Jennifer Maiden and Kate Middleton

In the last few years it has become increasingly clear that Michael Farrell's prior status as a wunderkind of poetic play and Oulipo-ish experimenta is evolving through multiple contexts into that of an indispensable poetic voice in Australian culture. This is due to the unforeseen but entirely welcome convergence of the brilliant ear Farrell has always had for the *bon mots*, slang and tripe of pop culture zones, and his increasingly literary fascination with the forgotten or smashed-up geologies of bush poetics.

It comes as no surprise therefore to find that Farrell's new collection *I Love Poetry* is a very Australian book, steeped as it is in the joys and complexities of artifice, fragmentation and the mocking of received opinions. I suspect it is also Farrell's most accessible collection, perhaps in part because it specifically addresses the issue that for many becomes the elephant in the room when they read his often paratactic work: the why, what, how, how come, and what the f__, of contemporary poetry and its world.

In the most obvious respect, *I Love Poetry* sits within a long tradition of book-length essays defending the usefulness of poetry, ranging

The Weekend Australian
Farrell, M 2017, *I Love Poetry*, Giramondo, Sydney; Maiden, J 2018, *Appalachian Fall: Poems About Poverty in Power*, Quemar Press, Sydney; Middleton, K 2017, *Passage*, Giramondo, Sydney

from Sir Philip Sydney's elegant *The Defence of Poesie* in the English Renaissance to Ben Lerner's rather quippy *The Hatred of Poetry* of more recent times. As Farrell's beautifully *naïf* title and book cover suggest, however, this is a decidedly less pedantic foray than anything I know of in that particular canon. The point here is that poetry is not so much the subject of Farrell's book, as its tricksterish main character. In the course of the collection it is Poetry itself that's shown to be a friend, a camouflage and also something of a royal without subjects. The ironic continuities don't stop there though, as it can also function as a rummageable rubbish skip, a way of not getting stuck in traffic, a groundcover, or ants on a page. Farrell in fact makes his own list of its utilities in the poem 'Put Your Helmet On', complete with an admission of the underlying consolatory purpose of the field:

> *These are the Uses of*
> *Poetry, it makes you warm, it replaces Cinema, it helps*
> *You put Words between Self and Heart. There's no*
> *original poem, it's all sequel as far back as We can*
> *remember. We embrace this, for the Loneliness is hard*
> *enough.*

One of the pleasures of *I Love Poetry* is the way that Farrell's perennially explorative style keeps finding itself on the shores of eloquence and aphorism. The trickster has not simply washed up here though, and it is stimulating to think about the ways in which ideas explored in Farrell's *Writing Australian Unsettlement : Modes of Poetic Invention 1796–1945*, have become embodied in *I Love Poetry*. The collection's opening poem 'A Lyrebird', for instance, is already classic, and it is no accident at all that such an evocative line-nest of not only the early iconography of Australian poetry but the hegemonic modes of poetic tradition itself comes from one who knows well how in our own post-canonic era,

> *The Great Poet*
> *assumes the mantle of kitsch*

Nevertheless, in the most playful of ways *I Love Poetry* can be read as something of a recruitment manual for a state of being, or even a way of living in our times, wherein landscapes both analogue and digital become live screens of endless poetic potential. In this way Farrell's work continues to be reminiscent of a Situationist *dérive*, but whereas Guy Debord and co. were derided for languishing in the sandpit of capitalism, Farrell's path to defragmentation is more a form of post-meridiem dreaming. It should be said too that if at times in the past the poet has left some readers behind with his sheer synaptic athleticism, here his trajectory necessitates a wider, more sequential, even readerly connection.

'It's as if you're writing for those who might not read you rather than those who might,' Farrell says in 'K in the Castle'. *I Love Poetry* does a lot with that impulse, yet one suspects that a key part of Farrell's gift is to always escape definition, closure or rust. In this he becomes that rather Tao-like thing: a live performer of the printed page. The fact that he is always freshening and laughing at the mere filling-in of poetic forms certainly makes his lines challenging, but it's also what makes them lines rather than posed lyrics, sawn-off sentences or mere functionaries of market expectations. Indeed, the lines about angels from the poem 'Pope Pinocchio's Angels' –

> ... *If*
> *you try to count them they turn into numbers. If*
> *you try to call them they turn into names*

could well serve as a summary of Farrell at his most accessible and syncretic, as he is here.

Like Farrell, Jennifer Maiden can be caustic, but never simply so. For decades now she has been conducting equipoised fictional dialogues in verse between characters both of her own imagining and of our culture's election. These dialogues, or pas de deux, pick up the slack, the huge and ridiculous slack foisted on us by a media industry caught in staccato cycles of press-release caricature and thumbnail gloss. Maiden the poet thus seems increasingly the corrective, serving as she does a profound community purpose in un-dumbing our political sphere not only by bringing an informed and emotionally intelligent sensibility to bear on duffer stereotypes we think we know, but by divining cadences of characterful intimacy from a sometimes benumbing public and parliamentary sphere.

Importantly, Maiden's alchemy is based on history work as well as studies of the zeitgeist. She uncovers the human strata behind celebrity via a symbolism of biographical particulars. Such work risks being merely entertaining, in the most puerile sense of that word, but no other writer in Australia, be it poet, novelist, playwright or short-story writer, combines narrative, demotic ear, social commentary and intellectual satire in such a uniquely readable blend as Maiden. In truth, she has observed long enough, and liminally enough, to know who these people, these media cut-outs are. In one scenario from her new collection *Appalachian Fall: Poems About Poverty in Power*, she seats Jimmy Carter beside the ghost of his 'distant cousin' Sara Carter Bayes, founding singer of the Carter Family, at the Trump inauguration in 2017. The Carter Family, in Maiden's words,

> *gave a voice to poverty so fatal*
> *it could only express itself in music*

and as a consequence the preternatural dialogue between the two cousins at the inauguration instantly provides us with a thrillingly unexpected commentary on the Trump constituency.

Like Farrell's, Maiden's new collection is also fascinating in its consciousness of her own, and other's, poetic lineages. This is perhaps best exemplified in 'The Thousand Yachts', a night-lit pas de deux on Sydney Harbour between the ghost of Kenneth Slessor and a critic who bears at least some resemblance to Maiden's former publisher Ivor Indyk. Despite the risks it takes with its rather in-house content, 'The Thousand Yachts' is surely one of Maiden's best poems, its layers of insight blended beautifully with the loaded provenance of its 'harbour-wet, slippery sublime' *mise-en-scène*. 'The Thousand Yachts' can read in multiple ways: as a time-fluxed interstice between the verses of Slessor's 'Five Bells', a canto from Dante's *Purgatorio* set on Sydney Harbour, or a numinous and heuristic piece of literary detection reminiscent of writers such as Susan Howe and Fleur Jaeggy.

In contrast to Farrell's alacrity and Maiden's quick associative magic, Kate Middleton's work has a deliciously slow and eliding quality. In her new collection, *Passage*, she is working with prior texts as foundries in two generalised forms: erasures and centos. One of these works is a now little-known collection of BBC radio broadcasts made by literary journalist and localist S.P.B. Mais, about his travels through Britain in the early 1930s. The stone-and-weather textures of Mais' published broadcasts, collected as they are in the book *This Unknown Island*, adhere to a lost sepia-toned regionality that helps to germinate Middleton's aesthetic. Her work is therefore engaged with reassembling, rearranging, regenerating, and is reminiscent of sound-art in the way its optical surface is mixed, blended and cut to create an exquisite response-ability in the receiver.

> *Outline the Welsh mountain in the fish lying in glass cases,*
> *A courtesy of perish weight*
> *And the river, white-faced, wearing a black hat of Bridge*
> *cut off from the other side of night*
> *Valley fog – so wide that it looks like the moor itself –*
> *ran down the windows*
> *A medley of bulrushes rose to the grey shingled roof*

There is a lot of space for the reader in these poems, and although the collection's title refers to the movement of time, Middleton dwells deeply in the vessels of moments wherein each line, each metaphoric verb, arises from a faithfulness to immersive stillness. There may be space but full attention, full and complete, is demanded and must be a pact sustained. Middleton occasionally falters, but what she is offering in *Passage* is, in her words, 'a tour through instinct' which after all 'needs a day of smoothest virtue. (It is very little visited).' The poet gives us a clue too when she declares,

My object was to copy the wildness of snow
climb the steepest way up into a deposit
of soft light, eventually piercing the loose
black shale of words. My consciousness:
the postman delivering a blizzard.

Middleton's then is a textual ambience where oblique sight knits with sound into a song of images, by route at times too of confessional touches that serve to buttress the fragmentation and allusiveness of the poet's slowed-down sight. Microrhythms are important, as in 'Prayer for any Morning', where meaning is emphasised by successive permutations of the phrase 'cherish the broken' running through the poem. A form of entrainment has been enacted upon us when after *(cherish / the broken)*, *(/ cherish the broken)*, *(cherish the / broken)*, the parentheses are finally released and *cherish the broken* stands free as a denouement of the poem's embodied theme.

This is a poet working not only with the sculptural potential of her 'black shale of words' but with attuned combinations of speaking and listening, and not only with listening but recording also, most particularly the timbral uprushes of the more-than-human world that lies at the heart of her maturing work.

Clear Elaborated Nectar:
the Poetry of Judith Beveridge

One of the advantages of having small children is that they return you to the earth-level existence of tiny animals like caterpillars, centipedes and insects. Suddenly, after walking along at adult height for so long, you are back down with your eyes to the ground, fascinated once more by the communitarian life of ants, the polka dots of ladybirds, and the furry wriggle of caterpillars. The poetry of Judith Beveridge can have the same effect. Her luminous and sympathetic art brings us up close again to the myriad creaturely realities that are equally important, clever, emotional and wondrous as our own.

For nearly forty years Beveridge's work has been enjoyed for its uncluttered lines and almost shamanic access to striking metaphors and similes. Now, in *Sun Music: New and Selected Poems*, which Giramondo must be roundly applauded for publishing and which really deserves the wide readership normally mustered by commercial releases at the pitch of a new Jane Harper or Tim Winton novel, we can see just how effectively these techniques have served her, and us, over the years.

Beveridge's first collection, *The Domesticity of Giraffes*, was published in 1987 to immediate acclaim. It scooped the prize pool, winning

The Weekend Australian
Beveridge, J 2018, *Sun Music: New and Selected Poems*,
Giramondo, Sydney

premiers' awards in both Victoria and her native New South Wales, as well as the Mary Gilmore Prize for a first book of poetry. In *Sun Music* there is a generous selection of eighteen poems from that collection, as well as similar-sized samples from all of her subsequent volumes, excluding the 2014 Buddhist verse sequence, *Devadatta's Poems*. The choice of work here bears testimony to a remarkable consistency across Beveridge's career, in technique, temperament and subject matter. Her writing transcends theoretical trends, paramours of the zeitgeist, and even its own obviously wide erudition, in favour of a determinedly focused investigation of our relationship with the natural world.

And a fraught and complex relationship it is – increasingly so. In a six-page author's introduction to the book, Beveridge takes the opportunity to describe how an almost pathological shyness as a child led to her close-up relationship with the world of animals and plants. She describes how even when she was older she 'dreaded catching a bus or train terrified someone would start talking to me and I would have to respond'. She reflects therefore on how 'the natural world didn't make demands on me to speak to it, so I found much solace and quietude there'. That of course is not an uncommon experience, nor is the often simultaneous realisation that it is the species of which we are a part that presents the greatest threat to these other life forms who bring us such consolation. This then is a key concern for Beveridge and one that has been playing out in her poems since the very beginning.

In the title poem of her very first collection we can immediately measure the potency of her gift by the way she drops us into the scale of a caged giraffe's magnificence, only to make real the anguish of its expropriation in the zoo.

> *Bruised-apple eyed she ruminates*
> *towards the tall buildings*
> *she mistakes for a herd:*
> *her gaze has the loneliness of smoke.*

In the prose poem 'Flower of Flowers', also from that first collection, she describes how wherever we go there is

> the smell of the earth raked, trodden-down, worked-over, battled-on. When we go out to the garden we feel like peasants whose bodies are the fruit of a plantation that is spoiling their whole lives.

This is just one of many instances in Beveridge's work where the awful bind between nature and human culture becomes explicit, but one also gets the sense that her gift is driven not by the quest for some idealised resolution of this tragic interdependence but by the sheer biophilic energy it provides. The repeated clarity of her similes in the poems gathered in this collection are ultimately evidence of that. Hers is an inverse poetry to that of Wallace Stevens, whose lines often sprang from a determination to resist comparison and restore things to themselves. By contrast, Beveridge's work seems largely underwritten by the almost totemic pleasure she takes in deep association and comparison, and a lonely yet swooning type of enthusiasm for life in all its forms.

There are so many animal poems here quietly awaiting their position in the canon of popular readership. There are major sequences and successful smaller poems about snails, elephants, spiders, caterpillars, bees, herons, egrets, bats, dogs, sharks, flying foxes, camels, crows and lyrebirds. All these poems combine the miniaturist literacy of that chronically shy girl with the mature gaze of the adult wordsmith.

Though these animal poems often protest against cruelty they are also celebrations from a lifetime of intoxicated attention. In the last section of thirty-three new poems, Beveridge reflects on the lineage of such delight with an ever increasing sense of its passing. Where occasionally her poems may risk too sentimental a rousing for their own meditative threads, or her simile-based descriptiveness begins to read as a default technique rather than as revelation, the best of this new work, such as the small poem for her Scottish father, 'Fogbow, Scotland', is not so easy to track.

A highlight of these new poems is surely 'Hymnal / Wild Bees', written in memory of fellow poet Martin Harrison. Here Beveridge walks a moist but foreboding landscape, past spoonbills *'poised, quiet as Gilbertine nuns'*, past *'bull ants talking chemically and incessantly to each other'*, to a wild bee hive whose supporting branch has shattered to the ground. Where once she had watched the bees *'swarm their weight towards the gum blossoms / in a light soot of yellow'* now all is silent. *'I'll never see again'*, she writes,

> the bees among the wildflowers, or see them busy
> in the depths among the stamens, moving from cup
> to cup as though they were flames lighting candles.

As sadness for the passing of a fellow poet entwines with the plight of the bees, her words take on a sacred and allegorical power:

> I'll never hear their lingering vibrato, a mind enamoured
> of its own music, getting right each thought's hum,
> its bearing and its course.

These lines cannot help but remind us also of what Judith Beveridge has been doing for over four decades now. Her life's response to the potencies of nature, her devotions to the bee-like ministrations of the poetic craft and to defending a more-than-human world against the protean haphazardies of her own species, has created a body of work as relevant as any in the land. In their *'clear elaborated nectar'* these poems can be read by everyone.

Darting Through Mesh

One likes to think that the era of mainstream Australia's almost complete disregard for contemporary poetry is coming to a close. But even with certain encouraging signs of late, the vicarious middle-class fantasy of what a poet or writer amounts to certainly does not include the possibility that he, or she, has spent time in prison for armed robbery. Notwithstanding heroic figures such as Osip Mandlestam in Stalinist Russia, Pramoedya Ananta Toer in Indonesia and Yannis Ritsos in the Greek Junta, and despite even the avant-garde chic assigned to Jean Genet in France, and the countless other poets and writers whose work has survived, or even flourished, behind bars, the contemporary reader still looks largely to lifestyle backdrops and escapist formations when fulfilling their writerly stereotypes.

Robert Adamson famously enjoyed and endured a wild young adulthood around the northern shores of Sydney Harbour before eventually being imprisoned, first in boys homes, and then in Long Bay Gaol in the early 1960s. Amidst the brutalisation of prison life he was given the task of bookbinding for the government printer, discovered poetry, and set out on a path, not necessarily of redemption but toward the joys and difficulties of art and illumination. Until *The Clean Dark*, his 1989 collection, in which he captured a wider readership by placing himself firmly in the tradition of fisherman-poets such

The Weekend Australian
Adamson, R 2015, *Net Needle*, Black Inc., Melbourne

as George Mackay Brown and Ted Hughes, he was largely known for his central and lively role as the editor of *New Poetry*, the magazine of the innovative Poetry Society of Australia. All along, but most successfully since *The Clean Dark* and the volume that followed it, *Waving to Hart Crane*, he has immersed himself in the world of both romantic and experimental poetics, constructing a long and rather Franciscan dialectic between trauma and beauty, between disgrace and fulfilment, in a body of work that deserves to be on every high school and university syllabus, and in every bait & tackle shop, in the country.

As is immediately evident from its title, *Net Needle* continues Adamson's signature art of romantic and realistic juxtaposition. The volume once again shows Adamson to be a beneficiary of the more protean aspects of modernism, an emotionally warm and compassionate poet whose scarifying disclosures are never made simply to shuck the past. Indeed, the past for Adamson, time as a whole in fact, seems too prismatic for such easy possibilities, so that if he is clean he is nevertheless still dark; if he carries the memory of a needle it can have more than one use. In this case the 'net needle' refers elegiacally to fishermen of his childhood, who have '*stitched their lives into my days*',

> their hands
> darting through mesh, holding bone
> net needles

The volume opens with a brief sequence of poems rich with declaration and inquiry. It is immediately clear we are reading a poet in a fecund stage of technical advancement but also one with a humility reminiscent of Dante before his guide. In Adamson's case the guide is environmental, and he inscribes his riparian context microscopically in these opening poems, absorbing us in spectral interiors of shadow and inflection, of dream and questioning. '*I'm looking hard*,' he tells us, '*my boat plows through fog*', and, as he peers, he asks:

What form shape or song
Might represent a soul? What words paint or mud
Resemble such an intangible glow?

A stain of mist hangs above a blackbutt,
Brushed by the wings of a grey-headed flying fox.

Prepared by such symbols we travel in Part Two back to the glare of the Sydney Harbour of his youth, a blue-water forge of touchstones, rebellion and lurid horizons. These poems formed part of a collaboration with linocut artist Peter Kingston in 2012, published as the limited-edition artist-book *Shark-net Seahorses of Balmoral: A Harbour Memoir*, which is available for viewing in the national and state library collections. The subject matter of these poems, in its eventfulness and powerful genius loci, is reminiscent of Adamson's prose memoir *Inside Out*. What would the pre-1788 peoples of the harbour make of this kindred latecomer? Such is the picture-forming power of the harbourscape in Adamson's work that the question springs to mind. Amongst the highly vocalised verse, some lines seem more etched into indisputable form, like the following from 'Sugarloaf Bay, Middle Harbour':

On windless mornings, the bay
stretched tight, a glass drum,
as if waiting for the vibration of an
unknown force, some dark fin that might cut
a pathway to civilisation.

One senses that Adamson, the Neutral Bay urchin, the zoo-thief, the crim, the poet, is often in league with the sharks. In fact what he represents is a type of moral authenticity that the newly captioned Team Australia increasingly pours down the drain. His work in Part Two of *Net Needle* sees him continuing his particularly vivid form of social history, in which the glamour intrinsic to starlit shores and turquoise bays has not yet been appropriated by the financially elite. Along with Kenneth Slessor and Christina Stead, as well as figures like the Sydney cave surrealist Les Robinson, Adamson is the voice of a harder, more mercurial and therefore more evocative harbour, a flawed place in which suicide-cliffs and fin-shadows coexist beside hope, poverty, and fluorescent birds. With the harbour now so polluted, the fish 'very scarce', it is part of his romantic narrative to have relocated that democratic landscape in the uplands, as it were, the less glary, less *lairy*, but equally profound riverscape of his grandfather's Hawkesbury. It is a measure of Adamson's talent for what is these days called 'place literature' that the enigma of the shadow-clad river, with its sucking banks and noirish lap-lap, seems a predestination for the middle-to-late-life poet, seeker like the river of the edges of things, fisher of images, archivist of the sensuous currents of truth.

Part Two closes with two poems from prison, or the 'black slot', as Adamson calls it here. The mix of humour and violence is just right, as when the inmates who form the Long Bay Debating Society are instructed by the governor in 1964 to debate the topic: 'Is the Sydney Opera House Really Necessary?', or when Adamson tells us

> *the prison doctor stitched*
> *my cut wrists*
> *without anaesthetic*
> *his idea of punishment.*

The third section of the volume contains poems referencing or inspired by other poets and writers, a collection of names reflecting Adamson's perpetual lookout on the constellations of modern poetry and also something of his own more personal combing of tradition: Randolph Stow, Francis Webb, Blake, Shelley, Sonya Hartnett, Michael Dransfield, Francis Thompson, St Augustine, Pierre Reverdy, Rimbaud. The list reads not like a curation but as a sincere series of links within his poetic project. In 'The Midnight Zoo' he declares:

> *Forget the warnings*
> *Though don't leave your place*
> *This isn't official history anymore.*

Through the agency of influence, Adamson not only displays a wider technical range in this section but also the fires of a despair not yet coddled into cosy old age. As he writes in 'Ballad of the Word Trauma':

Trauma can't be
contained in particular shapes, it eventually becomes
abstract fire, power, thought, light.

Adamson also declares, in 'The Sibyl's Avenue', that 'the sky isn't blue it's abstract'. Always the disciple of Rimbaud, always the amanuensis of something greater than himself, he speaks volumes in such a line for the potency of the form, the way poetry can leap the close guards of scientific empiricism to give us a simpler, brighter and more lasting idea of the truth.

In the fourth and final section, Adamson focuses on the transformative death of animals, in brief prose passages reminiscent of Yeats' Red Hanrahan stories. When he finishes the volume with his long-crafted ode to his wife Juno, 'The Kingfisher's Soul', the juxtapositions are alive again. Death and love, the bird-pulse of spirit, and its passing. There is a sense here of a poet leaving nothing behind, and that he will take precisely that with him when he goes. He will fly off again into 'new light', after praising life 'with broken words'.

Little Climates

With all the talk about the science of climate change we can sometimes too easily forget that each of us, in our mood and temperament, in the micro-environments we create as we live our lives, and in the way we respond to both adversity and good fortune, constitute a climate in ourselves. Climate then is not just meteorology but also personality, domestic arrangement, spirituality, social behaviour. You may, for instance, ask yourself whether your own personal climate, or atmosphere, is one that others would be comfortable to live in, or to be around. And you may look at the people you know, or at public figures, and think about them not in the usual psychometric frameworks of happy or sad, aggressive or loving, but rather as individual climates of their own. What for instance was the 45th President of America's weather like? Volatile, unpredictable and therefore dangerous? Or the current Queen of England's? Calm, moderate, but with a slight chill? If looked at this way, the global climate crisis soon becomes a crisis not only of energy use, of meteorology and technology, but also of human behaviour. And when the sum total of individual human climates becomes nothing other than the global climate, suddenly our relation to the physical world around us seems more enmeshed, intimate and networked.

The Weekend Australian
Neve, C 2020, *Unquiet Landscape:*
Place and Ideas in 20th-Century British Painting,
Thames & Hudson, London

Painter, novelist and art critic Christopher Neve's classic collection of essays on twentieth-century British landscape artists, *Unquiet Landscape*, takes this kind of view of how artists relate and represent the landscapes they paint. Apart from the unusual lucidity of Neve's aesthetic observations, and his talent for applying a philosophical approach to the description of pictures without the writing becoming too obtuse or academic, this focus of the book on the way we not only make the world around us but are in fact living ingredients of that world is surely the key reason for the timely reissue after thirty years of what was until now considered a quietly brilliant book about similarly quiet British painters.

The essays in *Unquiet Landscape* focus on a suite of artists, many of whom are these days either largely forgotten or, through the urgent refocusing of mainstream culture on the importance of our relationship to nature, newly resurgent. A number of these artists are associated with a most fecund period at the London Slade School of Design in the 1920s, when painters such as Paul and John Nash, Eric Ravilious, Enid Marx and Edward Bawden took the lessons of graphic pattern and transferred them to the visceral and aerial textures of landscape painting. Others painters Neve writes about, such as Joan Eardley, Ivon Hitchens and Graham Sutherland, found their way into the landscape in often stubborn and incontrovertible solitude.

The book is aptly divided into two sections, 'Tangible Places' and 'Intangible Places', a structure that reflects Neve's focus on the enigmas of psychogeography, the 'tangible' being the massed physicality of the seemingly impervious and supposedly 'objective' properties of landscape, and the 'intangible' being the extent to which our personal climate, or what Gerard Manley Hopkins called our 'inscape', determines any depiction of the world around us.

In the essay 'Seeing Becomes Feeling', Neve outlines a theory not only of looking at art, of making art, but also of experiencing landscape, or life, more generally. And yet there is nothing at all general about what he recommends. His insights are to do with the particularities of understanding place and 'seeing properly'. As he says, when it comes to art, sight in some way ought always to become insight.

In 'Seeing Becomes Feeling', Neve's own insights about the art of Kentish painter William Townsend are detonated by Townsend's love of physical structure, which he renders via a process as 'systematic as scanning and plotting electronically on a screen'. A network of objects in weight, shape, tone and perspective is delineated, and if the artist's seeing is clear enough, Euclidian enough, then the whole human experience of seeing is ensnared in the view. This goes beyond the triangulation of visible content to an aesthetic of feeling, although importantly, not to the extent that it risks the kind of Romanticism that 'trumps up feelings and overruns its audience with emotions they do not have'. Whatever the case, Townsend, along with many of the other artists featured in the volume, has found an eloquent interlocutor in Neve.

And yet Neve himself, as a painter as well as a writer, and who tells us that he makes a point of not writing about any picture he hasn't seen in the flesh, admits that 'the critic is a vandal'. Elsewhere too he quotes Walter Sickert: 'If the subject of a picture could be stated in words then there had been no need to paint it.' But herein lies the sensitivity of Neve's approach. It is not so much that he is attempting to paraphrase the subject of the paintings he writes about but rather that he is taking those subjects, in collaboration with their creators, as starting points for his own ideas on the inseparability of human creativity from our connection to place and our understanding of nature.

In an essay on abstraction that focuses largely on the St Ives modernist Ben Nicholson, Neve emphasises the fundamental mistake of realist painters who attempt to mimic what they see by assembling the material, or retinal, components. As he says, a successful painting emulates our experience of a landscape, as opposed to the landscape itself. Like Mondrian, Ben Nicholson has been accused of taking all that too far to the other extreme, but Nicholson's belief that 'blue can exist in a painting in its own right', without the need of sea or sky to validate its effect, does not dismiss the fact that none of these painters, himself included, are painting entirely fictional landscapes. A compelling ratio then between place and self, between retinal ingredients and felt sensation, is what all the painters in *Unquiet Landscape* manage to achieve.

The Glaswegian painter Joan Eardley is a case in point. Eardley's late art involves a miraculous transmutation of her sympathy for the homeless and disadvantaged children of the Glasgow slums into the high pictorial tension of the littoral shore and ocean around the fishing village of Catterline. Neve describes her work as having 'an innate emotional connection between sea and paint', which is another way of saying that what we are looking at is a process. And, as Neve rightly declares, 'a sense of process is characteristic of all great painting'. In Eardley's case the visibility of process becomes emblematic of both the compassion and the brutality of life, and is most successful when 'bits of reality, like the grit in a bird's gizzard, are an aid to digestion'.

The paintings of yet another Slade artist, David Bomberg, allow Neve to further this pursuit of a description for how an artist's personal climate generates a powerful sense of repeated motif. After his experiences of trench warfare in the Great War, Bomberg categorically rejected the machine age, declaring that he wanted his work to be 'part of the winds, the tides and ocean swell'. This he believed was the most 'humane proposition', a proposition so strong, Neve writes, that it constituted 'something of a crusade against a spiritually bankrupt audience'.

Given Neve's focus on the internal view, it is appropriate that a hallmark of his own style is a self-interrogation of the critic, to the extent that he includes himself in Bomberg's 'spiritually bankrupt audience'. But it's in this very idea that we locate the sensitivity of Neve's approach. It is not so much that he is attempting to capture the subject of the paintings he writes about but rather that he is taking those subjects as starting points for his own powerfully expressed ideas on the inseparability of human creativity and nature.

Unquiet Landscape then is in part a charting of Neve's own process as a viewer, which, after so much looking and travelling among the subject-lands of the artists he writes about, leads him ultimately to declare that 'to look in an artist's place for his inspiration is all but pointless'. Whether in the chalky downs of Sussex or the chanking seas of Scotland, Neve concludes that the real subject of these great paintings is not the outside world, not the roiling sea or the cauterised field, but the artist themselves. 'The birds have stopped singing in the lost lands,' he writes. 'The unquiet country is you.'

Afterword: What Jesus Wrote on the Earth

As a rebellious kid I often didn't take any notice of the gospels when we went to Mass, or as they were retold to us at school by our teachers. I preferred, perhaps with a child's innate distaste for hubris, to ignore the precis and commentaries of the priests and teachers in favour of trying to make my friends laugh, or to think about girls, or the footy, or absolutely nothing at all, which of course is another great talent of children: emptying the mind.

There was, however, one gospel story that cropped up from time to time which did grab my attention, though not perhaps for the usual reasons.

The story was the one in John 8:7, when the scribes and Pharisees present Jesus with a woman who has supposedly gone off and slept with someone else's husband. In response Jesus delivers his telling instruction regarding the casting of the first stone. What captivated me about this scenario was not the moral lesson but rather the fact that both before and after speaking to the men, Jesus is depicted as remaining down on his haunches, in a drawn-out and enigmatic silence, writing, or drawing, with his finger in the dust.

Faith Guide, Easter 2012

Despite the strength and repetition of the image we are never told what it is that Jesus writes on the ground, and it was this absence of information, along with what seemed to me to be the simple bush-familiarity of Jesus's gesture, that caught my childhood attention. A man down on his haunches drawing a map in the earth with his finger was a thing I'd seen many times in the Australia I grew up in. And so, once the story had pulled my attention away from the lisp of the priest, or Debbie Marrari in the next pew, it was with the natural curiosity of a pre-theological and local mind that I continued to wonder what the marks that Jesus made in the dirt may actually have been.

To be honest, I don't remember exactly what I imagined he may have written. Perhaps the directions to the pub at Glenburn, a crosshatch of a game of noughts and crosses, or how to find the track in to the duck ponds in the upper reaches of the Painkalac. Whatever it was back then, I've often speculated in the years following, through the static of a mind gradually filling with received opinion and cultural chatter, what it was he drew there in the dirt. Could he, for instance, have been inscribing the fate of his own iconic cross and the burden to come? Or was he referring to the inscribing of the ten commandments in stone by God's own finger in the Old Testament? Or perhaps, in the way of earthly realism, this chippy's son from Nazareth was merely doodling in the margins, as we are all prone to do by way of collecting our ideas, or visions, or thoughts?

The challenging thing, for child and adult alike, is that the search for meaning in this vignette from the gospels is left entirely to our own imaginations, be they moral or otherwise. Either as an oblique response to the self-righteousness of the Pharisees or as a rustic imprint of the essence of sage man on earth, it is quite literally up to us to draw the picture.

—

Recently a friend and I were walking along the Yarra River in the Melbourne suburb of Templestowe. We were in a gentle parenthesis from our normal lives, catching up and enjoying a remnant patch of riverscape in a rapidly burgeoning twenty-first-century town. We set off on the path from a bend where when I was a kid a local river-rope dangled from a gum-tree branch, then we crossed over a newly built concrete pedestrian bridge high above the river, before walking alongside the grounds of the Blessed Sacrament Monastery where my family would occasionally go to Mass when I was young, and which is now a drug rehabilitation centre.

My friend and I chatted happily as the river path wound in its meander past the ramshackle sheds and vegetable gardens and tennis courts of the drug rehabilitation centre. Eventually we came around again in a loop to the pedestrian bridge, which we crossed before walking up the worn rise over the roots of a big gum and along the downward slope beyond it, through a tangle of fallen limbs and glinting light on leaves.

It was then that I noticed an incongruous thing up ahead of us in the middle of the path, something that hadn't been there when we had come through that way only an hour or so before.

From a distance the object was nondescript, just a low blob on the tarred track, a lumpen shape, but as we drew nearer it began to take on a more distinct form, like that of a small creature. As we grew even closer still it became apparent, to our great amazement, that we were looking at a platypus.

To see a platypus swimming wild is always a riveting experience but to actually encounter one travelling under its own steam across the ground was a rare thrill.

Silently we expressed our amazement at each other with wide eyes, marvelling at how it had emerged from the river in the time it had taken us to walk the two or three kilometres along the path, across the foot bridge, around the old monastery and back. Both of us were thinking how unlikely that was. What was it doing? Why had it come up the steep bank from its burrow and the water? Was there another billabong or anabranch that we didn't know of that it was heading for?

Presuming it had frozen still on the track due to the threat of our approach, we also now stopped still to observe it. The platypus is one of those ancient animals whose unique adaptations have ensured its survival since the days of yore. To encounter one is to enter a time machine and, by doing so, to ironically gain a sense of something well beyond time, a numinous feeling for something vaster and deeper than our own brief lifespan on earth.

It is well documented how the first Europeans to arrive in Australia had been so flummoxed by the platypus that when they sent a specimen back to the British Museum, the scientists in London thought that someone was playing an ingenious colonial joke. The platypus and the echidna are, of course, the only egg-laying mammals on earth, but the Poms had never encountered such a creature before, and with its duck-like bill and otter-like body they couldn't quite fathom such diverse biological attributes being assembled in the one creature. With befuddled hands on white beards, those erudite minds suspected it to be a folly, a tricked-up collage sent back from the Antipodes by men who quite obviously had gone a bit troppo due to being so far from the dress coats and gentlemen's clubs of a well-upholstered England.

With all that racing in my mind, and knowing how unlikely it was to have the opportunity to observe a platypus so far out of the water, I began slowly to step sideways from the track to get a better angle. The platypus is visually blind in the water but navigates by the use of its electrosensitive bill, which now, like some peering, periwigged colonist, I was keen to observe up close.

I moved out wide at first but then when I took a few diagonal steps back towards the path the platypus had still not moved. Moving even closer, I encountered the same lack of reaction, until eventually I was hovering, with growing confusion, only a metre or so from where it lay.

Standing then right next to the marvellous creature I saw at last that the platypus was dead. But not only had it died right there on the track, around its flat broad neck was a red rubber band about a centimetre wide, like you might buy at your local newsagency. On even closer observation, down on my haunches now, I saw that the rubber band had slipped over its neck while it was swimming and, once there, had not been able to be removed. The animal's flesh had swollen, probably in the course of its desperate attempts to shrug the rubber band off, and I could see that so tight had it become around the fur that it had squeezed and cut into the flesh of the neck, exposing raw pink skin.

I stood up, stepped back. I looked in disbelief at my friend. Suddenly we were shadows without bodies over the dead monotreme on the ground beneath us. The platypus had choked to death.

In some distress we began to discuss the probable mechanics of the poor creature's death, including how stacked the odds were against the neck of a platypus, in all the moving volume of the old Wurundjeri river, slipping into the deadly noose of a newsagency rubber band. We fell silent again as we contemplated how in our lifetime those very odds had quite obviously changed. Right there we were sharing a condition I can only describe as species shame, a horrible state resembling a grimace of the soul.

What then were we to do? Looking up from the track I saw a thick piece of hard bark, with edges upturned by the curvature of the eucalypt trunk it had once clung to. Without thinking I walked over and picked it up.

Tentatively then I rolled the platypus with a stick from where it died on the newfangled concrete path, up onto the coarse furrows of the bark. Eventually it lay, flippers splayed, in a slight curve, almost like a small dog asleep. I picked up the bark, and carried it through the trees of the riverbank down to the water.

Searching about amongst wattles, leaning forward, it wasn't hard to find an indent in the eroded bank by which I could access the water.

I went down on my haunches again, this time with the intention of floating the platypus back out onto the river.

I lay the bark down, relieved that it did indeed float, and, spying a possible route through the tangle of snags and eddies, pushed it gently away from the bank. Luckily, the makeshift bier moved on an eddy, and began to slowly travel off downstream.

I remember I stayed crouched low by the water for some time, feeling as if the once-bright river trees were now whispering at me like chthonic spectres, ghosts of the past witnessing for the umpteenth time our ignorant conduct from above and beyond.

I've thought often since about whether I did the right thing. Either way it seemed all I could do in the moment was follow my instinct to treat the platypus as the most sacred of all living things, as high royalty in fact, a king or queen of the old and ceremonious river in a new world plagued by the careless dominion of *us*.

———

For me the memory of the dead platypus has become both prophetic and factual, which goes part of the way to explain why it has come to be, in a weird elision of time and place, the image I now imagine Jesus inscribing on the earth in John 8:7. But beyond that, it is the *traumatic* quality of the image, and our culpable relationship to it, that has seen the platypus begin to replace for me the central symbol of Christianity, Christ's gaunt and bloodied suffering on the cross.

I watch things morph and transform and clarify in my mind. Sometimes the platypus Jesus draws in the dirt is in the tragic mode of his own Passion, senselessly garrotted by a discarded rubber band from a suburban newsagency. At other times though it's living happily in clean water, flipping and duck-diving in arabesques on a stream. And other times still, when Jesus's own and very tangible melancholy seems to win out, the picture drawn in the dust has the overwhelming mood of a global requiem. A local motif, of all that is beyond our culpability and subsequent need for moral theory, lies on a thick piece of canoe-shaped bark. It floats downstream above swirls equally ancient and impure, travelling through a city too set in its ways to even notice it passing by.

It was not my conscious choice to insert this unspeakable death of the platypus into the baffling gaps of moral non-comprehension that are present in and seemingly intrinsic to our era. Nevertheless, because the power of its trauma has lived on in my imagination, and because there are so many of us with a strong belief that the human race must urgently befriend again the plants and animals of creation, I sometimes envisage, perhaps through the eyes of a child in the future, an alternative end to its destiny on the river.

I close my eyes to see the universal suffering of the creature re-animated, its wondrously diverse body reinvigorated, its miraculous electrosensitive bill resensitised, as it lifts its head above the regenerative furrows of the floating bark and quietly slips back into the waters of a city finally awoken from a devastating dream.

Sources

Author's Foreword: Where the Songs Are Made

Alan Garner's novel *Strandloper* was published in 1996 by The Harvill Press. Another take on the perspective Garner ascribes to his fictional Nullamboin, and which also has relevance to current debates over the outsourcing of memory to digital means, is from Plato's *Phaedrus*: 'If men learn this, it will implant forgetfulness in their souls; they will cease to exercise memory because they rely on that which is written, calling things to remembrance no longer from within themselves, but by means of external marks. What you have discovered is a recipe not for memory, but for reminder. And it is no true wisdom that you offer your disciples, but only its semblance, for by telling them of many things without teaching them you will make them seem to know much, while for the most part they know nothing, and as men filled, not with wisdom but with the conceit of wisdom, they will be a burden to their fellows.' (Plato's *Phaedrus* (c. 360 B.C.E.), 274c–275b, Reginald Hackforth, transl., 1952).

WB Yeats uses the phrase 'In dreams begin responsibility' as an epigram at the beginning of his book, *Responsibilities*, first published in 1914. He attributes the line to an 'Old Play'.

The David Unaipon information is from his *Native Legends*, published in Adelaide in 1929 by Hunkin, Ellis & King.

One: The Colours of the Ground

The Watergaw

The poem 'The Watergaw' appears in Hugh MacDiarmid's *Collected Poems*, published by Macmillan in 1962.

The recording of MacDiarmid's comments on the poem can be found at 'Hugh MacDiarmid', Penn Sound, writing.upenn.edu/pennsound/x/MacDiarmid.php.

The quoted census statistics are from Ian Clark's, *Aboriginal Languages and Clans: An Historical Atlas of Western and Central Victoria, 1800–1900*, published in 1990 by the Department of Geography and Environmental

Science, Monash University, Melbourne. It should be noted that there would be obvious reasons why many members of the Wadawurrung clans would not have consented at this time to have their population counted in this way. The reliability therefore of the numbers must be questionable. They nevertheless provide perhaps at least some indication of the decline, not only in the Wadawurrung population, but in their trust of the invaders.

The list of tuber and root foods is compiled from a blend of personal experience and from the valuable ethnobotanical research found in Beth Gott and John Conran's *Victorian Koorie Plants* – Gott, B & Conran, J 1991, *Victorian Koorie Plants*, Yangennanock Women's Group, Aboriginal Keeping Place, Hamilton, VIC.

The reference to language being 'an arena in which to gather' references Bruno Latour: 'Be not the one who debunks but the one who assembles, not the one who lifts the rugs from under the feet of the naïve believers but the one who offers arenas in which to gather.' http://modesofexistence.org

You can listen to an audio rendition of this essay at: https://www.griffithreview.com/articles/the-watergaw/

Summer On The Painkalac

For an introduction to Wadawurrung language a great resource is the Wadawurrung language app, published by the Victorian Aboriginal Corporation for Languages. The app is avaliable free online. For other written Wadawurrung language dictionaries and references used in these essays please see the Select Bibliography below.

The Colours of the Ground

The Peter Minter quote comes from his poem 'I just do eyes, j-j-just eyes', quoted in 'Bev Braune reviews Peter Minter and Nathan Shepherdson', Cordite Poetry Review, cordite.org.au/reviews/braune-minter-shepherdson

The Proust quote comes from Proust, M 2002, *Swann's Way*, trans. L Davis, Penguin, New York.

For information on the old Jarosite mine at Pt Addis see:

https://www.torquayhistory.com/brief-history-of-torquay/beaches-n-parks-2/jarosite-mine/

I found the Century Dictionary definition of 'jarosite' at Wordnik, www.wordnik.com/words/jarosite

Whoo-hoo Thinking

The Empson quote comes from his poem 'Aubade', written in 1937. I first came across it in Frank Kermode's review of Empson's *Complete Poems* in the LRB, www.lrb.co.uk/the-paper/v22/n12/frank-kermode/the-heart-of-standing-is-you-cannot-fly

Other quotes are from Christopher Neve's *Unquiet Landscape: Places and Ideas in 20th-century British Painting*, reissued by Thames & Hudson in 2020; John Cage's *Silence*, reissued by the Wesleyan University Press in 2011; the preface to Hegel's *Philosophy of Right*, which I found at 'Hegel and the Owl of Minerva', Hesiod's Corner, hesiodscorner.wordpress.com/2017/10/10/hegel-and-the-owl-of-minerva; Yeats, WB, 1937, *A Vision*, Introduction, www.ricorso.net/rx/az-data/authors/y/Yeats_WB/quots/quot9.htm – A Vision; and Erik Satie – A Learned Lecture on Music and Animals, archive.vanityfair.com/article/1922/5/a-learned-lecture-on-music-and-animals.

The definition of 'call' is my edited assemblage of the definitions given at www.lexico.com/definition/call.

Mere Scenery and Poles of Light

The Cézanne letters come from Danchev, A 2013, The Letters of Paul Cézanne, J. Paul Getty Museum, Los Angeles.

John Eliot Gardner's biography of JS Bach, *Bach: Music in the Castle of Heaven*, published by Knopf in 2014, is a great book on Bach, especially because it is written by a working musician and a brilliant conductor of Bach's music. Gardner's book is dedicated to 'fellow travellers through Bach's landscape'.

Barry Hill has written powerfully on William Buckley, particularly in his 1993 poetry collection *Ghosting William Buckley*. The comment I quote here is from Hill's essay 'Buckley, Our Imagination, Hope', published in 2008 in Gardner, Robyn (ed.), *Writings on the Shipwreck Coast*, Mattoid/Grange, Port Fairy.

For other titles dealing with Buckley's story see the Select Bibliography below.

The quote from Andrea Lauterwein comes from her wonderful volume: *Kiefer/Celan: Myth and Mourning*, published in 2007 by Thames & Hudson.

The quote from David Unaipon comes from his 1929 publication, *Native Legends* (see Select Bibliography below). I also drew on information about Unaipon in Philip Jones's important book, *Ochre and Rust: Artefacts* and Encounters On Australian Frontiers, published by Wakefield Press in 2007. Information on the story of David Unaipon walking through our district is discussed locally but is yet to be fully documented. My fictional imaginings here are triggered by local conversations sparked by Anna McIldowie's *Identifying the Gadubanud Narrative* project, and also by the excellent ABC Radio documentary of Unaipon: *On The Shore of a Strange Land: the Story of David Unaipon*, which can be listened to at: https://www.abc.net.au/radionational/programs/archived/hindsight/on-the-shore-of-a-strange-land-the-story-of-david/3028838

Moonah Mind

The definitions of 'sinuous' and 'tangle' come from Online Etymology Dictionary, www.etymonline.com

Gerald Vizenor's concept of 'natural motion' comes from his book, *Native Provenance: The Betrayal of Cultural Creativity*, published by University of Nebraska Press in 2019.

Two: The Ocean Last Night

The Ocean Last Night

The French composer Francis Poulenc's ability to move between playful experimentalism and an expression of the sacred has been a constant companion to me through the years of writing this book. The Poulenc quote here is from Gendre's 'Dialogues des Carmelites: the Historical Background, Literary Destiny and Genesis of the Opera', in *Francis Poulenc: Music, Art and Literature*, published by Ashgate in 1999.

The Peter Turchi quote is from his book, *Maps of the Imagination: The Writer as Cartographer*, published by Trinity University Press, San Antonio, in 2004.

Archie Roach's beautiful song 'A Child Was Born Here', first appeared on the album *Looking for Butter Boy* in 1997. A moving live rendition of the song can be viewed on the YouTube recording of the concert Archie Roach did with the Melbourne Symphony Orchestra in February 2022. https://www.youtube.com/watch?v=JEGmoD4LaAw

Susan Howe's essays and poems have long been a guiding light. The quote here is from her essay collection, *The Quarry*, published by New Directions in 2015.

The Unaipon quote is from *Native Legends*, published in Adelaide in 1929 by Hunkin, Ellis & King

The Lawson poem is called 'To a Fellow Bard Camping Out'. It can be found in the 1984 publication, *A Fantasy of Man: Henry Lawson Complete Works, 1901–1922*, edited by. L. Cronin, and published by Lansdowne in Sydney.

One True Note?

The list of different spellings of 'Wadawurrung' comes from Ian D. Clark's *Aboriginal Languages and Clans: An Historical Atlas of Western and Central Victoria, 1800–1900*, published in 1990 by the Department of Geography and Environmental Science, Monash University, Melbourne.

The John Berger quote is from, *Confabulations*, published in 2016 by Penguin Random House, London.

An interesting reference on the field of psychoacoustics is Joshua Leeds' *The Power of Sound: How to be Healthy and Productive Using Music and Sound*, published in 2010 by Healing Arts Press.

The quotes from Noam Chomsky are from his 2009 essay, 'The Mysteries of Nature: How Deeply Hidden?', published in the Journal of Philosophy, no. 4.

The quotes and ideas of David Abram come from his 1997 book, *The Spell of the Sensuous*, published by Vintage Books, New York.

The quote from Charles Taylor is from his book, *The Language Animal*, published in 2016 by The Belknap Press, Cambridge, MA.

I heard David Prosser speaking on ABC Radio National Word Up: David Prosser, on the AWAYE (Listen up) program. You can listen at: www.abc.net.au/radionational/programs/awaye/features/word-up/word-up/8746116

Scarry's idea of 'radiant ignition' is in her *Dreaming by the Book*, published in 2001 by Princeton University Press.

David Tournier's 'Magpie' is from *Nyernila Listen Continuously*, published by the Victorian Aboriginal Corporation for Languages and Arts Victoria in 2004.

Otway Taenarum

The music and sounds being listened to on the bungalow step are from Richard Connolly's 1988 ABC radio documentary, *Naples Part 2: A House on the Sea*. Retrieved 15 October 2017. http://www.abc.net.au/radionational/programs/elsewhere/naples-part-2-a-house-on-the-sea/3022814

The quote from Seamus Heaney is from his 1987 volume, *The Haw Lantern*, published by Faber and Faber.

There are different versions online of the Satie quote about being born very young in a very old world, and I'm not sure where I first encountered it – probably in his *Memoirs of an Amnesiac*!

The commendation from the Yeats Society of Ireland is from a citation written by Maura McTighe, President of the Yeats Society, Sligo.

The Stanner essay 'The Dreaming' is in *The Dreaming & Other Essays* by WEH Stanner 2009, published in 1953 and reissued in 2009 by Black Inc., Melbourne.

The quotes from Alan Garner in this essay are from his 2015 piece, 'Creation Myths: Revelations from a Life of Storytelling', New Statesman, nos 5255–56, pp. 74–77.

The fascinating Julie Baleriaux study on the mythological aspects of subterranean rivers was published in 2016 as: 'Diving Underground: Giving Meaning to Subterranean Rivers', in J McInerney & I Sluiter (eds), *Valuing Landscape in Classical Antiquity: Natural Environment and Cultural Imagination*, Koninklijke Brill NV, Leiden, The Netherlands.

There is much work being done, and still to be done, from the Gadubanud perspective, about La Trobe's incursion into Cape Otway in 1846.

The information about Lady Gregory's husband Robert Gregory is gleaned from Colm Toibin's 2003 book, *Lady Gregory's Toothbrush*, published by Picador, London.

The quote from Nicholas Jose is from his 2002 book, *Black Sheep: Journey to Borroloola*, published by Hardie Grant, Melbourne.

Being Here

For an introduction to Wadawurrung language a great resource is the Wadawurrung language app, published by the Victorian Aboriginal Corporation for Languages. The app is avaliable free online. For other written Wadawurrung language dictionaries and references used in these essays please see the Select Bibliography below.

For a good understanding of mycorrhizal symbiosis in fungi see *Entangled Life* by Merlin Sheldrake, published by Penguin Random House in 2020. Also *The Mycorrhizal Symbiosis in Mediterranean Environment: Importance in Ecosystem Stability and in Soil Rehabilitation Strategies,* edited by Hafidi and Duponnois, published in 2012 by Nova Science Publishers. Another great mushroom book is *Wild Mushrooming – A Guide for Foragers* by the wonderful Alison Pouliot and Tom May. From time to time Alison also runs excellent fungi workshops in the Otways in autumn.

Donna Haraway's 2016 book, *Staying with The Trouble: Making Kin in the Chthulucene*, published by Duke University Press, is a stimulating and insightful book on the the cultural shifts we need to make in the climate change epoch.

For a stimulating study of Thomas Berry's term 'ecozoic', see Kiplinger, A 2010, *Groping Our Way Toward A New Geologic Era: A Study Of The Word Ecozoic* Retrieved 5 January 2022
https://ecozoictimes.com/what-is-the-ecozoic/what-does-ecozoic-mean/

Harry Saddler's book, *The Eastern Curlew: The Extraordinary Life of a Migratory Bird*, was published by Affirm Press in 2018.

Alexis Wright's essay, 'What Happens When You Tell Someone Else's Story?' was published in Vol 75 of *Meanjin* in 2016.

The Bruno Latour quote is from his foreword to Despret's *What Would Animals Say If We Asked The Right Questions*, published by the University of Minnesota Press in 2016.

The David Abram quote is from his book *The Spell of the Sensuous*, published by Vintage, New York, in 1997.

The Maria Takolander quote is from *Catching Butterflies: bringing magical realism to ground*, published in 2007 by Peter Lang, Bern.

Select Bibliography

One of my favourite writers, the American poet and essayist, Susan Howe, calls herself a 'library cormorant', which is a phrase that comes from Coleridge. I've always been fond of the phrase for the way it breathes the air of instinctual estuarine life into the often interior mustiness of the library concept. For me a lot of reading happens outdoors.

Howe also writes about what she calls the 'telepathy of archives', the way the voices in books are never dead and can in fact reach across time and space to find uncanny and unforeseen connections with each other and with the world around them.

There's a note I made in one of my walking notebooks from 2008, about the land being a living text we all better learn to read well, and quick. Yes, this is an urgently needed literacy these days, and ironically it involves much slow work. *Festina lente.* In my experience this literacy is often well complemented by us diving like library cormorants into the seas of sound and meaning we print on paper leaves.

Words Are Eagles is an attempt to translate something of the living text of land and ocean in my hereabouts into a form a fellow library cormorant might enjoy. It would be remiss of me then not to include a list of some of the books that have helped me think about the nuances of the organic urge to write-sing-speak about a place so complex and beautiful as the one where I live. Here then is the list below.

Needless to say, I have done much diving into the pages of these books over the years, and much sitting afterwards on rock and branch to digest the nourishment they've given me. I should say too that this is the kind of natural 'wreading' process that ensures that no book ever stands alone. As with the life a cormorant feeds upon everything we write and read is always made up of a living community entirely dependent on the greatest teeming text of them all - Mother Earth.

Abram, D 1997, *The Spell of The Sensuous*, Vintage Books, New York

Adam-Smith, Patsy 1965, *Moonbird People*, Rigby, Adelaide

Adam-Smith, Patsy & Powell, John 1978, *Islands of Bass Strait*, Rigby, Adelaide

Addison, Marylyn (compiler) 1998, *King Island A Time of Change: An Oral History of King Island*, Marylyn Addison, Currie

Aireys Inlet Water Board 1991, *Annual Report*, Aireys Inlet Water Board, Aireys Inlet

Aireys Inlet Water Board 1992, *Annual Report*, Aireys Inlet Water Board, Aireys Inlet

Alsop, P 1982, *A History of The Great Ocean Road*, Geelong Historical Society, Geelong, VIC

Andrews, Munya 2004, *The Seven Sisters of the Pleiades*, Spinifex, North Melbourne

Arkley, Lindsey 2000, *The Hated Protector: The Story of Charles Wightman Sievwright Protector of Aborigines 1839–42*, Orbit Press, Melbourne

Ashcroft, B, Devlin-Glass, F & McCredden, L 2012, *Intimate Horizons; The Post-Colonial Sacred in Australian Literature*, ATF Press, Hindmarsh, SA

Baleriaux, J 2016, 'Diving Underground: Giving Meaning to Subterranean Rivers,' in J McInerney & I Sluiter (eds.), *Valuing Landscape in Classical Antiquity: Natural Environment and Cultural Imagination*, Koninklijke Brill NV, Leiden, The Netherlands, pp. 103–121

Ball, H 1996, *Flight Out of Time: A Dada Diary*, University of California Press, Berkeley, CA

Banivanua-Mar T & Edmonds, P 2010, *Making Settler Colonial Space: Perspectives on Race, Place and Identity*, Palgrave Macmillan, Houndmills, UK

Bardon, Geoffrey & Bardon, James 2006, *Papunya – A Place Made After The Story*, Miegunyah, Melbourne

Barker, J 2017, 'Why Did The Couta Leave Lorne Waters?,' *Lorne Independent*, no. 191, p. 9

Baudin, N 1974, *The Journal of Post Captain Nicolas Baudin*, trans. C Cornell Libraries Board of South Australia, Adelaide, SA

Berger, J 2016, *Confabulations*, Penguin Random House, London

Bernac, P 1977, *Francis Poulenc: The Man and His Songs*, V. Gollancz, London

Berndt Ronald M & Berndt, Catherine H 1989, *The Speaking Land – Myth and Story in Aboriginal Australia*, Penguin, Ringwood

Bird, E 2006, *Place Names on the Coast of Victoria*, retrieved May 24, 2017, www.bcs.asn.au/vic_coast.pdf

Bird, Eric CF 1993, *The Coast of Victoria: The Shaping of Scenery*, Melbourne University Press, Melbourne

Birregurra District Historical Centre 2003, *A Journey Through Time: Our District's Timeline* 1836–2003, Birregurra District Historical Centre

Birregurra District Historical Centre 2007, *Turkeith Farm Journals – An Introduction*, Birregurra District Historical Centre

Birregurra District Historical Centre 2007, *Warncoort & Mt Gellibrand History*, Birregurra District Historical Centre 2016

Blair, R 2012, 'Figures of Life: Beverley Farmer's The Seal Woman as an Australian Bioregional Novel', in T Lynch, C Glotfelty, & K Armbruster (eds.), *The Bioregional Imagination: Literature, Ecology and Place*, University of Georgia Press, Athens, GA, pp. 164–180.

Blake, BJ 1998, *Wathawurrung and the Colac Language of Southern Victoria*, Pacific Linguistics, Research School of Pacific and Asian Studies, Australian National University, Canberra.

Blake, LJ 1975, *Letters of Charles Joseph Latrobe, Victoriana Series no. 1*, Government Printer, Melbourne

Blay, John 2015, *On Track: Searching Out The Bundian Way*, New South, Sydney

Blum, Ron, *Anglesea to Aireys Inlet & Beyond*, Ron Blum, Oaklands Park, SA

Bloom, H 1997, *The Anxiety of Influence: A Theory of Poetry*, Oxford University Press, London

Bondi, L, Davidson, J & Smith, M 2007, *Emotional Geographies*, Ashgate, Aldershot

Bonfantine, Krista 2021, *Water Management from Basin to Biofilm*, Doctoral thesis, Deakin University, Geelong

Bonwick, James (1858) 1970, *Western Victoria: Its Geography, Geology and Social Conditions*, William Heinemann, Melbourne

Bonwick, James 1887, *Romance Of The Wool Trade*, Griffith, Farran, Okeden, and Welsh, London

Bonyhady, Tim 2000, *The Colonial Earth*, Miegunyah, Melbourne

Boyce, J 2008, *Van Diemens Land*, Black Inc, Melbourne

Boyce, J 2011, *1835: The Founding of Melbourne and the Conquest of Australia*, Black Inc, Collingwood, VIC

Boyce, J 2014, *Born Bad: Original Sin and the Making of the Western World*, Black Inc, Collingwood, VIC

Boyce, J 2020, *Imperial Mud: The Fight for the Fens*, Icon Books, London

Brougham Austin, G (1890) 2005, *Pen & Ink Sketches at Lorne*, Ferguson & Mitchell, Melbourne

Buckby, Pauline 2003, *David Howie: Devil Or Saint?*, Jamala Press, Tasmania

Bunce, Daniel 1859, *Language of the Aborigines of the colony of Victoria and other Australian districts with parallel translations and familiar specimens in dialogue, as a guide to Aboriginal Protectors, and others engaged in ameliorating their condition*, Thomas Brown, Geelong

Burns, Shirley 2006, *Onion People: The History of Onions in Victoria*, Shirley Burns, Colac

Cahir, Fred 2019, *My Country All Gone The White Men Have Stolen It: The Invasion of Wadawurrung Country 1800–1870*, Australian History Matters, Ballarat

Cahir, Fred, Clark, Ian D. & Clarke, Philip A 2018, *Aboriginal Biocultural Knowledge in South-eastern Australia: Perspectives of Early Colonists*, CSIRO Publishing, Melbourne

Canton, J 2013, *Out Of Essex: Re-Imagining a Literary Landscape*, Signal Books, Oxford.

Carson, A 2009, *Eros the Bittersweet*, Dalkey Archive Press, Champaign, IL

Carter, P 1992, *The Sound in Between: Voice, Space, Performance*, New Endeavor Press, Strawberry Hills, NSW.

Carter, P 1996, *The Lie of The Land*, Faber & Faber, London

Cecil, K & RV Carr 1986, *The White Queen: A History of the Split Point Lighthouse Aireys Inlet, Above the Eagle Nest Reef in Bass Strait, Victoria, Australia*, Neptune Press, Belmont, VIC

Cecil, K & RV Carr 1987, *Aireys Inlet – A History From Eagle Rock to Cranberry Hill*, Anglesea & District Historical Society

Cecil, K 1990, *The Great Ocean Road*, Anglesea & District Historical Society, Anglesea

Cecil, Keith L 1993, *Aireys Inlet School Centenary 1893–1993 – A History of State School no. 3195*, Anglesea & District Historical Society

Cecil, Keith L 1994, *Lorne (Volume 2) The Formative Years 1889–1922*, Lorne Historical Society, Lorne

Clark, ID 1990, *Aboriginal Languages and Clans: An Historical Atlas of Western and Central Victoria, 1800–1900*, Department of Geography and Environmental Science, Monash University, Melbourne.

Clark, Ian D 1995, *Scars in the Landscape: A Register of Massacre Sites in Western Victoria 1803–1859*, Aboriginal Studies Press for the Australian Institute of Aboriginal and Torres Strait Islander Studies, Canberra.

Clarke, Banjo (as told to Camilla Chance) 2003, *Wisdom Man*, Penguin, Melbourne

Chomsky, N 2009, 'The mysteries of nature: how deeply hidden? *The Journal of Philosophy*, no. 4, p. 167

Colac and District Historical Society 2004, *Colac: A Short History from 1837*, Colac Historical Society

Connolly, R 1988, *Naples Part 2: A House On The Sea*, Radio National, Retrieved 15 October 2017, http://www.abc.net.au/radionational/programs/elsewhere/naples-part-2-a-house-on-the-sea/3022814

Corangamite Dry Stone Walls Conservation Project 1999, *"If These Walls Could Talk"*, Corangamite Arts Council, Terang

Cougle, Paul 2018, *Murrangoork*, Arcadia, North Melbourne

Critchett, J 1990, *A Distant Field Of Murder*, Melbourne University Press, Carlton

Croll, RH 1946, *Smike To Bulldog: Letters from Sir Arthur Streeton to Tom Roberts*, Ure Smith, Sydney

Crosby, AW 1986, *Ecological Imperialism: The Biological Expansion of Europe, 900–1900*, Cambridge University Press, Cambridge

Dawson, J (1881) 1981, *Australian Aborigines: The Languages and Customs of Several Tribes of Aborigines in the Western District of Victoria*, George Robertson, Melbourne

Debord, G 1983, *Society of The Spectacle*, Detroit: Black and Red

Dearnaley, J 2019, *Wadawurrung Ethnobotany as synthesised from the research of Louis Lane*, Retrieved March 15 2021, https://dro.deakin.edu.au/eserv/DU:30134971/dearnaley-wadawurrung-2019.pdf

Di Lampedusa, G 1963, *The Leopard*, trans. A Colquhoun, Collins, London

Duyker, Edward 2006, *Francois Peron - An Impetuous Life*, Miegunyah, Melbourne

Edgecombe, Jean 1993, *Discovering King Island Western Bass Strait*, J.M. Edgecombe, Sydney

Edgecombe, Jean 1986, *Flinders Island and Eastern Bass Strait*, Edgekirk, Sydney

Edwards, Geoffrey, Smith, Geoffrey, Sullivan, Lisa 2016, *Land of the Golden Fleece - Arthur Streeton in the Western District*, Geelong gallery, Geelong

Farrell, M 2015, *Writing Australian Unsettlement: Modes of Poetic Invention 1796–1945*, Palgrave Macmillan, New York

Ferrier, Sue, *Wathaurong Medicines*, Sue Ferrier

Forrest Primary School 2013, *Characters: Forrest Victoria*, Forrest Primary School, Forrest

Fornaserio, J 2016, *Reflections of a Philosophical Voyager*, The Friends of The State Library of South Australia, Adelaide

Frank, AW 2000, 'The Standpoint of Storyteller,' *Qualitative Health Research*, vol. 10, no. 3, pp. 325–344

Gammage, Bill 2011, *The Biggest Estate On Earth - How Aborigines Made Australia*, Allen & Unwin, Sydney

Gammage, Bill & Pascoe, Bruce 2021, *Country: Future Fire, Future Farming*, Thames & Hudson, Port Melbourne

Garbutt, RG 2011, *The Locals: Identity, Place and Belonging in Australia and Beyond*, Peter Lang, New York

Garner, A 1996, *Strandloper*, The Harvill Press, London

Garner, A 2015, 'Creation myths: revelations from a life of storytelling,' *New Statesman*, no. 5255–5256, pp. 74–77

Garner, A 2007, *The Voice That Thunders*, The Harvill Press, London

Garner, H 2014, *This House of Grief*, Text Publishing, Melbourne

Geelong Field Naturalists Club 1987, *From Buckleys To The Break*, Geelong Field Naturalists Club, Geelong

Geelong Gallery & Filmer, Veronica 2004, *More than a memory - the art of Elizabeth Parsons*, Geelong Gallery, Geelong

Gibson, Ross 2012, *26 Views of The Starburst World – William Dawes at Sydney Cove 1788–91*, UWAP, Perth

Gordon, Harry 1962, *The Embarrassing Australian: The Story of an Aboriginal Warrior*, Lansdowne Press, Melbourne

Gott, B & Conran, J 1991, *Victorian Koorie Plants*, Yangennanock Women's Group, Aboriginal Keeping Place, Hamilton, VIC

Gran, A-B 2010, 'Staging Places as Brands,' in B Timm Knudsen & A Waade (eds.), *Re-Investing Authenticity: Tourism, Place And Emotions*, Channel View Publications, Bristol, pp. 22–37

Greenblatt, S 2011, *The Swerve: How The World Became Modern*, W.W. Norton & Company, New York

Gregg, Simon 2011, *Nicholas Chevalier – Australian Odyssey*, Gippsland Art Gallery, Sale

Gregory EB, Gregory ML, Koenig WL 1985, *Coast To Country: Winchelsea A History of The Shire*, Hargreen Publishing, North Melbourne

Griffiths, Tom 1996, *Hunters and Collectors: The Antiquarian Imagination in Australia*, Cambridge University Press

Griffiths, Tom 2001, *Forests of Ash: An Environmental History*, Cambridge University Press, Cambridge UK

Hack, Pema Lily & Hack, Juna Mani 2016, *The Christmas Day Fire*, Wye River

Hafidi, M, & Duponnois, R (eds) 2012, *The Mycorrhizal Symbiosis in Mediterranean Environment: Importance in Ecosystem Stability and in Soil Rehabilitation Strategies*, Nova Science Publishers, Hauppauge

Haraway, DJ 2016, *Staying with The Trouble: Making Kin in the Chthulucene*, Duke University Press Durham

Harcourt, Rex 2001, *Southern Invasion Northern Conquest: Story of the Founding of Melbourne*, Golden Point Press, Melbourne

Hardy, Sarah 2008, *Dame Joan Hammond Love & Music*, Allen & Unwin, Sydney

Hill, Barry 1993, *Ghosting William Buckley*, William Heinemann, Port Melbourne

Hill, Barry 2004, *The Enduring Rip: A History of Queenscliffe*, Melbourne University Press, Melbourne

Honan, Jodie 2009, *A Natural History of Port Fairy and District*, Port Fairy Historical Society, Port Fairy

Houghton Norman 2010, *Sawdust and Steam: A History of Sawmilling in The East Otway Ranges 1850–2010*, Norman Houghton, Geelong

Hounam, CE 1949, *Climate of the Western District of Victoria*, Commonwealth of Australia Meteorological Bureau, Melbourne

Howe, S 2015, *The Quarry*, New Directions, New York

Howe, S 2014, *Spontaneous Particulars The Telepathy of Archives*, New Directions, New York

Hunt, Ian C 1999, *Feel The Sea Wind*, Ian C Hunt, Lorne

Jennings, Pam & Trevor 2016, *Wymbooliel & Benwerrin Pioneers – Parish of Lorne Otway Ranges*, Pam & Trevor Jennings, Leopold

Jones, Freda & Sullivan, Tom 1989, *In The Path of the Roaring Forties: Memories of King Island*, Regal Publiscations, Launceston, Tasmania

Jones, John 2010, *Robert Dowling: Tasmanian Son of Empire*, National Gallery of Australia, Canberra

Jones, Jonathan (contributing editor) 2016, *barrangal dyara (skin and bones)*, Kaldor Public Art Projects

Jones, Philip 2007, *Ochre and Rust: Artefacts and Encounters On Australian Frontiers*, Wakefield Press, Kent Town, South Australia

Jones, P 2017, 'Beyond Songlines,' *Australian Book Review*, no. 394, Retrieved 20 October 2017, https://www.australianbookreview.com.au/abr-online/archive/2017/4223-beyond-songlines-by-philip-jones

Jose, N 2002, *Black Sheep: Journey to Borroloola*, Hardie Grant, Melbourne

Kaplan, Gisela 2004, *Australian Magpie: Biology and Behaviour of an Unusual Songbird*, CSIRO Publishing, Collingwood

Kenny, Robert 2007, *The Lamb Enters The Dreaming: Nathaniel Pepper & The Ruptured World*, Scribe, Melbourne

King Island Natural Resource Management Group 2000, King Island Flora: A Field Guide, King Island Natural Resource Management Group, King Island

Kiplinger, A 2010, *Groping Our Way Toward A New Geologic Era: A Study Of The Word Ecozoic* Retrieved 5 November 2017, https://ecozoictimes.com/what-is-the-ecozoic/what-does-ecozoic-mean/

Koenig, WL 1933, *The History of the Winchelsea Shire*, Winchelsea Shire

Kynaston, Edward 1981, *A Man On Edge: A life of Baron Sir Ferdinand von Mueller*, Allen Lane, Ringwood

La Capria, R 1991, *Capri Or No Longer Capri*, Thunder's Mouth Press, New York

Le Griffon, H 2006, *Campfires at The Cross*, Australian Scholarly Press, North Melbourne, VIC

Latour, B 1993, *We Have Never Been Modern*, Harvard Univesity Press, Cambridge, Mass

Latour, B 1999, *Pandora's Hope: Essays on the Reality of Science Studies*, Harvard Univrsity Press, Cambridge, MA

Latour, B 2016, 'Foreword: The Scientific Fables of an Empirical La Fontaine', in V Despret, *What Would Animals Say If We Asked the Right Questions?* Trans. B Buchanan, University of Minnesota Press, Minneapolis, pp. xii–xiii. Retrieved from http://www.jstor.org/stable/10.5749/j.ctt1c0gm8

Latour, B, Leclercq, C (eds) 2016, *Reset Modernity!*, ZKM Centre for Art and Media, Karlsruhe, Germany, The MIT Press, Cambridge, MA

Lawson, H 1984, *A Fantasy of Man: Henry Lawson Complete Works, 1901–1922*, Lansdowne, Sydney

Laxness, H 1966, *The Fish Can Sing*, trans. Magnusson, London: Methuen

Leahy, Cathy, Ryan, Judith, Crombie, Isobel, Patty, Megan (eds) 2019, *Colony – Australia 1770–1861 / Frontier Wars*, Thames & Hudson, Melbourne

Loney, JK 1971, *Otway Memories*, Ken Jenkin Print, Geelong

Loney, Jack 1979, *The Otway*, Jack Loney, Portarlington

Loney, Jack 2009, *The Mahogany Ship*, Jack Loney

Lowe, Pat 2007, *In The Desert: Jimmy Pike as a boy*, Magabala Books,

McCann, IR 1992, *The Coast and Hinterland in Flower*, Victorian National Parks Association Inc

McComb, Sandra 2021, *A Short History of Fishing in Lorne*, Lorne Historical Society

McDonald, Margaret (ed) 2009, *Flowers of Anglesea and Aireys Inlet*, Inverted Logic, Melbourne

McIldowie, Anna 2012, *Identifying 'the Gadubanud Narrative'*, Honours Thesis Latrobe University

McKenna, M 2016, *From the Edge: Australia's Lost Histories*, The Miegunyah Press, Melbourne

McLean, Ian 2016, *Rattling Spears: A History of Indigenous Art*, Reaktion Books, London

McPhee, Hilary 2001, *Other People's Words*, Picador, Sydney

MacKellar, Maggie 2008, *Strangers in a Foreign Land: The Journal of Niel Black and Other Voices from the Western District*, Miegunyah, Melbourne

Mathews, F 1991, *The Ecological Self*, Barnes and Noble Books, Savage, MD

Mayfield, Enid 2010, *Flora of the Otway Plain & Ranges 1*, CSIRO Publishing, Collingwood

Mayfield, Enid 2013, *Flora of the Otway Plain & Ranges 2*, CSIRO Publishing, Collingwood

Merleau-Ponty, M 1978, *Phenomenology of Perception*, trans. C Smith, Routledge & Kegan Paul, London

Millard, Ron 1987, *Bambra-Boonah*, Ron Millard, Bambra

Morris, Hugh 1964, *Murroon State School 940 and District 1868–1964*, Murroon State School

Morrison, GE (Duruz, R ed) 1979, *The Long Walk*, PAP Book Company, Warrnambool

Morrow, Jennifer & Grieg, Peter 2019, *Walking The Barwon River from Source to Sea*, Upper Barwon Landcare Network

Muecke, S 2004, *Ancient & Modern: Time, Culture and Indigenous Philosophy*, UNSW Press, Sydney

Murnane, G 2015, *Something For The Pain*, Text Publishing, Melbourne

Niall, I 1960, *The New Poacher's Handbook*, Heinemann, London

O'Donaghue, D 2016, 'Discussion of Part III: Image, Loss, Delay,' in A Tutter & L Wurmser (eds.), *Grief and its Transcendence: Memory, Identity, Creativity*, Routledge, New York, pp. 189–194

Olsewski, Peter 1980, *A Salute to the Humble Yabby*, Angus & Robertson, Sydney

Pascoe, Bruce 2014, *Dark Emu Black Seeds; agriculture or accident*, Magabala Books, Broome.

Pascoe, B 2003, *Wathaurong: The People Who Said No*, Wathaurong Aboriginal Co-Operative, North Geelong, VIC

Pascoe, B 2001, *Earth*, Magabala Books, Broome

Pascoe, B 2007, *Convincing Ground: Learning to Fall in Love with Your Country*, Aboriginal Studies Press, Canberra

Pavord, A 2005, *The Naming of Names: The Search for Order In The World of Plants*, Bloomsbury, London

Pescott, Trevor 1995, *The You Yangs Range*, Yaugher Print, Belmont

Plomley, NJB 1976, *A Word-List of the Tasmanian Aboriginal Languages*, Plomley in Association with the Government of Tasmania, Launceston

Poulenc, F 1991, *Echo and Source: Selected Correspondence 1915–1963*, trans. S Buckland, Victor Gollancz, London

Pouliot, Alison & May, Tom 2021, *Wild Mushrooming: A Guide for Foragers*, CSIRO Publishing, Melbourne

Poulter, Hazel 1985, *Templestowe – A Folk History*, Jim Poulter, Templestowe

Pybus, Cassandra 2020, *Truganini: Journey through the apocalypse*, Allen & Unwin, Crows Nest NSW

Rasula, J 2002, *This Compost: Ecological Imperatives in American Poetry*, The University of Georgia Press, Athens, GA

Read, P 2000, *Belonging: Australians, Place and Aboriginal Ownership*, Cambridge University Press, Cambridge

Read, Peter 1996, *Returning to Nothing: The Meaning of Lost Places*, Cambridge University Press, Cambridge

Reynolds, Henry (1981) 1990, *The Other Side of The Frontier: Aboriginal Resistance to the European Invasion of Australia*, Penguin, Melbourne

Reynolds, Henry & Clements, Nicholas 2021, *Tongerlongeter: First Nations Leader & Tasmanian War Hero*, New South, Sydney

Riches, Kenneth R. 2009, *Let There Be Flight: A History of Flying in Western Victoria*, Kenneth R. Riches

Robertson, C 1980, *Buckley's Hope*, Scribe Publications, Fitzroy, VIC

Robinson, GA & Presland, Gary (ed) 1980, *Journals of G.A. Robinson May to August 1841*, Ministry for Conservation, Melbourne

Rose, DB 2004, *Reports from a Wild Country: Ethics for Decolonisation*, University of New South Wales Press, Sydney

Scarry, E 2001, *Dreaming by The Book*, Princeton University Press, New Jersey

Schnur Neile, Caren & Behar, Ruth 2009, 'Between Textuality and Orality: An Interview with Ruth Behar', *Storytelling, Self, Society, vol. 5, no. 3*, Wayne State University Press, Detroit

Scott, Kim & Brown, Hazel 2005, *Kayang & Me*, Fremantle Arts Centre Press

Sheldrake, M 2020, *Entangled Life: How Fungi Make Our Worlds, Change Our Minds, and Shape Our Futures*, Penguin Random House, London

Slade, Gurney 1925, *The Pearlers of Lorne*, Thomas Nelson and Sons, London

Smith, Roger 2015, *The Redwoods of the Otway Ranges*, Lothis Custom Publishing, Melbourne

Stanner, WEH (1953) 2009, *The Dreaming & Other Essays*, Black Inc, Melbourne

Steiner, G 1989, *Real Presences*, University of Chicago Press, Chicago Stevens, Wallace 1990, *The Collected Poems*, Vintage, New York

Stepnel, Ken 1972, *Great Ocean Road*, Rigby, Adelaide

Stirling, D 2004, *Lorne: A Living History*, JD Stirling, Lorne, VIC

Stilgoe, JR 1990, *Shallow-Water Dictionary*, Exact Change, Cambridge, MA.

Stilgoe, JR 1994, *Alongshore*, Yale University Press, New Haven, CT

Stilgoe, JR 2015, *What Is Landscape?* MIT Press, Cambridge, MA

Sutton, Peter & Walshe, Kerryn 2021, *Farmers or Hunter-Gatherers: The Dark Emu Debate*, Melbourne University Press, Melbourne

Sydenham, George Francis (1896) 2013, *The Otways: Through the Magic Lantern*, Colac & District Historical Society Inc, Colac

Sykes, Patricia 2004, *Modewarre*, Spinifex, North Melbourne

Takolander, M 2007, *Catching Butterflies: bringing magical realism to ground*, Peter Lang, Bern

Taylor, A 2001, *Long Time Now*, Magabala Books, Broome

Taylor, C 2016, *The Language Animal*, The Belknap Press, Cambridge, MA

Taylor, R 2017, *Into the Heart of Tasmania*, Melbourne University Press, Melbourne

Burns, Creighton (ed) 1983, *Ash Wednesday...*, The Age, The Adelaide Advertiser and the Allied Trade Employers Federation, Melbourne, Adelaide

Thoreau, HD 1951 (1865), *Cape Cod*, Norton, New York

Toibin, C 2003, *Lady Gregory's Toothbrush*, Picador, London

Tribulato, Olga (ed) 2012, *Language and Linguistic Contact in Ancient Sicily*, Cambridge University Press, Cambridge UK

Turchi, P 2004, *Maps of The Imagination: The Writer as Cartographer*, Trinity University Press, San Antonio, TX

Unaipon, D 1929, *Native Legends*, Hunkin, Ellis & King, Adelaide, SA

Upfield, Arthur (1952) 1972, *The Clue Of The New Shoe*, Wm Heinemann, London

Vendler, H 1980, *Part of Nature, Part of Us: Modern American Poets*, Harvard University Press, Cambridge, MA

Victorian Aboriginal Corporation for Languages 2004, *Nyernila Listen Continuously*, Arts Victoria, Melbourne

Victorian Government Tourist Bureau 1956, *Victoria's South Western Riviera Australia*, Victorian Government Tourist Bureau

Village Well 2009, '*Point Grey & Slaughterhouse Place Essence Report,*' Village Well, Melbourne

Walling, Edna 2008, *The Happiest Days of My Life*, Barbara Barnes

Warren S 2015, 'Writing of the Heart: Auto-Ethnographic Writing as Subversive Story-Telling – A Song of Pain and Liberation,' in D Loads, T Peseta, J Rattray & J Smith (eds.), *Identity Work in the Contemporary University: Exploring an Uneasy Profession*, SensePublishers, Rotterdam, pp. 105–116

Were, Jonathan Binns (1964) 1990, *A Voyage from Plymouth to Melbourne*, The Craftsman Press, Burwood

White, Mary D 1989, *The Flowers of Anglesea River Valley*, Lutheran Publishing House, Adelaide

White, Mary D 1990, *Coastal Vegetation of Anglesea-Aireys Inlet Region*, Lutheran Publishing House, Adelaide

Whitehead, Jo (ed) 2013, *The Wadda Wurrung People: Did You Know?*, Jo Whitehead, Queenscliff

Whittaker, Alison 2018, *Blakwork*, Magabala Books, Broome

Whitworth, Robt. P (compiler) 1870, *Balliere's Victorian Gazetteer and Road Guide*, F.F. Bailliere, Melbourne

Williams, WC 1992, *Paterson*, New Directions, New York

Wilson, EO 1984, *Biophilia*, Harvard University Press, Cambridge, MA

Wilson, EO 1993, 'Biophilia and the Conservation Ethic,' in S Kellert & EO Wilson (eds.), *The Biophilia Hypothesis*, Island Press, Washington, pp. 31–41

Winch, Tara June 2019, *The Yield*, Penguin Hamish Hamilton, Sydney

Wordsworth, William 1823, *A Description of The Scenery Of The Lakes In The North Of England*, Longman, Hurst, Rees, Orme,and Brown, London

Wright, A 1997, *Plains of Promise*, UQP, St Lucia

Wright, A 2017, *Tracker: Stories of Tracker Tilmouth*, Giramondo, Artamon, NSW

Wright, A 2016, 'What Happens When You Tell Someone Else's Story?', *Meanjin*, vol. 75, no. 4, retrieved 12 October 2017, https://meanjin.com.au/essays/what-happens-when-you-tell-somebody-elses-story/

Wynd, I 1992, *Barrabool Land of the Magpie*, Barrabool Shire, Torquay

Acknowledgements

I've done so much walking on so many tracks and had so many conversations over the years with all kinds of people that have resonated with me long afterwards. They've all contributed to this book. For instance, the voices of my childhood are always, even now, singing in my ears. Naturally then there are too many people to mention here but in particular I'd like to express my gratitude to Sian Marlow and our sons Patrick and Jamesie, for their love, understanding and support. I'm also deeply grateful to Antoinette Hanna, Mick Matthews, Maria Takolander, David Tournier, Christos Raskatos, Bruce Pascoe, Patrick Mangan, Geordie Williamson, Amanda George, Richard Collopy, Hilary McPhee, Peter McPhee, Ian Chater, David McCooey, John Clarke, Simon McLean, Wendy Haslem, Carrie Tiffany, Peter Steven, Corinna Eccles, Lindon Pearce, Krista Bonfantine, Peter Downie, Ian Murray, Mick Sowry, Jock Serong, Nick Day, Robert MacFarlane, Anna McIldowie, Meg Parker, Cecilia Hartigan, Clare Price, Jennifer Abel, Ashley Hay, Robert Ashton, Jane Grant, Eliza Feely, as well as my brothers Bill, Peter and Tim, our sister Madeleine, and all our extended family across the generations, especially our father, Adrian, and our mother, Patricia.

All these people have given me the heart to write these things down.

I'd also like to thank my agent, Jeanne Ryckmans, my publisher Terri-ann White, my editor, Nicola Young, and all the other supportive editors who have published these essays in various journals and newspapers over the last few years.

And to all the true singers, teachers and deep scholars of our home inlet and surrounds, to the wimba-wallabies, the eels (including the footy-playing eels), the gang-gangs, the heath, wattle and ngangahooks, the bluetongues and bristlebirds – this book's to let you know we're still listening.

Thank you to all journal, magazine and newspaper publications for permission to use essays and reviews previously published by them.

About Upswell

Upswell Publishing was established in 2021 by Terri-ann White as a not-for-profit press. A perceived gap in the market for distinctive literary works in fiction, poetry and narrative non-fiction was the motivation. In her years as a bookseller, writer and then publisher, Terri-ann has maintained a watch on literary books and the way they insinuate themselves into a cultural space and are then located within our literary and cultural inheritance. She is interested in making books to last: books with the potential to still be noticed, and noted, after decades and thus be ripe to influence new literary histories.

About this typeface

Book designer Becky Chilcott chose
Foundry Origin not only as a strong,
carefully considered, and dependable
typeface, but also to honour her late
friend and mentor, type designer Freda
Sack, who oversaw the project. Designed
by Freda's long-standing colleague,
Stuart de Rozario, much like Upswell
Publishing, Foundry Origin was created
out of the desire to say something new.